The American Indian
and the
Problem of History

The American Indian and the Problem of History

Edited by

CALVIN MARTIN

New York   Oxford
Oxford University Press
1987

Oxford University Press

Oxford   New York   Toronto
Delhi   Bombay   Calcutta   Madras   Karachi
Petaling Jaya   Singapore   Hong Kong   Tokyo
Nairobi   Dar es Salaam   Cape Town
Melbourne   Auckland

and associated companies in
Beirut   Berlin   Ibadan   Nicosia

Library of Congress Cataloging-in-Publication Data
The American Indian and the problem of history.
Bibliography: p.
1. Indians of North America—Historiography. 2. United States—
Historiography. 3. Canada—Historiography. I. Martin, Calvin.
E76.8.A47   1986   970.004'97   86-8425
ISBN 0-19-503855-X (alk. paper)
ISBN 0-19-503856-8 (pbk. : alk. paper)

"The Metaphysics of Writing Indian-White History" by Calvin Martin
originally appeared in *Ethnohistory* 26 (Spring 1979): 153–59. Reprinted with
the kind permission of the American Society for Ethnohistory.

9 8 7 6

Printed in the United States of America

Will

Preface

The authors herein have been remarkably patient with me throughout the (unexpectedly) arduous process of putting this book together. So, too, has my editor, Sheldon Meyer, and literary agent, Georges Borchardt, both of whom could surely give Job some advice on the art of being longsuffering. What I originally imagined to be a simple and swift enterprise turned complex and lengthy as the collective impact of the essays registered with me. Engrossed with the phenomenon of "time"— to me a novel subject (yes, ironic for an historian), whose mysteries, disguises, subterfuges, and precincts I now sought in reading and thought—I wound up expending vast amounts of that very substance in pursuit of it. Time surely had its revenge. I have come to sympathize with Aldous Huxley's castigation of time as "evil." Yet so fascinating.

The inspiration for the introduction and epilogue was slow in coming, but when it came, it did so powerfully and voluminously. My thoughts in these two essays are admittedly not perfect; I expect that others will improve on them. I would like that. In these two essays I indulged that most human urge to grasp the big picture, the panorama, and express it as a theory. A risky business. Time and one's critics are not kind to theories, especially in the social sciences, it seems. Yet during their brief summer theories are often fruitful. I would like to think that what I have said in these two essays, together with the theories and views expressed by the eighteen other authors herein, will prove inspirational and useful to a broad spectrum of readers.

Specialists in this field will wonder why certain individuals have not contributed to the table of contents. Chances are I am wondering, too. A number of scholars turned down the invitation to write. For the most part their reasons are obscure to me, but I respect their wishes. Those who did accept and whose essays follow come from a variety of disciplines and speak for as many points of view. I feel strongly that this diversity of training and perspective is one of the book's greatest strengths and appeals. Taken together, the essays give a remarkably thorough treatment of the issue: the "metaphysics" of writing Indian-white history.

I ought to point out that I gave my authors complete freedom in choosing the context and style in which to convey their thoughts. I set the theme and circulated my "Metaphysics of Writing Indian-White History" article (reprinted herein) as a stimulus—as my version of the assignment. The results follow. Moreover, I did a minimum of editing; I felt it would be instructive to give the reader each contributor's unadulterated view. I regard each essay, including my own, as a primary source, to be scrutinized for its biases, tactics of persuasion, cogency of logic, evidence, and, ultimately, metaphysic.

Yet even while exercising these critical faculties, one should not lose sight of the fact that each of us herein is trying to comprehend a deep mystery. Respect the book for that. There is, perhaps unfortunately, no final, divine arbiter in these matters. Nor will "history" play that role. We, singly, are the arbiters. This is part of the reason why I have sought such a broad range of viewpoints and commitments: to present the reader with a lot to choose from in forming his or her own ideas and conclusions.

I began this project while on a two-year leave of absence from Rutgers University, the first year as the recipient of a National Endowment for the Humanities Senior Fellowship for Independent Study and Research (July 1981–June 1982), and the second year as a John Simon Guggenheim Memorial Foundation fellow (July 1982–June 1983). Both fellowships were awarded to assist in the research and writing of a book I have tentatively called *The Biological Conquest of the North American Indian* (Oxford University Press, forthcoming). *The American Indian and the Problem of History* started out as an escape from the long hours and intensity of the "biological conquest" project; in a sense, this book began life as a form of re-creation. The fellowship leave from Rutgers during those two years thus aided implicitly in the completion of this edited volume, and I would like to thank both of these fellowship agencies for their indirect assistance. I would also like to applaud the administration of Rutgers University for its generous fellowship leave program.

To those many students at Rutgers and at Dartmouth College who (in most cases unknown to them) stimulated my thinking in the preparation of this book, I offer, too, my gratitude. More personally, J. Wesley Martin provided expert and thoughtful editorial assistance, for which I am appreciative. Finally, and most important, I wish to thank my eighteen colleagues herein for their stimulating and illuminating views. They taught me much. So, too, have Nina, Lindsey, and Forrest, though in a rather different realm. With them I have so often escaped "time."

Princeton, N.J.   C. M.
October 1986

Contents

Contributors   xiii

Introduction   *An Introduction Aboard the* Fidèle   3

1   *The Metaphysics of Writing Indian-White History*   27
CALVIN MARTIN

2   *Cultural Pluralism Versus Ethnocentrism in the New Indian History*   35
ROBERT F. BERKHOFER, JR.

3   *American Indians and American History*   46
NEAL SALISBURY

4   *Thoughts on Early Canadian Contact*   55
CORNELIUS J. JAENEN

5   *Demographics of Native American History*   67
HENRY F. DOBYNS

6   *Pagans, Converts, and Backsliders, All: A Secular View of the Metaphysics of Indian-White Relations*   75
MARY YOUNG

7   *Revision and Reversion*   84
VINE DELORIA, JR.

8   *Distinguishing History from Moral Philosophy and Public Advocacy*   91
WILCOMB E. WASHBURN

9   *Indians on the Shelf*   98
MICHAEL DORRIS

10   *The Metaphysics of Dancing Tribes*   106
RICHARD DRINNON

11 *On the Revision of Monuments*   114
FREDERICK TURNER

12 *Envision Ourselves Darkly, Imagine Ourselves Richly*   120
CHRISTOPHER VECSEY

13 *Fox and Chickadee*   128
ROBIN RIDINGTON

14 *I May Connect Time*   136
PETER IVERSON

15 *Present Memories, Past History*   144
PETER NABOKOV

16 *Personal Reflections*   156
N. SCOTT MOMADAY

17 *White Buffalo Woman*   162
HENRIETTA WHITEMAN

18 *From a Native Daughter*   171
HAUNANI-KAY TRASK

19 *Socioacupuncture: Mythic Reversals and the Striptease in
Four Scenes*   180
GERALD VIZENOR

Epilogue   *Time and the American Indian*   192

Cumulative Bibliography   221

Contributors

Professor Robert F. Berkhofer, Jr.
Department of History
University of Michigan
Ann Arbor

Professor Vine Deloria, Jr.
(Standing Rock Sioux)
Department of Political Science
University of Arizona
Tucson

Dr. Henry F. Dobyns
Center for the History
of the American Indian
The Newberry Library
Chicago

Professor Michael Dorris
(Modoc)
Native American Studies
Dartmouth College
Hanover, New Hampshire

Professor Richard Drinnon
Department of History
Bucknell University
Lewisburg, Pennsylvania

Professor Peter Iverson
Department of History
Arizona State University West
Phoenix

Professor Cornelius J. Jaenen
Department of History
University of Ottawa
Ontario, Canada

Professor Calvin Martin
Department of History
Rutgers University
New Brunswick, New Jersey

Professor N. Scott Momaday
(Kiowa)
Department of English
University of Arizona
Tucson

Peter Nabokov
Department of Anthropology
University of California
Berkeley

Professor Robin Ridington
Department of Anthropology
and Sociology
University of British Columbia
Vancouver, British Columbia

Professor Neal Salisbury
Department of History
Smith College
Northampton, Massachusetts

Professor Haunani-Kay Trask
(Native Hawaiian)
Department of American Studies
University of Hawaii at Manoa
Honolulu

Dr. Frederick Turner
Old Santa Fe Trail
Santa Fe, New Mexico

Professor Christopher Vecsey
Department of Philosophy
and Religion
Colgate University
Hamilton, New York

Professor Gerald Vizenor
(Chippewa)
Native American Studies
University of California
Berkeley

Dr. Wilcomb E. Washburn, Director
Office of American Studies
Smithsonian Institution
Washington, D.C.

Professor Henrietta Whiteman
(Cheyenne)
Native American Studies
University of Montana
Missoula

Professor Mary Young
Department of History
University of Rochester
Rochester, New York

The American Indian and the Problem of History

An Introduction
Aboard the Fidèle

It was on an April Fools' Day a little over a century ago that Herman Melville took his compatriots on an excursion down the Mississippi aboard a steamer ominously named *Fidèle*, there to expose the nation's bigotry and hypocrisy through the machinations of a confidence man, actually a series of them, each professing the cardinal Christian virtues of love, hope, and charity. Melville had each preach a philosophy of optimism, concern, philanthropy, and benevolence. Yet all were frauds, as indeed each of these sentiments was a fraud, he felt. Melville had assembled a gallery of individual and ideological knaves taking advantage of a shipful of fools. *The Confidence Man: His Masquerade* (1857) is on its surface a treatise on misanthropy, yet underneath, in the final analysis, is a compassionate and humane assessment of the plight of us all.

The culmination of the narrative occurs in Chapter 26, "Containing the Metaphysics of Indian-Hating, According to the Views of One Evidently as Prepossessed as Rousseau in Favor of Savages," and Chapter 27, "Some Account of a Man of Questionable Morality, But Who, Nevertheless, Would Seem Entitled to the Esteem of That Eminent English Moralist Who Said He Liked a Good Hater." The two chapters recount the tale of Colonel John Moredock, legendary Indian-hater on the Illinois frontier who devoted himself to "quenching" not just the "band of Cains" who murdered his kin but, having accomplished that grisly errand, would spend the rest of his born days hunting Indians in general (1954:174). Being Indian was provocation enough for this rugged individualist who, incidentally, when not out bushwhacking his victims was at home being the model husband, father, yeoman farmer, soldier, and member of the territorial council. A sturdy Jeffer-

3

sonian, with just this one peculiar pathology. Yet, as rendered by the narrator, a confidence man ironically named Charles Noble, Moredock's behavior is really not a pathology at all. A quirk, a bit of an overreaction perhaps, but the man's actions were basically righteous. Moredock was a good and decent individual, a pillar of the community, even a candidate for governor (declining to run because of his conflict of interest). It is the Indian, rather, who is forever and incorrigibly diabolical. Indians, avers Noble, are fired by the same predatory instincts which inflame the panther. There is no such thing as a good specimen of either species.

Charles Noble, whose sleight-of-hand ennobles the dispossession of the American Indian, protests he is merely retelling a story, rather, a *history*, which he has heard repeatedly from his "father's friend, James Hall, the judge, you know" (1954:161). These are not actually his sentiments, Noble contends, but Judge Hall's. Melville did not invent this Judge James Hall; there was indeed such an individual (1793–1868), who rode as circuit judge in Illinois and wrote extensively on Indians and frontiersmen. In fact, Melville based his narrative, almost verbatim, on Hall's "Indian Hating—Some of the Sources of This Animosity—Brief Account of Col. Moredock," found in Hall's *Sketches of History, Life, and Manners, in the West* (1835).

On reflection one realizes that Herman Melville conjured up more than just the "metaphysics of Indian-hating" in this little tale; more importantly, in his own way he confronted the "metaphysics of writing Indian-white history." Charles Noble, the Mississippi operator (confidence man), indeed uttered the words, but they are really of the historian, Judge Hall, "who judges what is to be impressed on impressible minds" (Adler 1972:425). The historian is the real object of Melville's scrutiny, and so shall he and she be in the essays which follow.

By comparing Melville's discourse on Indian-hating to its source, it becomes apparent that he took certain liberties with Hall's text, making the historian a rather unvarnished bigot. By stripping away Hall's formulaic expressions of sympathy for the Indian and augmenting Hall's narrative, Melville damns him as a swindler. Posing as a patron and benefactor, historian Hall is in reality a symbolic, literary slayer of Indians. Though he speaks the words of benevolence, charity, and sympathy, his philosophy, his metaphysics is mischievous and ultimately destructive. Hall cloaks his ignorance of these people, truly a metaphysical ignorance, in platitude, irrelevant goodwill, and shallow and meaningless charity—a liberal smokescreen. Noble casually ob-serves that the judge "was a great smoker" (1954:172). In truth Hall's Indians are nothing more than savages. By manipulating Hall's text Melville ruthlessly drives that stark message home (Adler 1972; Melville 1954:lxvi–lxx).

It is a telling passage where narrator Charles Noble offers to reveal Judge Hall's philosophy to his rapt listener, Frank Goodman (the cosmopolitan, another confidence man): " 'Shall I give you the judge's philosophy, and all?' " To which Goodman replies that he is uneasy about entertaining another man's philosophy for fear it might not square with his own school of thought, but urges Noble to go ahead nonetheless. " 'Of what school or system was the judge, pray?' 'Why, though he knew how to read and write, the judge never had much schooling. But, I should say he belonged, if anything, to the free-school system. Yes, a true patriot, the judge went in strong for free-schools.' 'In philosophy?' " asks a bemused Goodman, disappointed both by the absurd answer and shabby credentials. He continues, " 'The man of a certain mind, then, while respecting the judge's patriotism, and not blind to the judge's capacity for narrative, such as he may prove to have, might, perhaps, with prudence, waive an opinion of the judge's probable philosophy. But I am no rigorist; proceed, I beg; his philoso-phy or not, as you please' " (1954:161–62).

Whereupon Noble proceeds with his narrative. I, however, would like to pose that question anew, and this time, unlike the convivial Frank Goodman, look carefully at the responses given. "Of what school or system was the historian, pray?" In commissioning the essays for this collection I was tacitly asking each author to tip his or her hand on this precise issue. I chose individuals with considerable standing in this discipline; each has published and taught extensively on the subject of Indian and white relations (Trask on Hawaiian-white relations). Each one having handled the material in one fashion or another for years, I was now asking everyone to stand back and survey the whole five-hundred-year panorama of joint Indian and white history. I wanted an analysis of the entire forest: the large contours, and what it all means. I instructed all eighteen to distill what they considered to be the essence of the Indian-white dialogue, and to render that vision in ten to twelve typescript pages—alas, some went over. The essays were to be written with candor and style, with the overriding question being, How well have we, how well *do* we, render the history, the meaning of Indians and whites in concert? For surely in recounting that history we inevitably confer upon it some sort of meaning, explicit or implicit, deriving from one's particular frame of reference.

Frame of reference. All of the authors in these pages graduated from something more substantial than the "school of hard knocks," where James Hall seems to have earned the bulk of his education. Formal education is not at issue for these eighteen scholars. At issue, rather, is level, or type, of perception and understanding. To what degree do these authors, or, for that matter, any of us who practice this craft, understand the worldviews of these two societies, Indian and white, which we presume to chronicle? To answer that question we must pose an even more fundamental question—a question behind a question: What is the ontological, phenomenological, and epistemological agenda each of us brings to bear on the history of Indian-white relations? What are the mental filters, prisms, and mirrors we individually lock into place as we put pen to paper? And to what degree do those filters, prisms, and mirrors permit us to render these people as *they* comprehended themselves and construed the world? In sum, What *is* our metaphysics of writing Indian-white history, and how accurately does it convey the metaphysics of those individuals and groups of individuals we seek to describe?

As I ask myself these questions, I despair that this discipline has not improved much since Melville's day, when he, too, posed them. Many of us in this profession are still, I fear, tenacious and unconscious confidence men. Regarding the Indian side of the Indian-white couplet, one finds platitudes still expressed and condolences extended—expressions of concern and benevolence. But then what? From there on the Indian is usually shoehorned into the dominant culture's paradigm of reason and logic, its calculus of viewing the world and manipulating its parts. The traditional historian colonizes the Indian's mind, like a virus commandeering the cell's genetic machinery. The typical procedure is to make Amerindians into what might be termed a "people of history," such as we have become in our civilization. Let it be said bluntly and forcefully that Native Americans traditionally subscribed to a philosophy of history, and of time, profoundly different from ours and that of our forebears. The reverberations are enormous.

There is also, of course, the problem of understanding the white side of the equation. How well have we comprehended and rendered the world as the Euro-Americans perceived it? In general, not well. Cornelius Jaenen, Neal Salisbury, and to a somewhat lesser extent, Mary Young, have wrestled with this theme in their respective essays. As Jaenen sees it: "If historians have paid insufficient attention to Amerindian realities, values, and ethos at the time of contact between European and Amerindian, it may be equally true that insufficient thought has been given to European realities, values, and cosmography of the colonial period. . . . While it is important to understand the hunting rituals and the deep sense of symbiosis of hunter and hunted, men and animals [among American Indians], . . . it is equally important to understand the intellectual constructs and philosophical frameworks into which Europeans fitted their observations and received accounts of Amerindian life." Jaenen concludes, "I have discovered our historiography to be as burdened with myths and stereotypes on the European side of the equation as on the Amerindian side." Indeed.

Despite our shortcomings in the way we have portrayed the European and American (including Canadian) side of the Indian-white dialogue, I am convinced we have erred far more egregiously in rendering the Indian side. For here we have created canons of reality, truth, credibility, and evidence of what constitutes fact, and identified and interpreted certain points of reference within the human psyche, which we have packaged and enshrined by calling the whole thing "social science." Equipped with this intimidating analytical tool we have then marched into the Indian realm determined to measure everything there in the algebra of its logical and conceptual circuitry. It is truly a dazzling machine, this behavioral-intellectual spectrophotometer of ours: a broad-band instrument whose program is Aristotelian, Augustinian, Calvinist, Baconian, Cartesian, Newtonian, Darwinian, Marxist, and many others, or combinations thereof. It furnishes us with both our questions and our interpretations of the responses we believe we receive.

But this is surely the wrong intellectual probe. We wield it not out of malice, but ignorance—an ignorance that is fired by a kind of ethnocentric righteousness: we believe our science of humankind is the most powerful analytical tool yet invented. I concede that. But in a larger sphere of performance and perception it is terribly destructive. And the truth of the matter is that *Homo sapiens* functions within a sphere larger than that which this analytical system is presently capable of assessing. It is truly a biological, or biohistorical, sphere, a realm which we in the Western cultural tradition, with our science, are only beginning to understand in relation to ourselves. We are novices—"completely amateur sorcerer[s]," was Loren Eiseley's assessment (1978: 179)—in comprehending such biological terms and relationships.

Let us pause in this great mission of ours to remind ourselves that in studying the American Indian we are dealing with a member of the species who has survived equally as long as we have on this planet, survived for all those millennia with a refinement of intellect, level of insight, and sophistication of perception second to none. These people and their ancestors scrutinized and pondered the great cosmic and existential issues and produced answers just as complete and satisfactory as ours. Perhaps even more satisfactory than ours. Away back then something prompted them to key their speculative philosophies to an overarching and undergirding biological system. Western European speculative philosophy, on the other hand, is nowhere near as primally biological. It tends to be, at least from medieval times on, anthropological, a perspective given further impetus with the discovery, exploration, and conquest of exotic lands beyond European shores. The biological focus bequeaths to its adherents and practitioners a profoundly different set of definitions, interests, values, and goals. Ethical questions differ radically between the biological and anthropological outlook, as do questions such as what is meaningful, what is worthwhile, what one does with one's time and energy, who we are, what constitutes reality, and the question of cognition. All of the key and fundamental questions of human existence tend to be asked differently and yield different answers on the basis of this anterior point of reference.*

The point to be made is that the (what I am calling) biological orientation of American Indian cultures was every bit as reasonable and practical (if one wishes to use these terms and concepts) as the Western anthropological paradigm. The proof is that Indians survived; they reproduced and thrived. When Europeans reached these American shores the indigenous population was demographically stable. If survivability of the species is the ultimate criterion of success for any philosophical system, and I would argue that it is, then the biological model obviously worked. Of course it worked at other levels of behavior and

---

*By "anthropological" I am, yes, referring obliquely to the academic discipline of anthropology, while at the same time I am using the word to mean something more subtle and pervasive than the term "anthropocentric" can convey. For me, the word "anthropological" is another way of saying "the world according to, for, and about humanity." It is the *logos*, word, of and about and directed at *anthropos*: humanity.

activity, too; it furnished more than just room and board, just as the European system of thought furnished a meal ticket and more.

My purpose in raising these issues is that they provide insight, I believe, into why some of us historians are so taken with American Indians, a point I shall come back to shortly. First, it is important to get a sense of historiographical context. While reviewing recent Indian-white historiography, Reginald Horsman observes, "Native American history [by which he seems to mean Indian-white history] has never quite thrown off the parochial air that dominated it when it was merely a subfield of an equally parochial frontier history." By "parochial" he means that Indian-white historians have generally lagged behind other historians in employing "the new approaches and techniques that have begun to transform writing on other areas of American history" (1982:242). Indian-white history occupies a backwater status in this profession for more reasons than this, however. Horsman's complaint is surely legitimate, but even more interesting is the yawning disinterest of non-Indian-white historians in the subject. The majority of American historians seem to regard the whole issue as an endless tale of woe and atrocity committed mostly against Indians, a litany many find redundant, tiresome, and depressing. More pointedly, the Indian experience is viewed, and so treated, as a curious, even quaint sideshow within the larger panorama of Anglo-American performance and achievement in North America (see Hoxie 1985).

Indian-white history thus floats in a backwater both because of the unimaginativeness of its practitioners (as Horsman argues) and because it is sequestered there by the remainder of the profession, for whom it is largely irrelevant. Actually, they are right: it is irrelevant. Ultimately it is so, I believe, because the two core philosophies in operation here, the biological and anthropological, are fundamentally antagonistic and irreconcilable, at least as presently practiced. There are two very different cosmic errands being carried out here. Those individuals who take it upon themselves to write Native American history, which generally translates into the history of Indian and white relations, with few exceptions do so consciously or unconsciously from an anthropological perspective and commitment that inevitably does violence to the biological perspective and commitment of traditional American Indians, and as a result renders them in caricature. To use a biochemical analogy, it is as though one thought structure is fat soluble, the other, water soluble. Ironically, in writing histories of colonization we are proceeding by way of ideological colonization.

Thus the Director Emeritus of the Newberry Library's D'Arcy
McNickle Center for the History of the American Indian, Francis
Jennings, recently wrote a book appropriately titled *The Ambiguous
Iroquois Empire*, dealing with the seventeenth- and eighteenth-century
English–Iroquois Covenant Chain (alliance) and the Tributary System
between the Iroquois and their Indian allies. Yet Jennings has scarcely a
clue as to what the Iroquois and their allied tribes had in mind in all of
this. He fills the void by supplying the Indians with a Western outlook
and course of action, speaking volumes about his knowledge of American Indians when he waves aside their mythic world as a "weird kink in
Indian mentality" (1984:81; Martin 1985a).

Another recent study, *Changes in the Land: Indians, Colonists, and
the Ecology of New England*, by William Cronon, depicts beaver
aboriginally as merely some kind of "resource"—"an object of use,
conserved [before the advent of the European-inspired fur trade] because the need for it was slight" (1983:165–66, 105). Cronon "simply
does not understand" the Indians' world, I wrote in my review of the
book. "The spiritual matrix of the hunt, indeed, of the entire food
quest, the likelihood that major game animals were regarded as superior in skill and intelligence and power and that it was *they* who 'owned'
the land, and that Nature conserved *Homo* rather than vice versa—all
of this is a metaphysics Cronon either does not comprehend or refuses
to acknowledge" (Martin 1984:507). "The essential lesson for the Indians," Cronon explains carefully, "was that certain things [those "resources"] began to have *prices* [his emphasis] that had not had them before.
In particular, one could buy personal prestige by killing animals and
exchanging their skins for wampum or high-status European goods"
(1983:97). New England's furry creatures were thus nailed to the wall
through habitat destruction as well as "by having a price placed on their
heads" (1983:108). After ruminating on all of the above I concluded
that Cronon's Indians "could work on Wall Street."

What is important in these studies, each representative of what is
considered to be the most sophisticated and successful blending of
Indian and white history, is that the native is equated with the white at
the level of basic human motivation and self-interest. The equation is
specious, a card trick. At the core of their thinking Jennings's Indians
were, in his words, "as rational as Europeans," "human in the usual
simple and complex ways," and "rational persons" (Jennings 1984:6,
xix, 81). No one disputes that rationality; the problem is they are being
assigned someone else's rationality (Martin 1985a:20). Cronon does the

same thing with his New England Indians, who espouse what Marshall Sahlins facetiously calls "The Business Outlook" (1972:186n).

Probably no one demonstrates the chilling potential of this fallacy more than the anthropologist Eric Wolf does in his popular treatise, *Europe and the People Without History*. Wolf's goal was to show how the mode of production of "the people without history" (Native Americans, Asian Indians, Africans, and Chinese) became tied to and largely supplanted by the mode of production of the industrializing West (Western Europe and America) from 1400 onward. Thus the history of these non-Western societies became welded to Western history and, indeed, to global history from that point onward.

Wolf begins by observing, "Social historians and historical sociologists have shown that the common people were as much agents in the historical process as they were its victims and silent witnesses. We thus need to uncover the history of 'the people without history'—the active histories of 'primitives,' peasantries, laborers, immigrants, and besieged minorities" (1982:x). He then shows in some detail how each of these unsung societies became folded into the economy, and hence history, of the Western world, so that by the end of his ambitious exercise Wolf can look back and exclaim:

> As we unraveled the chains of causes and effects at work in the lives of particular populations, we saw them extend beyond any one population to embrace the trajectories of others—all others. . . . Ultimately, these chains of causation and consequence encompassed whole continents, and brought together the Old World and the New. . . . Drawn by these forces into convergent activities, people of diverse origins and social makeup were driven to take part in the construction of a common world. They included the European sea merchants and soldiery of various nationalities, but also native Americans, Africans, and Asians. In the process, the societies and cultures of all these people underwent major changes. These changes affected not only the peoples singled out as the carriers of "real" history but also the populations anthropologists have called "primitives" and have often studied as pristine survivals from a timeless past. The global processes set in motion by European expansion constitute *their* history as well. There are thus no "contemporary ancestors," no people without history, no peoples—to use Lévi-Strauss's phrase—whose histories have remained "cold" (1982:385).

In one sense Wolf is correct: there has been and continues to be such a joint, shared history; native peoples did indeed deal with whites. There was no choice. But that intercourse, economic or otherwise, cannot alone be hailed as their history. For in truth they were hijacked during the course of their own conceived historical "trajectory," to use Wolf's vivid expression. More accurately, for American Indians at least, the past five centuries have been a lesion upon an older history (though "history" may not be the best word to use here). The point is that they conducted themselves in the course of that coerced intercourse attentive to the strains of an older, more ancient muse. An older voice, an older song. (Again, "history" is probably not an adequate word in this context.) *That* is the missing ingredient in Jennings, Cronon, and countless other studies dealing with Native Americans.

What we scholars do, deliberately or inadvertently, is delete the coercive aspect of that joint history by performing the card trick mentioned above: by insisting that Native Americans were on the same intellectual/mental trajectory as were Europeans, by furnishing them with the same fundamental, unfolding existential premises and agenda we Westerners have subscribed to over the centuries. In short, we maintain that their approach to life was as human-oriented and human-comprehended, as human-engineered and human-interventionist—as anthropocentric—as ours. We maintain that they, like us, did taste the fruit "of the tree of the knowledge of good and evil" (Genesis 2:17) and that they, too, were expelled from the Garden into a world where *Homo* is convinced that survival is a ceaseless struggle with a mute and indifferent cosmos.

Wolf does this through Marxist anthropology (actually Biblical anthropology): "To demonstrate the global interconnections of human aggregates is one task; to explain the development and nature of these connections, however, is another. I have taken the position that no understanding of these connections is possible unless it is grounded in the economic and political conditions that generated and maintained these connections. To explicate the material underpinnings of these linkages, I have drawn freely on concepts taken from the storehouse of Marxian ideas. *I have taken from Marx the basic notion that social life is shaped by the ways human beings engage nature through production*" (my emphasis) (1982:385–86).

Ideology-making supposedly occurs by the same process. According to Wolf, "The ability to project symbolic universes may well be located in the structure of the human brain, driven . . . to resolve the irresolvable contradiction between Nature and Culture. . . . This contradiction is dealt with not in pure thought alone ('myth thinking man'), but in the active transformation of nature through the social labor of human beings. Contrary to those who believe that Mind follows an independent course of its own, I would argue that ideology-making does not arise in the confrontation of Naked Man thinking about Naked Nature; rather, *it occurs within the determinate compass of a mode of production deployed to render nature amenable to human use*" (my emphasis) (Wolf 1982:388). "The manner of that mobilization ["the deployment of social labor, mobilized to engage the world of nature"] sets the terms of history, and in these terms the peoples who have asserted a privileged relation with history and the peoples to whom history has been denied encounter a common destiny" (1982:391). Thus at the very core of human perception is this fundamental conviction that Nature must be wrestled to the mat to render it "amenable to human use"; human philosophies of life spring forth from "the active transformation of nature through the social labor of human beings." It is a premise, a mandate, a calculus, a code of human life and human survival which each of the unchronicled societies, including Amerindian, allegedly shared with one another and with Europeans. From such a common point of departure it is now a simple matter to harmonize the "histories" of Indians and whites: Indians can be mustered in with other peoples of history because they are a priori anthropocentric in their behavior and anthropological in their thinking. It is by virtue of this basic congruency of philosophical and ideological orientation and assumption—of cultural fabric—that both groups can be stitched together into the same tapestry.

I disagree. Marshall Sahlins, in what he calls "an anthropological critique of the idea that human cultures are formulated out of practical activity and, behind that, utilitarian interest" (1976:vii), speaks of a "privileged institutional locus of the symbolic process, whence emanates a classificatory grid imposed upon the total culture." This "dominant site of symbolic production . . . supplies the major idiom of other relations and activities" (1976:211). "In bourgeois society," he explains, "material production is the dominant locus of symbolic production; in primitive society it is the set of social (kinship) relations" (1976:212). Or again, "The peculiarity of Western culture is the institutionalization of the process in and as the production of goods, by comparison with a 'primitive' world where the locus of symbolic differentiation remains social relations, principally kinship relations, and other spheres of activity are ordered by the operative distinctions of kinship" (1976:211). "In the Western plan," he elaborates further,

the relations of production constitute a classification reiterated throughout
the entire cultural scheme, inasmuch as the distinctions of persons, time,
space, and occasion developed in production are communicated throughout, to kinship, politics, and the rest, despite the discontinuities in institutional quality. At the same time, as the accumulation of exchange-value
proceeds by way of use-value, capitalist production develops a symbolic
code, figured as the meaningful differences between products, which serves
as a general scheme of social classification. And this economic integration
of the whole, the transmission of both grid and code, social differentiation
and objective contrast, is assured by the market mechanism—for everyone
must buy and sell to live, but they can do so only to the extent that they are
empowered by their relations to production (1976:212–13).

Finally,

We speak as if we [in Western society] had rid ourselves of constraining
cultural conceptions, as if our culture were constructed out of the "real"
activities and experiences of individuals rationally bent upon their practical
interests. . . . Marx wrote that primitive society could not exist unless it
disguised to itself the real basis of that existence, as in the form of religious
illusions. But the remark may be truer of bourgeois society. Everything in
capitalism conspires to conceal the symbolic ordering of the system—
especially those academic theories of praxis by which we conceive ourselves
and the rest of the world. A praxis theory based on pragmatic interests and
"objective" conditions is the secondary form of a cultural illusion, and its
elaborate empirical and statistical offspring, the "etic" investigations of
our social sciences, the intellectual titillation of an "emic" mystification.
. . . What is finally distinctive of Western civilization is the mode of symbolic production, this very disguise in the form of a growing GNP of the
process by which symbolic value is created. But such institutionalization
of the symbolic process only makes it more elaborate, as well as less subject
to control and more dangerous. More elaborate because it encourages all
the human capacities of symbolic manipulation within a single social order,
and thus generates an enormous cultural growth. More dangerous, then,
because in the interest of this growth it does not hesitate to destroy any
other form of humanity whose difference from us consists in having discovered not merely other codes of existence but ways of achieving an end that
still eludes us: the mastery by society of society's mastery over nature
(1976:220–21).

Europeans ranked, classified, and comprehended Native Americans
within this grid right from the start. By construing them as a people of
"material production" we were able to make them into "a people of

history," rendering them intelligible in our terms—turning their behavior into *our* behavior under hypothetically similar circumstances. Yet theirs was a different code of existence, a different cultural universe, taking its cue from a very different "site of symbolic production." Sahlins argues that kinship relations formed this primary "locus of the symbolic process," whereas I see something deeper, more pervasive, something embracing kinship relations—something literally biological.

If we do extricate American Indians from our philosophy of history, by which I mean disengage them from our concepts of contingent, anthropocentric reality and practicality, from our fixation with the unfolding human and individual experience, where, then, does that leave them? In eternity, I believe.

In his slender volume, *The Savage Mind,* Claude Lévi-Strauss cautions against the reification and sanctification of "history." "History," he argues, "is tied neither to man nor to any particular object. It consists wholly in its method. . . . It is . . . far from being the case that the search for intelligibility comes to an end in history as though this were its terminus. Rather, it is history that serves as the point of departure in any quest for intelligibility. As we say of certain careers, history may lead to anything, provided you get out of it" (1966:262). I will argue that we historians need to get out of history, as we know it, if we wish to write authentic histories of American Indians. Lévi-Strauss continues, "This further thing to which history leads for want of a sphere of reference of its own shows that whatever its value . . . historical knowledge has no claim to be opposed to other forms of knowledge as a supremely privileged one. We noted above that it is already found rooted in the savage mind, and we can now see why it does not come to fruition there. The characteristic feature of the savage mind is its timelessness; its object is to grasp the world as both a synchronic and a diachronic totality" (1966:262–63).

I shall reserve for the epilogue of this book the explanation of how and why this was done; the point I wish to establish here is that despite our profusion of monographs we have in truth largely missed the North American Indians' experience and meaning of it. We have missed their "time" as they construed and sought to live it. Instead, what we have captured in print is more akin to posed, still photographs—"images," says Vizenor acidly, which form "discontinuous artifacts in a colonial road show." As Edward Curtis did in his photographs, clothing and posing his subjects in preconceived compositions and then freezing them in "camera time," we historians define them in and confine them to the terms of historic (i.e., anthropological) time. Vizenor is amused by Curtis doctoring his film on discovering an alarm clock in one of his shots, perched there next to his "aborigines." He excised it from the negative, and in so doing denied them "time" (anyway, it was the wrong time). Whereas we historians do the reverse: we quite deliberately *insert* an alarm clock in our posed scenes of Indians—and likewise furnish them with the wrong time. That is, we make them into a "people of history": assign them our terms and conception of living in time and space, our commitment to changing reality and changing humanity over the ages. We, too, pose and then doctor the negatives, refusing them "a theater for tribal events in mythic time" (Vizenor). "Historians have hidden the cyclical world of myth under our linear writings," charges Drinnon, "and have thereby robbed tribal people of their reality." Through such an interpretation and application of "history" we surely strangle these people.

The appeal of American Indians for many of us scholars, for many of the authors herein, has precisely to do with their astounding ability to annul time, their remarkable capacity to repudiate systematically time and history. The essays in this volume are novel in that they all in one fashion or another raise the question of whether we can write about North American Indians while adhering to the canons of formal, Western history. In the course of asking this, many of these authors have delineated the mythic world once fully occupied by American Indians and obviously still exerting a tremendous magnetic pull on them. They have delineated that world both to underscore its distinctiveness from our Western model of the universe and the functioning of man and woman within it, and, just as important, to express awe in its presence. It is an awesome phenomenon. Indeed, read this collection and realize that perhaps the majority of these authors, together with countless individuals not published in these pages, are implicitly engaged in a "revolt against time" (Wood 1982:1–25), against time and history, and they are finding in the American Indian a source of inspiration.

It was in *Henry IV* that Shakespeare pronounced life to be "Time's fool, / And Time, that takes survey of all the world, / Must have a stop" (Harrison 1962:87). The words were of the mortally wounded Hotspur, in bitter anticipation of his own imminent death. Time must indeed have a stop, echoed Aldous Huxley in another context. "'The most intractable of our experiences,'" he vehemently declared, "'is the experience of Time—the intuition of duration, combined with the thought of perpetual perishing. . . . By merely elapsing time makes nonsense of all life's conscious planning and scheming.' The passage of time ensures that everything significant a man has done will 'vanish the way everything [else] vanishes and changes,'" prompting him to exclaim: "'Time is evil'; it is 'the medium in which evil . . . lives and outside of which it dies'" (Wood 1982: 141–42). Similarly Carl Jung, glancing down the corridor of historical time at the spectacle of "'unending growth and decay of life and civilizations,'" was seized by the "'absolute nullity'" of it all (Wood 1982:181). While Dean Inge denounced as "'superstitious'" our "'belief in the automatic progress of humanity'" through time (Wood 1982:201).

Jung, Huxley, and T. S. Eliot are among the throng of novelists, poets, philosophers, theologians, and mystics who have made the supreme effort to transcend "duration," the seemingly meaningless passage of time; to grasp an unchanging reality, an eternal reality, of which we are all a part; to connect themselves individually and collectively to a timeless reality. The point of departure for many was the conviction that "true time, nonchronological time, consists of an ever-moving, eternally flowing present which contains its own past" (Wood 1982:17). The goal was to abolish, or transcend, history, with its seemingly random, even chaotic concatenation of events, so as to restore "the vision of existence under the aspect of eternity" (Wood 1982:20).

Eliot was convinced that our obsession with time has prevented us from seeking God—from understanding "'what has happened'" (Wood 1982:92). He thus sought and found, he believed, what he poetically called the "'still point . . . The point of intersection of the timeless/With time,' where temporal history is 'transfigured, in another pattern'—'a pattern/Of timeless moments'" (Wood 1982:111). Here, writes Douglas K. Wood in *Men Against Time*, was the "Great Time or Eternal Now, which is reached by periodically annulling time" (1982:87). "Man's destiny," both Eliot and Huxley agreed, surely "lies outside time" (Wood 1982:119).

Huxley was transfixed by the notion of timeless reality, and, more, of participating in such an eternity. "Reality cannot be segmented," paraphrases Wood, "it cannot be analyzed into subjects and predicates. Nor can it be categorized in terms of temporal relations; there is no before or after, change or succession, in eternity. Reality is timeless and spaceless, an all-inclusive unity of spirit, something an individual can get to know only by pursuing the ideal of non-attachment. Only then will he realize, in 'a non-personal experience of timeless space,' that his self is not really a separate entity but a part of the universal Self which is indistinguishable from the Absolute and divine Ground of all being" (1982:136). For Huxley, Wood claims, "Every thing is really One and the same, absolutely identical and synonymous. Language and our own egos create the illusion of separateness—of time and space, causality and individuality" (1982:137). The goal was to ignore the chronometer, to crack through time, to tune one's ear to a nonchronological reality—to those realities which moved in a different pulse, in a different rhythm, to a different tempo. One aimed to insert oneself into a realm where the categories of reality follow what novelist Ursula Le Guin calls "the meter of eternity" (1974:221).

Huxley was adamant that language was an impediment, preventing us from detecting the transcendent and eternal reality whose presence he felt was palpable, while the symbol and sensation of time, of linear chronology which became duration, kept us from understanding eternity around and within us. "Language allows man to create culture and survive," summarizes Wood, "but it excludes—or at least reduces—his awareness of reality. Time itself seems to be nothing more than a product of symbol-formation, and as such, it reduces or irrevocably precludes one's ability to perceive eternity" (1982:155). As is well known, Huxley resorted to Vedantism and mescaline in an effort to find a nonchronological configuration in life—find those immutable, eternal themes and categories within which we all function, which we all experience, and yet whose true (and truly powerful) nature we do not fully appreciate. In *Island*, Huxley has Will Farnaby deliver himself from time through the "metamorphic" effect of a hallucinogen: "'ONE, TWO, THREE, FOUR,'" recalls Farnaby, "'THE CLOCK IN THE KITCHEN struck twelve. How irrelevantly, seeing that time had ceased to exist! *The absurd, importunate bell had sounded at the heart of a timelessly present Event, of a Now that changed incessantly in a dimension, not of seconds and minutes, but of beauty, of significance, of intensity, of deepening mystery* [my emphasis]. . . . There was a *tempo*' during his experience, 'but no time. So what was there? Eternity.' Eternity and not real duration," clarifies Wood (1982:157).

Where Huxley combined drugs and Eastern mysticism and Eliot embraced Christian ritual to flee time, the Swiss psychoanalyst Carl Jung invoked myth—personal myth. Myths for Jung were "manifestations of timelessness in time." A myth, elaborates Wood in delineating Jung's thinking, "is an embodiment, a concrete manifestation, of a timeless and constantly repeated motif of human experience. It is the symbolic product of an unconscious archetype, which, insofar as it is reexperienced, allows the perceiver to participate in a mode of experience that subsists beyond time. It is a nonrational and numinous universal which, when experienced as a meaningful and living reality, unites the individual with the timeless wisdom of the human species," giving one, in Jung's words, "'the security and inner strength not to be crushed by the monstrousness of the universe'" (Wood 1982:165–66). The key was to make the corporate, collective myth personal: "Although a person may find an ancient myth meaningful, he must incorporate it within his own field of consciousness; he must, in other words, stamp the timeless themes of mythology with his own identity, create his own myth from the archetypal motifs common to all humanity. . . . An individual mythology allows a person to express what he is under the aspect of eternity. It permits him to integrate himself with the cycle of the aeons and the phylogenetic content of human experience—to identify himself with the eternal core of meaning concealed in the heart of life" (Wood 1982:166, 180). "A personal myth," Jung stressed, " . . . subsists above the temporal process, above change or creative evolution" (Wood 1982:181).

One goes about creating his or her own personal myth through a process Jung called "individuation," where "the time-bound ego" is replaced by "the transcendental self" (Wood 1982:177). This new self "'senses itself as the object of an unknown and superordinate subject.' It feels that it has been united and transformed, that it has become complete and whole by communing with and participating in a higher reality" (Wood 1982:180). Behind this lay Jung's conviction that "'our world, with its time, space, and causality, relates to another order of things lying behind or beneath it, in which neither "here and there" nor "earlier and later" are of importance.'" There exists an "'uncomprehended absolute object' which, operating through the archetypes of the collective unconscious, 'affects and influences us'" (Wood 1982:196). Having himself experienced individuation, Jung could describe this eternal phenomenon ("when 'the imperishable world irrupted into this transitory one'") as follows: "'Everything that happens in time had been brought together into a concrete whole. Nothing was distributed over time, nothing could be measured by temporal concepts'" (Wood 1982:181, 182).

Eliot, Huxley, Jung—all were moved by the realization that "the modern world has experienced a forgetfulness of Being . . . and that the future of humanity . . . depends upon our relearning the 'forgotten language' of Being, God, or the timeless Ground." Each was haunted in his own way by the conviction that "without contact with eternity we are destined to destroy ourselves" (Wood 1982:199).

The "terror of history," is how Mircea Eliade described the sensation and our state of affairs (1959:139–62). It is a theme I see embedded in many of the essays in this volume. Expressed very explicitly in those of Drinnon, Nabokov, Turner, Vecsey, and Whiteman. More subtly, perhaps, in essays by Iverson, Momaday, Ridington, Trask, and Vizenor, and my own. As I read what these particular individuals have written I find that they all seem to be engaged in a quest. They are not looking for, nor looking to compose, "history," as it is conventionally understood: the collection and interpretation of facts and data in the service of academic knowledge. Rather they are looking for timeless meanings, for themselves and our civilization. More pointedly, they are looking for *connections*: connections with nonchronological time in order to experience and know nonsegmented reality, that "divine and absolute Ground of all being," what Yeats called the "'magical dance'. . . which stimulates the Great Memory" (Wood 1982:137, 153). They seek connection with the "timeless wisdom of the human species," "the phylogenetic content of human experience" (Wood 1982:166, 180).

Each performs his or her task as historian or anthropologist or writer not in the pursuit of yet more abstract, sterile, academic knowledge on the American Indian (or Native Hawaiian, in Trask's case), but because each detects a certain "coiled intentionality" (as Nabokov puts it) in these materials: "Here, however, I had tasted histories premised upon purpose. A sense of coiled intentionality underlay these recollections, myths, and prophecies. . . . They were designed as actions, not pieces of evidence. Pertinence replaced dates as their index of utility. Their past was not prologue but the unfolding present. . . . As I hunted in the library stacks I seemed to be moving through shelves of rifled medicine' bundles, their voices and motives released only by beliefs and imperatives my society did not share." Elsewhere Nabokov calls it history "premised on spiritual renewal," confessing, in the end, "It was within the Indian world where I was finding the ways that made sense. What else could I do? It was in Native American places where I was learning the truth of Paul Radin's conviction, 'No progress will ever be achieved . . . until scholars rid themselves, once and for all, of the curious notion that everything possesses an evolutionary history; until they realize that certain ideas and certain concepts are . . . ultimate for man.' . . . In attitudes and stories and house-fronts and cave roofs from this native land I had come upon such ideas and concepts, meanings and connections, and they were becoming mine whether I liked it or not." "The inevitability of timeless history," he calls it.

It must be emphasized that this "Great Memory," this "timeless wisdom of the human species," this "phylogenetic content of human experience" is, at its core, biological, not anthropological. There are animals in this realm, in the audience, as Vizenor's fictional character, Tune Browne, realizes during the course of his ritual striptease. Bumping and grinding his way out of the garments of white invention, Tune, the "dreamer who lost his soul for a time and found his families in still photographs," discovers himself in the realm of myth again.

> He lowered his arms, spread his stout fingers like birds in flight and released several feathers from his vest. The lights were dim, the audience in the conference center was silent. Crows called in the distance, an otter slid down a river bank and snapped back in mythic time. . . . Tune turned the projectors off and the captured [photographic] images died when he dropped his trousers in a sovereign striptease. The audience burst into wild cheers and peals of animal laughter in the dim light, even the cats and crows called from the crowd. Tune listened to the birds over the trees and when he removed his wristwatch the dichotomies of past and present dissolved one last time. The inventors and colonialists vanished with the striptease.

For Frederick Turner, the Great Memory is the memory that

> our necessary human condition is to be a part of the total living universe, that we cannot be anything other than part of this gigantic organism, and that spiritual health is to be had only by accepting this condition and by attempting to live in accordance with it. If there is one theme that unites the hundreds of aboriginal cultures of North America, it is this one. . . . For more than a thousand years in the West, whites have been walling themselves off from an acknowledgment of the interconnectedness of all things, from an acceptance of the fact that there neither is nor ever can be any such entity as "human nature" considered apart from the rest of creation. . . . Immured thus in a prison of our own devising, we have almost forgotten who and what we are, and so have recourse to terms like "pagan," "primitive," and "animistic" to label those who have believed themselves part of a cosmos that nurtured many forms of life. . . . Compared to this aboriginal life-view, ours is a shockingly dead view of creation. We ourselves are the only things in the universe to which we grant an authentic vitality, and because of this we are not fully alive.

Clearly many of these authors have found something more meaningful, more portentous than what the concept we call "historiography" normally implies—or delivers. Frederick Turner put his finger on it when he acknowledged the "strange, compelling power" of a way of life that manages to connect *Homo* to the cosmos in a way that is both convincingly timeless and convincingly participatory. Could it be that these scholars are looking for their own "captivity narrative"? Nabokov calls himself "a mixed-blood caught in a captivity narrative, searching to reinhabit this land." In an eerie way these people seem to want to be possessed by the place—the landscape and elements—much as Whiteman says her Cheyennes were "owned" by the land. "In brief," she writes, "Cheyenne history is a continuum of sacred experiences rooted into the American landscape, with Bear Butte their most sacred and most powerful place." Trask, a Native Hawaiian, is forthright in declaring, "Land is inherent to the people; it is like our bodies and our parents. The people cannot exist without the land, and the land cannot exist without the people." Land forms the key to her people's history, she says; the land and the people are inseparable, incomprehensible without one another. One must inhabit the land as traditional Hawaiians did, one must feel the power, pungency, intimacy, the sensuality of the land, in order to comprehend and communicate *their* history.

All of this goes against the grain of Western history, observes Frederick Turner in *Beyond Geography*: "No. The thing to do was to *take* possession without becoming possessed: to take secure hold on the lands beyond and yet hold them at a rigidly maintained spiritual distance. It was never to merge, to mingle, to marry. To do so was to become an apostate from Christian history and so be lost in an eternal wilderness" (1980:238). But "'you are sunk in this ground here up to your armpits,'" counters a Crow spokesman in graphic admonition to another. And "so were they all," adds Turner, casting his eye over the aboriginal Plains, "and even deeper than that, for the lands were the very stuff of their dreams and visions. . . . In dreams and in visions the lands manifested the presence and abiding concern of the Great Spirit. So the people actively courted such states as ways of remaining attuned to the divinity that brooded in the wind and clouds and grasses, that vivified both human and animal existence. This was their kind of possession, and they celebrated it in their medicine bundles, their songs, stories, and communal ceremonies, down through the years of the Winter Counts into a season harsher than any of them could imagine" (1980:278–79).

Possession. This is more than topophilia. Thoreau was staggered by it at the top of Mount Katahdin: "'What is this Titan that has possession of me? Talk of mysteries!—Think of our life in nature,—daily to be shown matter, to come in contact with it,—rocks, trees, wind on our cheeks! the *solid* earth! the *actual* world! the *common sense! Contact! Contact! Who* are we? *where* are we?'" (F. Turner 1980:272). Lost for words, he established and maintained this "contact," experienced this "possession" in his life largely through intimacy with the American Indian (Sayre 1977). Robin Ridington, trying to convey the "connecting," "possessing" quality of myth, matter-of-factly explains, "I can be a frog or a fox and still be a person. I can know them as I know myself. If I am Indian I can be led toward a place where this knowledge will come naturally."

But what if we are not an Indian (or Thoreau)? Can we still "be led toward a place where this knowledge will come naturally"? Ridington thinks so. Although he warns, "Historians must be wary of dreaming up other cultures . . . they can, perhaps, dream into the rich store of information that hunters have given us about themselves." This is what he has done with the multitude of Indian stories he has heard in twenty years of fieldwork: "I have studied them, dreamed them, told them, taught them, and made them my own." Vecsey, too, takes possession of the same sorts of stories, and they possess him: "By retelling the stories of Indian lives, stories which are, I contend, our own stories, and by imagining ourselves as humans . . . instead of contemporary, white Americans, we can make manifest some crucial latencies of our human nature. Indian traditions have something to offer us non-Indians: values we have repressed or never known regarding environment, society, and the spiritual world. Their texts offer us insights concerning the possibility of human systems that we might recover or attain. The study of American Indians, I have found, challenges us in our Americanness and enriches us in our humanness, permitting us—as N. Scott Momaday has recommended—to 'imagine ourselves richly,' to know ourselves well."

Turner appears to agree when he admonishes us to "surrender . . . what we take to be our humanity to the magic and mystery of a universe no less alive in any of its phenomena—earth, stones, water, stars—than we ourselves are alive. . . . Surrendering to magic, to mystery, to a universe pulsating with vitality would seem to be to give up the long history of our own 'rise to civilization,' and in some sense this really would be the case. To most, including most professional historians, this surrender is neither necessary nor desirable. Yet I do not see how anything less than this can allow us to create the new and durable sequences we should be seeking." He calls it writing "from the *inside* of the lodges." And Drinnon believes that by learning "to speak a new language, the secret language of the body, as Martha Graham called the dance," we too might experience the primordial and eternal connections, such as those of which American Indians partook. For Nabokov, searching "for a pure home base," it was a tremendous breakthrough to realize that the American Indians he was scrutinizing did not "hold any exclusive claim to archaic verities. All our ancestors had reenacted mythic history. . . . It was within the Indian world where I was finding the ways that made sense."

One senses in all of this the American Indian wearing the mantle of savior, rescuing us from the disastrous course of history, or at least our rendition of it (see especially Turner and Drinnon). Indians of course have a long and distinguished career in the service of European and American causes, from their duty as "noble savages" at the hands of French *philosophes*, to surrogate slaves in the fervent rhetoric of antebellum abolitionists, to lost souls in the imaginations of numberless missionaries, to a cohesive influence in the "frontier thesis" of Frederick Jackson Turner and his disciples, all the way up to ecological gurus in the environmental scare of the 1960s. In each instance, Indians are pulled and twisted into a grotesque shape, a caricature of the genuine article, by those purporting to speak for or about them, or using them for this or that cause. We tend to invent Indians for all seasons; it's one of the interesting quirks of our culture.

And is that what is going on here—are we inventing a "biological" Indian? I think not. If many of the authors (Indian and non-Indian) in the following pages have concluded that American Indians have a message for the rest of us, that decision was reached after examining them on *their* terms—their metaphysics. Sequence is important here. None is foisting a preconceived set of terms, or agenda, on the American Indian. As several authors take pains to explain, insights were gained after a lot of listening, watching, and, in some cases, repudiating distorting and ill-fitting preconceptions. As Vecsey explains, "I started out as an historian looking for the stories about our mistreatment of Indians, in order to understand the darkness of our American heritage." Yet as he became more familiar with their "texts about themselves" he detected there was more going on than he had anticipated, and it was of an instructive nature: "The ways Indians have lived their lives, and the ways they have examined their lives . . . transcend the terrible lessons of Indian-white history. Their existence transcends our contact with them, stretching as it does into deep prehistory, into the glacial past." Vecsey found more than mere chronological depth; he eventually discerned transcendence of the anthropological and "historical" perspective as well: "John Beaver taught me that to Indians (at least the Ojibwa), human life depends upon other-than-human persons who give up their lives so humans can live, and who deserve and demand human respect."

"As I came to know the Indians I began to widen my own ways of thinking," recalls Ridington, in a similar vein. "I saw a connection between people and environment that could not be represented by legal documents alone." Working with Athapaskan Indians for his doctoral dissertation, Ridington at first refused their suggestions that they tell him their authentic stories, which were "much more interesting than the ones I wanted them to make up in response to the set of standardized pictures I had brought with me. . . . These stories were not the scientific data I required." Then he met Japasa ("Chickadee"), who "needed moosemeat, wind, stars, his language, and his relatives, rather than the narrow white [hospital] bed on which I had seen him perched cross-legged, like a tiny bird." By the end of his tale Ridington declares, "When I heard old man Japasa speak in 1964 about his medicine animals, I knew with absolute certainty this man was neither lying nor deluding himself. It was I who indulged in self-delusion when I persisted in asking for data in a form that could not accommodate Beaver Indian reality. In his last days on earth, the old man gave me his vision of that reality." For Peter Iverson, three years of teaching at the Navajo Community College "regenerated my life and my career. It altered how I taught, how I wrote, and what I wanted to write about. . . . I learned about silence and many other things, I believe, during those years. Many of the deepest impressions had nothing to do directly with the research that I ultimately would undertake. Yet in one way or another they influenced clearly what I wanted to say. . . ."

Surely this is not the mode of operation, the method of a ventriloquist—or confidence man. Melville, I think, would be genuinely pleased. Vizenor, embellishing on Gregory Bateson, concludes that "photographers and colonists are the faucets, historians hold the word-gates, and we are the energies of the tribes that run like dreams in a dance with the morning sun over wet meadows." Charles Noble manipulated the word-gates aboard the *Fidèle* on that April Fools' Day over a century ago; we historians hold them today in the essays that follow and in writings elsewhere. Do we truly know how to communicate those tribal dreams and energies? No, not entirely to our satisfaction. But we are genuinely learning; these essays make that clear. It is a momentous, if slow, act of discovery, surely rivaling that of the Christ-Bearer in 1492. And equally as exciting (see F. Turner 1980:118–19; Watts 1985).

1

The Metaphysics of Writing
Indian-White History

CALVIN MARTIN

The writing of Indian-white history by European-Americans is profoundly vitiated by our continuing ignorance of who our Native American subjects are. Those of us in the majority society who scrutinize the
past still have very little idea of *the Indian mind*, of *the Indian thoughtworld*, if one may be permitted to indulge in monolithic terms and
straitjacket Native American cultural diversity for the sake of conven-
ience;[1] we have only the most rudimentary understanding of native
phenomenology, epistemology, and ontology. We presume to document and interpret the history of a people whose perception of the
world for the most part eludes us, whose behavior, as a result, is
enigmatic.

I am referring of course to "ethnocentric bias": the tendency to
interpret another culture using the norms and values of one's own
culture as a point of reference. Admittedly, there is nothing novel about
decrying this tendency among historians, many of whom would doubt-

This essay previously appeared under this title in *Ethnohistory* 26 (Spring 1979 [calen-
dar year Winter 1981]): 153–59, and is reprinted here with the kind permission of the
American Society for Ethnohistory.

Many readers will be disappointed to see the male pronoun employed throughout
the essay, where male and female pronouns should rightly have been used. Thus North
American Indians are referred to in the singular as "him" or "he." It is a mischievous
usage, and I regret having rendered the text as such. Yet I have left it here, in the
reprinting, so to remain faithful to that original text and as a statement on my thinking,
then and now.

I am happy to say that I have avoided such exclusively male usage in the Introduction and Epilogue of this book.

less protest that they are faithfully reproducing the literary record of the Indian-white experience. Fair enough. But we should quit deluding ourselves about the significance and explanatory value of such history, for it is essentially white history: white reality, white thoughtworld. As such it has its place, certainly, but the point is that it has subtly transgressed its explanatory boundaries to pose as the sole or only valid or only serious explanation of what transpired when Indian and white met. White history (excuse the oversimplification)—i.e., retrospective white reality, retrospective white thoughtworld, or even the straightforward repetition of reality as perceived and rendered by white observers over the centuries—must be measured against an Indian history (another forgivable generalization)—an Indian reality, an Indian thoughtworld, as these may be reconstructed using ethnographic analogy. Historians are now in a position to rewrite virtually the entire pageant of Indian-white relations from the perspective of another, equally valid, equally serious reality—an American Indian reality—using the ethnohistorical approach.*

One begins by cultivating an appreciation for the metaphysics of the Native American lifeway. The first principle is that these people traditionally lived in a world dramatically different from the one we perceive, products as we are of the Judeo-Christian, rationalistic, empirical, scientific tradition. The Indian was a participant-observer of Nature, whereas we in the Western cultural tradition tend to be voyeurs. We keep our distance from Nature; we plunge into it enveloped by an arsenal of protective paraphernalia or admire it through a picture frame or scrutinize it through a microscope lens—antiseptically, removed from the Power of it all. In the fourth quarter of the twentieth century we seem still afraid of encountering Pan. Unlike young Ike McCaslin in Faulkner's "The Bear" (1961), we are unwilling or unable, it is debatable which, to rise at dawn and walk into the forest stripped of our civilized accouterments to confront the great primeval Bear. The result is that the Bear has nothing to teach us—about who we are and what is meaningful in life—because the wilderness has been either suffocated ("conquered," "subdued," "tamed," etc.) by Christianity and its technological offspring, or if it has a residue of Power remaining in it we find its speech incomprehensible—unintelligible. We may listen to Nature

*Since publishing this essay several years ago, I have come to believe that the ethnohistorical approach (marrying ethnographic analogy and ethnology with history), while still valuable, is not sufficient in illuminating the "American Indian reality" I refer to. See the Introduction and Epilogue for further thoughts on this issue.

but we cannot make out what it says. Our wilderness has become a proverbial Tower of Babel.

The anthropologist-poet Loren Eiseley, Benjamin Franklin Professor of Anthropology and the History of Science at the University of Pennsylvania at the time of his death in the summer of 1977, eloquently described our peculiar cultural orientation vis-à-vis the rest of creation in an essay titled "The Innocent Fox." He writes of an experience on a desolate stretch of beach with a fox cub whose den he had just spied beneath the overturned hull of a wrecked vessel. He had been looking for a miracle—"I had a growing feeling that miracles were particularly concerned . . . with the animal aspect of things" (1978:57)—and found it cavorting with a fox pup. "It was then I saw the miracle. I saw it because I was hunched at ground level smelling rank of fox, and no longer gazing with upright human arrogance upon the things of this world." Contemplating the fearless pup, Eiseley was reminded of an aphorism: "It has been said repeatedly that one can never, try as he will, get around to the front of the universe. Man is destined to see only its far side, to realize nature only in retreat." Such is the dilemma of Western man, in any case.

Meanwhile, it had become clear the pup wished him to play, and his instincts compelled him to oblige. "On impulse, I picked up clumsily a whiter bone and shook it in teeth that had not entirely forgotten their original purpose. Round and round we tumbled for one ecstatic moment. We were the innocent thing in the midst of the bones, born in the egg, born in the den, born in the dark cave with the stone ax close to hand, born at last in human guise to grow coldly remote in the room with the rifle rack upon the wall."

The miracle had come and gone; the universe had momentarily swung "in some fantastic fashion around to present its face." But the lesson remained and reverberated: "The universe as it begins for all things . . . was, in reality, a child's universe. . . . Sitting on my haunches before a fox den and tumbling about with a chicken bone" Loren Eiseley sensed he, that we, were somehow kinsmen to fox—to Nature. "For just a moment I had held the universe at bay." For just a moment Eiseley had experienced something of the mythic world familiar to North American Indians (1978:63–65).

The chief aim in life in virtually all North American Indian societies was to be saturated with the primordial Power of Nature which seemed to pulsate throughout all creation. Hence the vision quest, the dreaming, the magical songs, the drumming, the use of hallucinogens, the use of ancient tobacco. All of Nature was alive, populated by all sorts of beings—animal persons, plant persons, etc.—beings upon whom the Indian relied for physical and spiritual sustenance. Perhaps most important, he learned who he was by listening to the wisdom of the bear, the beaver, the eagle, the elements, and so forth. Nature talked to him in a way we may never fully comprehend—in a way that Eiseley only glimpsed. He truly lived in another realm. It is essential for the historian to grasp this, to understand that the Indian of the fur trade, the Indian of the Spanish mission system, the Indian of the Tecumseh revolt or Wounded Knee Creek—that all were individuals who lived more or less in what we would call a mythic world.

Robin Ridington, a British Columbia ethnologist, has captured the quintessence of this mythic world in an extraordinarily perceptive passage on the Beaver Indian vision quest. Having just finished describing the young person's experience he asks:

> What does it mean? I can only begin to answer that question just as a Beaver child newly returned from the experience can only begin to learn the answers over the rest of his life. However it is clear that the experience goes far deeper than learning the habits of animals and attaining a rapport useful for hunting in later life. Although it is all these things, it is also and more fundamentally the beginning of a path of seeking to understand his own humanity. They do not find animals in themselves, but rather begin to find themselves in the natures of animals. Each species has its unique and distinctive nature, and people can see in themselves qualities that are most like the qualities of a particular animal species. Animals, besides being themselves, are symbols for men of the varieties of human nature and a man can learn his combination of qualities through getting close to the qualities of animals.[2]

Further on, Ridington explains that around age thirty the Beaver male begins for the first time to see the deeper meanings inherent in his youthful vision quest; he now begins to recognize that he *is*, in fact, the animals of the stories (myths, legends) and of his dreams.

> When a boy-man becomes one of the core adults of a band and has his own children . . . the experience of his pre-adolescent vision quest and post-adolescent maturity come together in a powerful symbolic synthesis. He dreams. Of course he has always dreamed and known that dreams are crystalizations of reality, but these first dreams of maturity are special because they show him his medicines with the clarity of wisdom that adds a

new direction to the innocence of childhood and to the illumination of the vision itself. This clarity and wisdom can only come when he has entered responsibly into the lives of others and learned to see himself in them. He has always in a sense known his medicines, but now he knows what they mean. . . . In the dreams he sees himself as a child living in the bush and knows that the stories he has both taken for granted, and taken literally, are about *him*. When he entered the world of animals as a child he also entered into the stories. The animals he knows and *is*, are the animals of the creation (1971: 122–23).

The Sioux holy man Black Elk recalled a similar visionary experience with the Spirit of the Earth. "I stared at him," he remembered, "for it seemed I knew him somehow; and as I stared, he slowly changed, for he was growing backwards into youth, and when he had become a boy, I knew that he was myself" (Neihardt 1972:25).

One might pause here and reflect on the implications of all this for the writing of Indian-white history. It seems to me that the entire text of that history—all five hundred years of it—must be rendered so as to include this cosmological perspective, only briefly described here, if Indian behavior is to make any sense at all. Surely we have not been remiss in interpreting our joint history from our Western worldview. And yet it cannot be emphasized enough that the Indian simply does not make sense when measured against our cognitive yardstick. Even today the traditional Indian and even the moderately acculturated Indian remain largely a caricature of white ways. So long as he subscribes to the promptings and messages of the mythic world of his ancestors he remains a misfit in ours.

At the same time it should be recognized that under the white dispensation the Indian has had tremendous difficulty communicating with and sustaining his faith in the mythic world described above. When a group of irate Algonkins accosted the French Jesuit, Paul Le Jeune, and declared "'that since prayer has come into our cabins, our former customs are no longer of any service; . . . our dreams and our prophecies are no longer true,—prayer has spoiled everything for us,'" they were expressing what they knew to be the most calamitous consequence of European contact. Le Jeune described his accusers as "obstinate" in this conviction and "furious" with him—on the verge of assaulting him (Thwaites 1896–1901, 24:209–11, 213). Christianity, no doubt in league with European-imported disease, had rendered the mythic world in which they had formerly thrived more or less inarticulate. The anguished lament of Le Jeune's critics rolled down through the centuries to be uttered by an illiterate Naskapi interviewed by the ethnologist Frank Speck in the early years of this century. Basil sensed that "'the times have changed. With the coming of the whites and Christianity the demons of the bush have been pushed back to the north where there is no Christianity. And the conjuror does not exist any more with us, for there is no need of one. Nor is there need for the drum'" (Speck 1935:172).

Speck's informant and Le Jeune's detractors were all talking about the same phenomenon: spiritual powerlessness (Powerlessness). Indeed, the erosion, the dissipation of Indian spiritual power over the centuries and his sometimes desperate efforts to regain his grip on the mythic world—witness a whole series of revitalization movements from the Pueblo revolt under Popé to the message of the Delaware Prophet on the eve of the Pontiac rebellion to the vision of Handsome Lake through the Tecumseh revolt through the Ghost Dance religion to peyotism today—this ebb and flow of Power can in truth be said to form the warp and woof of the Indian-white experience.

European-Americans have in truth fashioned and imposed a new reality, a new thought pattern, a new perception on this continent which in many ways is the antithesis of the traditional mythic reality perceived by the Amerindian. Our European ancestors called into being a new intellectual order on this land which has tended to silence the mythic realm of the Indian, who is thus rendered incapable or handicapped in expressing his preferred epistemology and ontology. One is reminded of the melancholy Columbia River Indian, Chief Broom, in Ken Kesey's novel, *One Flew over the Cuckoo's Nest* (1962), a deaf-mute (self-imposed, admittedly) in the insane asylum ruled over and defined by Big Nurse. Historians might entertain the proposition that the world we have generated and defined for the Indian at large is also a kind of insane asylum in which he is more or less spiritually impotent, frustrating his efforts to communicate with either the mythic world or our Western world. He lives, perforce, in limbo, much as does the young Kiowa, Abel, in N. Scott Momaday's *House Made of Dawn* (1968). Quite possibly the greatest dilemma confronting contemporary Native Americans is "their inability to define themselves to whites," in the words of a spokesman for the North American Indian Ecumenical Movement (an effort at pan-Indian spiritual rejuvenation) (Stanley 1977:242)—because the two, Indian and white, still cleave to what at least appear to be mutually irreconcilable, mutually antagonistic, mutually unintelligible worlds. Professional historians should understand that the Indian is and always has been very much a creature of this other, mythic world, even though it may tend to elude him, compromised as he is by white influence.

The fact is there is a powerful, dual metaphysics—one Indian, one white—inherent in the writing of Indian-white history. To ignore the Indian thoughtworld is to continue writing about ourselves to ourselves. Indian-white history thus becomes white history because it expresses our or our forebears' perception of reality. This sort of historiographic colonialism is no longer tenable. Let us have the courage and humility to recognize another reality to what happened between Indians and whites. The place to begin is by appreciating the mythic world outlined above—but that is only a start. What we will emerge with, years hence, is a bicultural view of the dynamics of the fur trade, of King Philip's War, of Indian Removal, of the Plains Indian Wars—of the whole sweep of it all.

There is more involved here than antiquarian titillation. Historians can lead the way in dismantling the white paternalistic mind-set, that in its expression has always crippled the Indian, by admitting that there is another legitimate way of interpreting our mutual past—by admitting that Indian-white history is the process of two thoughtworlds that at the time were more often than not mutually unintelligible. Surely this is the most poignant message of Indian-white relations: five hundred years of talking past each other, of mutual incomprehension. Although the situation still prevails it may not still be inevitable, as it perhaps was the majority of the time. It comes down to this: If we are to understand the contemporary Indian we must first understand the historic Indian. That means giving him an historic voice—his own this time, not the ventriloquist's. And that will take us back to 1492 again, to the beaches of San Salvador, where the Western world allegedly discovered *los Indios*. It is a piece of fiction, of course: the West did not "discover" the Indian then; it discovered the European in caricature. That is where the discontinuity began, when our forefathers rejected the Indian claim to a legitimate vision of existence as a burlesque, a parody of the "true" and "divinely sanctioned" reality. (Indians felt similarly about the European thoughtworld, incidentally.) The time is auspicious to equip ourselves with the linguist's and ethnologist's tools and to return to the sources and find the Indian as he defined himself and his world. Perhaps in the

process of finding him we will discern another meaning for this land, as
well. In a very real sense the meaning of the New World still awaits our
discovery.

Notes

1. *The White Man's Indian: Images of the American Indian from Columbus to the
Present*, by Robert F. Berkhofer, Jr. (1978) is highly recommended as a stimulating and
erudite study of Native Americans—*the Indian*—in five hundred years of white imagination. See, in particular, his epilogue (pp. 195–97).

By referring to Native Americans as *an Indian* collectivity I am in a sense, I suppose,
perpetuating a pernicious image and stereotype of these people, who were and are in
many respects culturally and socially diverse. I agree with Berkhofer's sentiments on
this—that *the Indian* is an artifact of white imagination. But Berkhofer and I are
talking about two fundamentally different issues: he is interested primarily in docu-
menting the often fanciful, white ethnocentric image of Native Americans, whereas I
am trying to install a more ethnographically informed image in the minds of historians.
I doubt that Berkhofer would deny that it is possible and under certain didactic
conditions desirable to refer to and discuss an overarching cosmology, or worldview,
seemingly distinctive to Native American societies—all of them—just as one may
describe Western thinking in similarly gross terms. Let it be understood, then, that the
collective *Indian worldview* described in these pages is a convenient and candidly
artificial abstraction, or distillation, of certain pivotal sentiments and a distinctive
outlook on life shared by the members of these legion societies.

2. Ridington tells me it is now clear to him that Beaver children of both sexes engage
in the vision quest.

2

Cultural Pluralism Versus Ethnocentrism in the New Indian History

ROBERT F. BERKHOFER, JR.

When I entered the field of American Indian history as a graduate student in the 1950s, I was told by a noted historian of the United States's past that Indian history was not part of American history. If I persisted in writing a dissertation on Protestant missionaries to the American Indians from the 1770s to the 1860s, he said, I would never gain acceptance in my chosen profession of American history. Even though that historian wrote about Indians as peripheral to his interest in frontier whites, he was probably correct that I should have written about a topic more traditional to the profession at that time, if I wished a good job and scholarly recognition. Certainly the person who classified completed dissertations for listing in *Dissertation Abstracts* agreed with the noted historian. Although I requested that my dissertation be listed under American religious history, it was placed under the anthropology heading. The anonymous classifier knew better than I that anthropologists, not historians, studied Indians.

Since then Indians have become a legitimate concern of the historical profession. In fact, the publication of books on Indian history by historians has become so common that it resembles a cottage industry. One of the major journals in the history profession now lists completed dissertations in American Indian history under that heading, so numerous are doctoral studies in the field. What happened in the last quarter century that made for such a dramatic reversal in the historical profession that allows writing on Indian history to advance from a marginal topic at best to one in the mainstream of historical thinking and research? Certainly the past itself has not changed so drastically as to warrant such a reevaluation of Indians as subject matter. Surely, the emergence of the Third World to prominence and the claims of minority persons in America's cities to full-fledged citizenship broadened professional historians' perspectives to include peoples in the United States's past hitherto excluded entirely from the history books or relegated to the background, in the march of American society to industrial might and world power. American historians, in general, turned more to the study of Indians when they noticed also blacks, women, ethnics, and other groups omitted from the mainstream of Anglo-American history.[1]

The application of new ideals of cultural pluralism came to the history of the American Indians first in ethnohistory and then in what I christened the New Indian History.[2] Both ethnohistory and the New Indian History aim to see beyond traditional white prejudices and scholarly specialities so as to portray native peoples in their own right, acting for their own reasons in light of their own cultural norms and values. To accomplish this goal the New Indian historians search beyond the traditional white-produced documents of past Indian contact to locate new sources in oral history and artifact. Moreover, the New Indian historians try to tell the history of Indian tribespeople not in relation to white visions, policies, and confrontations but as integral to the tribe itself. This new Indian-centered history moves Indian actors to the front of their historical stage, as opposed to subordinating them to be simple background actors reacting to white expansion. Thus the New Indian History seeks the dynamics of a tribe's history before white contact and then proceeds with how its leaders and others coped creatively with the altered circumstances of the tribe over time. Such history, in opposition to the traditional view of the role of Indians in United States history, does not begin with white contact, does not last only so long as whites confront a tribe in their acquisition of its lands, and does not end when the tribal members scatter, remove, endure as reservation communities, or are left to shift for themselves in modern times. The change of focus lengthens the time span of Indian history as it puts Indian actors in the forefront of the action. Along with these altered approaches to the sources and nature of the story goes a changed moral outlook. Not only do the New Indian historians hope to eliminate the older ethnocentrism so common in the earlier history of frontier conflict between Indians and white Americans, but they also bring a moral outlook neutral or sympathetic to the Indian side of the story. The goals of the New Indian History therefore can be said to embrace moral as well as methodological ends in the effort to be fairer in the portrayal of Indians in their own history and American history in general.

By espousing an ideal of cultural pluralism as the heart of its method and morality, however, the New Indian History falls prey to the contradictions between that principle's cognitive and ethical dimensions. Moral sympathies assume ethical commitments that transcend the very cultural bounds presupposed in the idea of cultural pluralism. Adoption of an Indian "viewpoint" questions the fundamental assumptions upon which the New Indian historians practice their craft and understand the past. As the New Indian historians attempt to eliminate the ethnocentrism of the older approach to Indians and history, they therefore pose certain dilemmas of interpretation for themselves.

Even the meaning of the phrase "American Indian history" shows the dilemmas of cross-cultural interpretation. The words *American*, *Indian*, and *history* are all non-Indian in origin, and so the conceptions behind those words that designate the very subject matter of what we seek to understand are grounded in Anglo-American thinking and its larger context in Western civilization. Each of the words has its own history and a cultural context that is basic to its conceptualization and understanding. The big question is: To what extent can the meaning of these words be changed to reflect the goals of the New Indian History and to what extent must the achievements of the New Indian History remain rooted in the culture of the professional historian?

Although *American(s)* originally referred in European languages to all the native inhabitants of the Western Hemisphere and later to the white Europeans as well who settled (or invaded, depending upon one's interpretation), *American* was narrowed by the citizens of the newly-independent United States of America to mean themselves as opposed to the other Americans of the hemisphere. Thus the phrase "American Indian history" has two definitions today in the minds of Europeans and even Canadians and Mexicans. *America* took on the dual meaning of the space of the United States as well as of the New World continents. *American* Indians are thus those Native Americans who reside in the bounds of what was and is the United States, as opposed to, say, Canada and Mexico. The geography of American Indian history follows the white-originated conceptions of nationalism. Just as the European nations once partitioned the New World according to their political orientations and imperial ambitions, so modern historians now divide American Indian history by contemporary national boundaries and by tribes—or what once were called *nations*. Even the concept of tribe derives from a double sort of ethnocentrism combined with the power of military force and political negotiation. Efforts to pass beyond such nationalistic biases create problems of focus and subject in the structure of the historical narrative.

In its most ethnocentric usage, *American* meant the ideal Anglo-American citizen of the United States. Whether this meaning derived from ideals of racism or merely ethnocentrism, it always measured other persons by the yardstick of middle-class American values of religion, politics, family life, education, and appearance. Thus *Indian* referred to those people deficient at best and antagonistic at worst to what Americans were supposed to be, ideally. As a result, native tribespeople needed, according to this definition of Americanism, to be converted to the ideal life through mission example or military force. Either way, they would be eliminated from American society figuratively, if the policy worked, or literally, if necessary, to preserve the ideal America envisioned according to middle-class values. Native children were kidnapped from their homes to be transformed into such ideal Americans; adult natives were forced upon reservations or even killed in the name of Americanization. I first came across this zeal to Americanize native tribespeople in the letters of Protestant missionaries I read for my dissertation. Later I discovered that such attitudes permeated Anglo-American thinking. It is this meaning of *American*, of course, that the New Indian historians hope most to repudiate morally, conceptually, and methodologically in their writings.[3]

The term *Indian* is a word of European origin as well. The many tribal peoples who lived in the area that became the United States and elsewhere in the Western Hemisphere did not know themselves as a collective entity. These peoples, like societies everywhere, usually referred to their own group as "the people" or "true people." Only the contact between European people and Native American people caused both "sides" to recognize that the original people of the Western Hemisphere should bear the misnomer, *Indian*, as Columbus applied it to them, in his belief that he had encountered inhabitants near Japan. If the Indians had no collective reference for each other, then what is the collectivity that historians gather together under the rubric of American Indian history? The very term conceals the nature of tribal reality from the historical observer. To change the terminology to *Indians* or *Native Americans* mitigates without solving the problem of reference. The who and where of the New Indian History is still affected by the traditional white-originated conceptualization of the Indian derived from national-istic biases.[4]

The problem remains in the idea of a tribe. Who are the historical actors designated a *tribe*? How and when did they come to be denominated and delineated as that entity? I first learned of these difficulties late one night at the Library of Congress when I was reading *Proceedings of the Commissioners of Indian Affairs, Appointed by Law for the Extinguishment of Indian Titles in the State of New York* (New York [State] Commissioners of Indian Affairs 1861). The accounts of the treaty proceedings after the American Revolution spoke of tribes and chiefs in negotiations and as signatories, but I knew many of these treaties were subsequently repudiated by other chiefs of the same tribe or other tribes. I soon learned there was a consistent pattern of factionalism that explained the divisions of the so-called tribes and their alliances with English and American officials.[5] Ever since, I have been wary of who is said to be a chief, who is said to be represented, and what is said to be represented. The internal politics of the tribe led me to reconsider what was generally designated a tribe. It was not as simple as implied by the nicely delimited areas on maps in history and anthropology books of the 1950s. The formation and continuation of what came to be called a specific tribe has its own history, still far too little explored.[6] Often tribal peoples received their modern-day white-designated names from their native enemies telling white explorers, officials, and others about tribal societies to the west, inland, or elsewhere.

Which persons constituted a tribe and how they saw themselves had its own history which became hypostatized, first, by white contact and confrontation, then on official maps, and subsequently in the books of anthropologists and historians. Thus a history of a tribe has to cope with the changing boundaries of ethnic identity as well as territorial base over time. We cannot presume aboriginal genesis of a tribe any more than we can assume that some stable once-and-for-all designation refers to a specific kind of society. In fact, the ethnocentrism of a tribal people in combination with the ethnocentrism of other tribal and Euro-American peoples determined who constituted a tribe as an ethnic identity. The power of the respective peoples vis-à-vis each other then delimited the territory and at times the lifestyles of what came to be called a tribe. Thus the historical space as well as the tribe itself are the objects of research, for the semantics of tribal identity was created through and by history.[7]

Even the word *history* reveals its ethnocentric or provincial origins when we look at its use. The way we use *history* implies a particular manner of conceiving of the past and the fashion in which we write about it. The ambiguity of the word in English implies that the past and the way we look at it are the same. History-as-once-lived and history-as-now-understood-and-written are described by the same word, yet they are very different undertakings. The merging of the past-as-once-lived and the past-as-now-conceived involves assumptions specific to our culture and time, namely: the past was real and can be represented in a way that corresponds to that reality; the reality was dynamic and not static; the reality was factual according to our criteria, and not mythical; finally, the reality was objective enough to be readily understood now, in the same manner and by all human beings. Thus the past is *re-presented* and *re-created* in modern professional or formal history-writing. Given current practices of the history profession, formal history presumes that there is one basic, external, and real flow of events in the past-as-once-lived that can be fitted into one story about that flow. This formal history also presumes that events exist apart from the interpreters' minds, so the story seems to be told as if from an omniscient, godlike view that can be considered objective and impartial.[8]

Cultural pluralism challenges all of these premises. Plurality of viewpoints, of stories, of social realities (and, in effect, of realities), and of cognitive styles pervades modern social understanding. Furthermore, the moral ideal of cultural pluralism asserts that such plurality ought to pervade the understanding of such understandings. In these senses variant histories no longer add up to one flowing narrative, and understanding, of the past. No amount of further "research" will compromise the different ways of looking at the past. Under this view, the past-as-once-lived and the past-as-now-conceived are harder to synthesize into history-as-written; the various histories cannot become versions of just one history. Thus the use of cultural pluralism as moral guide challenges, through cultural pluralism as intellectual fact, the traditional understanding and doing of history as ethnocentric.

If the New Indian historians aim to change the meaning of *American* and *Indian* in American Indian history, must they not also transform the way we understand and practice *history*? The dilemmas of achieving a New Indian History are revealed in the problem of how the historian plots the tale told. From whose viewpoint should the narrative be cast? How should the events be ordered: a triumphal march of progress, a tragic decline or loss of community, or some other customary narrative plot in history? Should the tone of the historian be sardonic, ironic, romantic, tragic, or humorous regardless of the explicit plot? From whose categories of reality should the facts of history be derived? Do these culturally biased categories of reality determine the facts and therefore the nature of history-as-conceived and -as-written? If all would allow that the older history was extremely ethnocentric, can the New Indian History be radically pluralistic?

At its most extreme, the New Indian History would redefine the ordering of events in past time and even what constituted facts in the past-as-once-lived. American Indian history might then be defined as some tribal people said it was. It would entail the adoption of a different time sense, and an acceptance of the way some tribal people say their cosmos was (and is). Some spokespeople for such a view posit a "primal mind," to use Jamake Highwater's phrase. Such an approach to the native peoples of America seems to be a mirror image of the extreme ethnocentrism of the white citizens who so long dominated the American history books, for it postulates a common outlook or "Indian consciousness" that shaped all native peoples. Moreover, that outlook denies any understanding of formal history as we know it in favor of a mythic understanding and a radically different sense of time that stresses the eternal and the recurrent over the dynamic and temporal.[9]

Without predicating such a primal mind, one can see the difficulties of cross-cultural history if one turns to the role of origin stories in the history of a tribe. Whether traditional stories of a tribe's origins should be accepted as factual in regard to those origins is a question that quickly shows the different presuppositions about the nature of reality that underlie formal, or professional history in our society, versus folk, or native traditional, history. The first volume of *Navajo History*, issued by the Navajo Curriculum Center (Yazzie 1971), is a version of that society's stories of previous worlds and the beginnings of the Navajo people themselves, their division into clans, and the peopling of neighboring regions by other tribes. Should these stories be accepted as the prehistory of the Navajo or do they belong to the realm of mythology? The issues are summarized well, I think, in a long-standing argument that I have with a well-known Indian scholar. To make his point about the reliability of Indian origin stories he argues thus about the Puritans: the Puritans believed in the Christian Bible as fact; in order to understand the Puritans one must therefore understand the Bible. He and I agree on these points. We part ways on his conclusion: if the Puritans accepted the Bible as factual early history, then we too must accept the

Bible as a factual account of Christian prehistory. I think our differences on this point show the limits of cross-cultural cognition as opposed to cross-cultural ethics. One can believe that others believe certain things as facts, but one need not accept those versions of the past as factual in one's own cognitive system, even if one extends moral sympathy and understanding. In that sense, I suppose one ethnocentricity must be juxtaposed with another, and so one form of history must be accepted over another with all its implications for factuality and the ordering of past reality.[10] For this reason some have argued that professional, or formal history, is a form of bourgeois perception that arose during the late eighteenth century and continues today. The historical narrative and the novel both used some of the same assumptions about the nature of reality, the mode of narrative development, and the acceptable form of explanation. On these points, Marxist and non-Marxist formal history share assumptions about ordering the past, although they may diverge radically on the moral judgments embodied in the interpretation of that past.

That moral judgments need not alter the nature or focus of the narrative can be seen in some recent books on Indian history. Moral sympathy for the plight of the Indians in the face of Anglo-American expansion does not automatically transform the focus of the story from white to Indian actors, a major goal of the new Indian-centered history. In the first part of his highly acclaimed *Invasion of America* (1975), Francis Jennings argues at length for revised moral judgments on Puritan and Indian interaction, as well as for greater attention to the native participants in the drama of white-Indian relations. He accuses the Puritan leaders of total duplicity in their dealings with the native tribal leaders, but he rarely tells us who those leaders were, let alone what they were doing to guide the destiny of their tribespeople during the contest for the territory of New England. In the latter regard, Alden Vaughan's *New England Frontier* (1965), which Jennings accuses of justifying the Puritan conquests, offers far more information than Jennings does regarding who was who among native leaders and what they were doing to confront Puritan expansion.[11]

When we turn to intertribal history or the history of all American Indians, the difficulties of applying the goals of Indian-centered history are only compounded. Moral outrage or moral neutrality serves no better to shift the focus of the narrative from white policies and actions than does the older ethnocentric stress on the march of white society westward. Whether in textbook or in classroom, it is difficult to avoid periodization according to white policy and expansion and, therefore, a fundamental presentation from a white perspective in the end according to white historical practices. Although Arrell Gibson adds material on the archeological, linguistic, and religious foundations of Indian societies in his *American Indian: Prehistory to Present* (1980), the majority of his story embraces the traditional divisions by European colonial powers and subsequent periodization by United States policy changes. Likewise, *Subjugation and Dishonor: A Brief History of the Travail of the Native Americans* (1981), by Philip Weeks and James B. Gidney, whose title suggests its sympathies, nevertheless follows the traditional time frame common to (white) professional Indian history. Models not morals dominate these histories as they must if the writers would produce history as we know it, with narrative development supplied by some sort of central focus to join together the parts of the story. Perhaps the most innovative effort to break out of this traditional paradigm, with its problem of focus, is Edward Spicer's *Short History of the Indians of the United States* (1969). As the title implies, Spicer tries to concentrate upon the entire American population, from aboriginal to contemporary times, by focusing upon approximately concurrent events in many native societies, between 1540 and 1967. Although he does not always succeed in wresting the history of Native Americans from white policies and activities, he does show how far an attempt to write an Indian-centered history of all native tribes can go. If it is difficult to move Indian actors to the center of the historical stage in tribal and intertribal history, it is far harder to fit Indians into United States history in general, for the focus of such history does not even pretend to revolve about native tribespeople. At best, they are pulled in as supporting actors to demonstrate a larger point about morality, foreign policy, or politics, according to the purposes of the author. In this sense, Indians suffer the same disadvantages of focus in history common to all minorities.[12]

The discussion so far only hints at the dilemmas in eliminating ethnocentrism from formal history as practiced by professional historians today. Yet can any less be called for than the complete overturning of the traditional paradigm of historical understanding if a truly New Indian History is to achieve a cross-cultural history that embraces as well as sympathizes with Indian viewpoints? Such efforts so far have encountered limits imposed by the premises of reality and the focal theme demanded by the modern conception of formal history. Only the end of writing formal history as we know it can truly accomplish the cross-cultural goals implied by the metaphysics of writing Indian history. Can we, however, throw out the ethnocentric bathwater of Indian history without also tossing out the baby of history? While cultural pluralism expanded the horizons of traditional history and historians, it also placed certain conceptual constraints upon its transformation. History-as-understanding and history-writing are parts of specific cultures, hence ethnocentric in their presuppositions about the nature and ordering of the past-as-lived. Without these constraints, there can be no formal history-as-now-understood; with those constraints there can be no New Indian History as some envision its larger goals of cross-cultural respect and understanding.

Notes

1. Have Indians, however, been as significant as blacks in history books or in making a "name" for a historian? Is the Civil War more important than the French and Indian War in determining the destiny of Anglo-Americans? The former generally receives far more extensive treatment in historical surveys of the American past than the latter.

2. I use this term in my essay, "The Political Context of a New Indian History" (1971). A recent essay on ethnohistory by James Axtell, in chapter 1 of *The European and the Indian* (1981), provides references to theoretical articles and statements in the field.

3. The specific word "America" derives from Amerigo Vespucci. The evolution of this term is described briefly in my book, *The White Man's Indian* (1978), which treats white understandings of Native Americans. My research into missionary letters culminated in *Salvation and the Savage* (1965). Interestingly, in light of the goals of the New Indian History, I was not allowed by the editor at that press to put the term *savage* in quotation marks or italics, to signify the ironic or peculiar use of the word for the Indian.

4. I have explored some of the implications and difficulties of the effort to eliminate the ethnocentrism of the traditional Turnerian approach to the American frontier in "The North American Frontier as Process and Context" (1981). Neither a concentration upon stages of acculturation as found in American anthropology in the 1950s, nor the repudiation of white domination of the acculturative process and the corresponding stress on the creativity of the dominated under acculturation in the 1960s, nor even the exploration of the implications of the Capitalist World-System in our decade really solves the problem of designating the who and where of tribal peoples without recourse to white-based concepts of nationalism and political understanding, much as their moral proclivities might diverge.

5. My thinking on the post-Revolutionary peace treaties eventuated in "Barrier to Settlement: British Indian Policy in the Old Northwest, 1783–1794" (1969).

6. A notable exception is James A. Clifton's *Prairie People* (1977)

7. See, for example, Charles Hudson's *Catawba Nation* (1970), which traces through history the definition of that tribe.

8. Some of the presuppositions of formal history today are exposed in *The Writing of History* (Canary and Kozicki 1978), especially in the essays by Hayden White and Louis Mink.

9. Jamake Highwater's *Primal Mind: Vision and Reality in Indian America* (1981) is an interesting and controversial statement of its theme. Compare the past-as-lived and the past-as-interpreted in *A Basic Call to Consciousness: The Hau de no sau nee Address to the Western World* (Akwesasne Notes 1978), which postulates "a consciousness of the Sacred Web of Life in the Universe" common to all peoples 2500 or more years ago and still kept alive by tribal peoples around the world today.

10. Particularly pertinent to this point are the remarks of Indian scholar Dave Warren on the "Indian Weltanshaung" paraphrased in *Red Men and Hat-Wearers*: "[I]n the Indian world view, the past is dominated by concern with the origin and destiny of the people. . . . To him the Indian world view of history approaches a metaphysical level in which statements and events are justified by means of myths, creation legends, and stories coming directly from the tribe. To explain the tribe's history, then, demands a unique set of terms and references which may not be familiar to non-Indian scholars" (Tyler 1976:135). Contrast the various chapters of this book by white scholars with the brief section on history by Indian scholars (Tyler 1976:135-37).

The tribal histories produced by the tribes themselves embrace a wide range of historical presuppositions about the past-as-lived and the past-as-interpreted and -as-written.

Peter J. Powell, in *Sweet Medicine* (1969), offers an interesting combination of Christian and Cheyenne religious commitment and formal and oral history that shows both the possibilities and limits of cross-cultural history models. Note particularly the poignant introduction, the overall organization, and the specific contents of each chapter.

11. Vaughan addresses the criticisms of his book in a long introduction to a new edition, published in 1979. It is instructive on what is at issue in the conflicts over morality and facts in Indian history; in addition, the volume provides an excellent bibliography on both sides of the argument as it pertains to New England history.

12. Gary B. Nash, in *Red, White and Black* (1974), offers an ambitious effort to incorporate Native Americans and Afro-Americans into colonial history with Euro-Americans. The latter are treated at far less length than the former two peoples, but the framework of the story remains traditional.

Dorothy V. Jones, in *License for Empire* (1982), exemplifies the reorientation to the Revolutionary period we get from the fusion of Native American with European and United States diplomacy.

I have pointed out some of the difficulties of understanding the history of Indians as a minority, particularly in relation to the overall history of the United States, in "Native Americans and United States History" (1973).

3

American Indians
and American History

NEAL SALISBURY

When Europeans began their invasion of America, they sought to understand, legitimize, and elevate their actions through a mythology in which they juxtaposed themselves as "civilized" Christians to the "savage," heathen natives. In so doing they maximized the differences between themselves and the Indians in moral, biological, and cultural terms. It is not surprising that these myths informed historical as well as first-hand and imaginative representations of Indian-white relations for several centuries; what is surprising is their staying power among contemporary scholars supposedly emancipated from the religious and racial superstitions of the past. For while the convention of distinguishing Indians and whites as two different species of humanity is largely outmoded, a vestige of it survives in the assumption that Indians have not participated in "history," except in their encounters with the whites who actually "made" that history.

Many historians, anthropologists, and archeologists work from a methodological inconsistency which cannot be justified by recourse to any currently acceptable scientific or humanistic premises, one which implies that Indians lack not only a past of their own but a present and a future as well. This implication might bear debating were it not for the wealth of evidence against it, much of it produced by these very scholars. At the heart of the inconsistency is the scholars' inability to break their myth-rooted habits once and for all and, instead, approach Indian

The author wishes to thank Dana Salisbury for her constructive comments on an earlier draft of this essay.

history as historians supposedly approach other subjects, that is, by envisioning events in past time as occurring in multifaceted contexts, and by bearing in mind that history consists, quite simply, of the processes of change and continuity over time, processes from which no human or collection of humans can be exempt. This means, first, casting aside the patently ahistorical notions of "prehistory," "ethnographic present," "historical baseline," and "protohistory," all of which qualitatively differentiate the Native American past from the European past and prevent us from seeing it on its own terms and as a continuum. By the same token it means laying aside the assumption that linguistic, cultural, and political boundaries served to isolate Native Americans from one another until Europeans came along and obliged them to interact. Scholars do not make such assumptions about other people in the absence of supporting evidence; yet they make them about Indians without ever looking for evidence. In so doing they fragment native people in space just as, in the previous case, they do so in time. Finally, it means retaining the complexity of each people's historical background when describing relations between Europeans and Native Americans rather than flattening them into monolithic "whites" and atomized but equally simplified "Indians."

The task for scholars is to come to terms with Native American history in its entirety, as revealed in archeological, oral, documentary, iconographic, ethnographic, and all other forms of evidence. What would be the outlines of a history based on this record? A good start was made more than a decade ago by D'Arcy McNickle in a generally overlooked essay, "Americans Called Indians," in which he distinguished New World "beginnings," an "Archaic Mode," the onset of agriculture, and a transition "from prehistory to history" (1971). Accounting for the additional evidence and interpretation produced since McNickle wrote, particularly by archeologists and ethnohistorians, it is possible to build on his work and identify five distinct phases based on the varying relationships of indigenous peoples with external—environmental and cultural—influences. Because of regional and local variations and exceptions, not to mention vast lacunae in the evidence, the chronology of this outline is intended to be neither precise nor final. Its purpose is rather to encourage thinking and discussion about the Indian experience in historical terms.

The earliest of these phases might be termed the "Beringian" (ca. 40,000 to 12,000 B.C.), for it centers on the now-submerged Bering Land Bridge that linked Siberia and Alaska during most of the final stage

(Wisconsin) of the last Ice Age. It was during Wisconsin times that nomadic Siberian hunting bands, existing at the very margins of an expanding Eurasian population, began crossing into what is now Alaska, in pursuit of such familiar big-game mammals as reindeer, caribou, long-horned bison, and woolly mammoths. Though hints of earlier human activity throughout the hemisphere have been found, the oldest in-context evidence is a kill site about 27,000 years old at Old Crow Flats, Alaska. Eight thousand years later, if not before, some of these people had moved with their favored prey beyond the limits of glaciation, as evidenced by an extensive campsite uncovered at Mead-owcroft Shelter in eastern Pennsylvania. Despite having moved this far, Beringian peoples continued to utilize the tool kits and hunting me-thods of their Siberian ancestors, who in turn had drawn on traditions extending both to East Asia and to Europe and the Near East. In every sense, the "discovery" of the New World was in reality the expansion of the Old. Yet it did serve to carry many of the migrating bands into new environments in which their descendants would fashion their own distinctive cultures.

A second, or Paleo-Indian, phase of Native American history (ca. 12,000 to 6,000 B.C.) is marked by the appearance all over the continent (and indeed the hemisphere) of a number of distinctively New World adaptations and innovations. The most significant technological devel-opment was the variety of delicately flaked and "fluted" points for spears and other projectiles, manufactured in special camps near rich quarries. This systematic use of native materials reflects a new relation-ship between humans and their American environments. The points are found in association with—often still embedded in—familiar Pleisto-cene mammals at large kill sites. Some of the sites were used for several millennia, indicating that cyclical movements within delimited territo-ries had replaced Beringian nomadism. The size of both the base camps and the flint-processing camps, and the evidence that entire herds were now being trapped and slain, shows that Paleo-Indian bands were larger and more complexly organized than their forerunners. Finally, variations of the fluted point and associated subsistence and settlement patterns are found all over the continent, indicating that while Eurasian influences continued to operate, a distinctively Native American culture was beginning to emerge.

That emergence was propelled by the rapid environmental changes marking the end of the Ice Age. Over the last four millennia of the Paleo-Indian phase, the earth's climate grew warmer and drier, bringing about the major regional environments and the range of flora and fauna that have prevailed, except where disturbed by humans, until now. Though the casualties of these changes included the great Pleistocene mammals upon which the Paleo-Indians were so dependent, change was in the long run enormously advantageous for the human inhabitants.

During the Archaic phase (ca. 6,000 to 500 B.C.), autonomous, kin-based, egalitarian bands moved into virtually every ecological niche and learned to exploit the full range of available resources in each through carefully calculated seasonal rounds. Though the results varied from the arid deserts of the west to the lush forests of the east, there was everywhere a tendency toward larger populations, central village sites occupied for much of the year, and the proliferation of bands as new groups split off from older, overpopulated ones. Moreover, regional exchange networks made possible the distribution of technology, subsistence practices, local materials, and religious ideas over vast distances so that cultural boundaries transcended those based on politics, ethnicity, and language. Archeologists are now coming to recognize that the Archaic phase had a fairly uniform, continent-wide development. The descendants of Siberian nomads had made North America their own and were increasingly recognizable as "a people."

The combination of increasing populations and the meshing of exchange networks with those of Mesoamerica, where agriculture, urbanization, and state-level social-political organization had been established, eventually led to the modification of, and crises within, many Archaic societies. What distinguishes the post-Archaic phase (ca. 500 B.C. to A.D. 1500) above all is the variety of strategies employed by Native North Americans to maintain traditional norms in the face of demographic and environmental pressures and Mesoamerican cultural influences, and the relative success of those strategies. During the first three centuries A.D., groups of eastern communities established cult-based "Hopewellian" and other networks through which raw materials and finished goods moved. As a result, members maintained their sedentary settlements in the face of growing populations and limited or varying food resources. The networks eventually grew so elaborate that elite administrators arose to oversee them. For Hopewellian communities in the northeast, the tendencies toward centralization and stratification apparently proved too high a price to pay, for the participants eventually abandoned the networks, recovered their autonomy, and reverted to smaller-scale reciprocal exchanges. Elsewhere, especially in the southeast, Hopewellian modes of redistribution were intensified, giving rise to highly stratified and centralized Mississippian chiefdoms of the type encountered by de Soto and other Europeans in the sixteenth century. Yet even the Mississippian tendency had limits, imposed by some combination of environmental constraints and cultural preferences, which are most clearly revealed in the thirteenth-century decline of Cahokia, pre-Columbian North America's only urban marketing center.

Despite the obvious advantages of agriculture for coping with problems of population increase, post-Archaic Americans never became so dependent on it as to alter entirely their traditional lifeways. The modern obsession with the "inevitability of progress" has led some to speak of an "agricultural revolution," overlooking the facts that plant domestication remained a subsidiary subsistence activity, even where a "revolution" was possible, for up to a millennium after its introduction, and that a major development in hunting—the introduction of the bow and arrow—more or less coincided with the shift to agriculture as a primary subsistence activity in most of North America. Thus Native Americans maintained the subsistence diversity and, hence, the balanced relationship with their natural environments that had enabled them to prosper since Archaic times.

Where environmental constraints precluded such diversity by single groups, it was maintained through reciprocal exchanges between hunters and farmers. This is especially apparent at the perimeters of the agricultural zone in the northeast, Plains, and southwest. As with the Archaic phase, but on an even larger scale, evidence from all regions points increasingly to patterns of far-flung exchange, supra-local political association or integration, and, in some areas, warfare. Even the "tribelets" of California are no longer viewed by archeologists as the simple, self-contained entities once postulated by A. L. Kroeber and others. As the post-Archaic phase drew to a close, North America was a land of about ten million people and characterized by a vast array of social and political arrangements, languages, customs, and beliefs. Moreover, most individuals identified themselves first as members of lineal families and then, through those families, as members of economic-political-religious communities in which everyone participated through tradition-carved roles and activities. But identification with the particular and the traditional was simply the means which enabled Native Americans to expand their cultural horizons almost indefinitely without forgetting who they were and whence they had come—to be simultaneously many people and one.

The maintenance of equilibrium by communities with their natural and social environments and their pasts has continued to characterize Native Americans since the onset of the European phase (ca. A.D. 1500 to present). Indians initially approached European visitors as they customarily approached strangers, with offers of hospitality and exchange. In many cases, disillusionment came quickly when the visitors took advantage of the hospitality to kidnap and/or inflict violence on their hosts. In other cases, initial exchanges led native groups into complex trade arrangements which lasted for years, decades, or centuries, often leading to radical cultural changes, but eventually ending when the furbearing animal populations were exterminated or when Europeans developed other priorities. Indigenous trade routes and relationships facilitated not only the activities of explorers and traders but the spread of diseases for which Native Americans lacked immunities and which rendered them and their lands vulnerable to conquest.

The variety of Indian responses to European-imposed conditions over the subsequent five centuries have been efforts to locate the proper balance between past and present, and between indigenous tradition and foreign innovation, in dealing with the colonizers. A few well-known examples will suffice to illustrate the range of these responses: resistance movements, such as those led by Pontiac and Tecumseh; the military and diplomatic strategies of the Creek and Iroquois during the colonial period; the shift to equestrian nomadism by tribes driven onto the Plains by an expanding fur trade; the "compartmentalized" posture of the Pueblos; the Ghost Dance and peyote movements. Even the Cherokee in the early nineteenth century, though deeply divided in their attitudes toward white political and cultural hegemony, agreed that preserving their nation's integrity and autonomy in the face of expansionist pressure was the highest priority. Similar motives, however misguided or futile, have characterized other "progressives" before and since. The point is that the disruptions and destruction of peoples and their ways of life over the past five centuries have deterred few surviving natives from their identities as Indians.

However, the European phase can be fully understood only by examining the processes that propelled the invaders as well as the invaded. Historians of Western Europe have customarily described the early modern period (roughly the fifteenth century through the eighteenth) in terms of its dominant institutions and most dynamic developments—the Renaissance, the Reformation, the rise of nation-states, and the commercial and maritime revolutions. Against this background, expan-

sion into the Americas and the overrunning of native people is easily
understood in terms of dynastic and religious rivalries, and desires for
material and spiritual fulfillment. And as an explanation for the dynamics of Indian-white relations, the customary approach makes sense,
since the contrasts between expanding Europe and the kin-based, face-
to-face communities of North America could not be more striking. But
social historians during the past few decades have presented quite a
different picture of early modern Europe and the preceding late medieval period. The world they describe consisted primarily of peasants
living at the level of subsistence, oriented toward kin and local communities, exchanging goods through barter, and believing in a wide range
of sources of supernatural power, unconnected, if not actually counter,
to Christian teachings. Though there was obviously a wealth of difference between a traditional village in France or Ireland and one in
Huron or Cherokee country, what these historians describe suggests a
Western Europe with striking parallels to North America and one
hardly expansive in its ambitions or potential.

Of course, both historical portraits of Western Europe are accurate
and must be seen in combination to gain a full picture of the region just
before and during its overseas expansion. For it is internal conflict that
underlies early modern Europe's domestic history *and* its overseas
expansion. Spurred by the kind of population growth in relation to
resources which North Americans had likewise confronted, "progressive" elements in Western European society sought to conquer and
thereby escape from traditional Europe, with its array of seemingly
static customs and beliefs, as they groped toward a new order. Their
efforts both impelled overseas expansion and shaped the attitudes and
policies of colonizers toward the people they encountered. For example,
the lifting of customary restraints on the quest for wealth and on the
uses of land and labor, making the latter commodities to be bought and
sold; the expanded powers and claims of territorial nation-states, particularly notions of sovereignty and the duties of subjects; the rise of
commercial classes and associated claims as to the rights of property;
the efforts to eradicate "pagan" and other heresies in favor of one or
another official variety of Christian monotheism; and the emergence of
prescribed lifestyles stressing "civility" and the value of work—all are
equally evident in the efforts to transform Western Europe and North
America from "traditional" to "modern" societies.

The result on both continents was the geographic and cultural dislo-
cation of peoples, but with sharply differing consequences. Europeans

traveling to America carried lethal microbes causing plague, smallpox, and other diseases which they had contained among themselves but which found "virgin soil" in the previously unexposed populations over here. As a result, the land of dislocated and depopulated Native Americans was seized for occupation by dislocated and multiplying Western Europeans, beginning principally, in the case of North America, with the English. By the seventeenth century population growth and the rise of capitalism in both countryside and city had combined to throw thousands of English families off the land altogether and to render the futures of many more highly tentative. The opening up of colonies in Ireland and the West Indies as well as continental North America offered real alternatives to landlessness, alternatives which were presented in a variety of packages so as to attract settlers from all but the very extremes of wealth and poverty in the English social structure. With land as the attraction and its distribution in the hands of colonial elites, dislocated English generally made common cause with their more affluent countrymen rather than with dislocated natives, reinforcing the widespread perception (then and now) that cultural differences were the principal cause of Indian-European contention. As colonial populations rose and the availability of land shrank, social and economic tensions mounted, beginning with Virginia and New England, at several points in the seventeenth century, and finally spreading throughout the colonies from the 1750s onward. Just as the replacement of white indentured servitude by black slavery in the southern colonies united whites of all classes, so geographic expansion united speculators and farmers who focused on adjacent Native Americans as the highly visible symbols of their common discontent. Thus was perpetuated the precedent, established with initial colonization, of Indian lands as a solution to domestic social and economic problems.

As a sizable chunk of British North America became the United States of America, the implications of this ideological blurring of social tensions multiplied. The new nation was proclaimed an "empire for liberty," in which the availability of land for farming would preclude the tensions and regimentation associated with industrialization. In fact, the capability and willingness to seize Indian land enabled the United States to have its cake and eat it, too—to become a major producer of both agricultural and manufactured products. It wasn't "Americans" in the abstract who were spared the factory but independent Protestant farmers and planters from the eastern United States and northwestern Europe, while unskilled factory and construction work was relegated primarily to landless peasants from Ireland, China, and, later, southern and eastern Europe and the southern United States. Meanwhile, the conquest and settlement of the "frontier" became the basis of a national identity and mythology which celebrated Euro-American deracination as "individualism" in contrast to the backward communalism of Indians and others who refused or were unable to abandon their own cultures and values for those of the dominant class.

Over the past century the shift from entrepreneurial to corporate capitalism in the United States has resulted in a shift in interest in Indian lands from their seizure for use by individual non-Indians to the exploitation of their water and mineral wealth by large private interest groups. Throughout this period, federal policy has vacillated. Liberal administrations have fostered tribal governments which would operate according to the principles of managerial science so as to mediate between traditional people and the outside interests, private and public, with whom they must deal, while conservative ones have sought to terminate all federal protections so as to place the dwindling resources of Indian people at the mercy of those seeking to profit from them. At this writing, the pendulum has swung further than ever in the latter direction so that Native Americans, by all indices the country's poorest as well as smallest minority group, now face large energy and other corporations without the disinterested aid of the federal government. While some Indians see their tribal holdings as sources of wealth and security, many others recognize that nothing could more directly counter traditional native values than acquiescing in schemes which would destroy their land. Some of these Indians have moved beyond pan-Indianism to establish links with native and tribal people around the world who, like themselves, are powerless subjects of large nation-states. They advocate lessening or abandoning reliance on the "special relationship" with the federal government and rediscovering sources of real autonomy, free of dependence on non-reciprocating centers of power and rooted in traditional values. In so doing, they return to the kinds of solutions implemented repeatedly by their forebears long before Columbus's "discovery," reminding us, academic parochialism notwithstanding, of the richness and depth of America's history.

4

Thoughts on Early
Canadian Contact

CORNELIUS J. JAENEN

I backed into Amerindian history. Before I knew it, my research interest in early French colonization in North America found me as much concerned with the Amerindian participants as with the French intruders. France had started to implant her industry and institutions in an inhabited continent. It was no more possible for me to ignore those native inhabitants than it was for the early French fishermen, traders, and missionaries to ignore them. As they had become the central figures in the French drama of New World exploitation so they little by little became the central figures in my attempts to recreate the activities of that historical period.

Before long I found myself challenging, at least intellectually if not vocally or in print, every premise and every pronouncement that had become part of the accepted truth and traditional history of that contact experience. But I am not a radical or revolutionary by nature. It is just that I cannot abide unfounded assumptions or misrepresentation.

Many ethnohistorians today err, as a result of their often compulsive desire to understand the world view of the Amerindians at the time of initial contacts, in the direction of assuming that our "white" contemporary world views and our complex, technological, and largely urban-centered civilization, represent the ethos of French and British peoples of the colonial era. Indeed, in many respects, European views of nature, its fauna and flora, and of the "natural men" who inhabited this New World, may have been closer to Algonkian and Iroquoian views and values of that period than they are to today's generalized views.

There are indications from the French sources that this may have been the case and that our castigations of what we now assume to have been the Judeo-Christian, rationalistic, and "scientific" tradition are sometimes quite wide of the mark. If historians have paid insufficient attention to Amerindian realities, values, and ethos at the time of contact between European and Amerindian, it may be equally true that insufficient thought has been given to European realities, values, and cosmography of the colonial period. Ethnohistorians have always been aware of the hazards of the upstreaming methodology borrowed from the anthropologists, at least in terms of it being intellectually dangerous to assume a relatively static Amerindian society over the historic period. Now, this judiciousness needs to be exercised in terms of European cultures, and anthropologists need to be warned about this historical weakness.

My assessment of where our historiography is going is that we are beginning, perhaps just beginning, to understand better the Amerindian cosmography, their myths, their values, and belief systems. My own research concentrates on the early periods of contact between Europeans (notably the French) and Amerindians, and therefore I am much aware that European views of native societies can be understood properly only in terms of the intellectual constructs and conceptual frameworks of the sixteenth, seventeenth, and eighteenth centuries (Jaenen 1978, 1980). So, too, Amerindian societies must be judged by their values and concepts which dominated in the past.

While it is important to understand the hunting rituals and the deep sense of symbiosis of hunter and hunted, men and animals, as Calvin Martin (1978) and Frederick Turner (1980:11–13) have demonstrated, it is equally important to understand the intellectual constructs and philosophical frameworks into which Europeans fitted their observations and received accounts of Amerindian life. Knowledge of and communion with nature, the regard for all creatures as basically equal, and the identification with animals and birds were all clear evidence to Europeans, accustomed to visualizing creation according to a Chain of Being, that the native people of America were little better than animals, that they were in the infancy of mankind, and that a long process of civilizing would be required to make them men on an equal footing with Europeans, capable of participating fully in the arts, letters, science, and religion of the Old World.

Furthermore, historians consider it useful to explain European interpretations of observed "facts" and of acquired knowledge of the New World, whether from official correspondence, travelers' tales, missionary publications, interviews with public officials and visiting natives, according to the known intellectual and philosophical frameworks, and the theological and scientific postulates, that were part of the European classical, Judeo-Christian, medieval, and Renaissance heritage. Just as the new knowledge acquired from the classical times to the Age of Discoveries had been melded into a unified world view, so the new information and impressions of the New World and its apparently "new men" were incorporated into this holistic and almost sanctified view of the unfolding universe. Such traditional concepts as the Lost Paradise, the impending Golden Age, the discovery of the Lost Tribes of Israel, and the establishment of the Millennial Church in the New World were accorded fresh credence because they seemed to explain some characteristics or qualities of the incredible discovery of a hitherto unknown world inhabited by exotic men, living like Adam in the days of his innocence before the Fall, as one Jesuit missionary permitted himself to write (Thwaites 1896-1901, 32:283).

Of course Adam in such a pristine state should have required no conversion. Hence, Catholic missionaries were quick to establish that American man was more like Adam after the Fall, in need of salvation and the cloak of God's righteousness. But was he capable of receiving divine grace? The Church, like many other European institutions, was self-perpetuating. Its mission was premised not only on the sinful state of mankind, but also on the optimistic conviction of the effective operation of divine grace. Divine grace and human evangelization could produce regenerated man, even in the Americas. Thus, Amerindian man was defined as a rational being in humanistic terms, and a spiritual being capable of receiving divine grace in religious terms.

Our historiography has not been liberated yet from the savagery/ civility dichotomy which Bernard Sheehan (1980) has restated recently. Civilized men lived in a world of order and discipline under established authorities, labored for their bread, pacified their sexual urges in marriage, formed complex social arrangements, and so on. Amerindians appeared to live free of the complexities and limitations of such a regulated world and so were esteemed to be in the early stage of social evolution. Concomitant with the image or stereotype of "savage men" were such value judgments on their way of life as idleness, improvidence, infidelity, immorality, and probably an inherent incapacity to take on the responsibilities and privileges of an ordered European Christian lifestyle. Many explanations were offered in colonial times for the apparent nomadism and undisciplined manner of living, ranging from the supposed effects of the New World climate and virgin (un-tilled) environment through the speculations about people in the infancy of mankind, undeveloped and immature (hence requiring guardians and tutors), or else degenerate people who had declined in spirit and in physical energy as they removed themselves in space and time from their point of origin. The most optimistic view of their "uplifting" and integration into human *civility* was through rendering them sedentary agriculturalists, at the level of French peasants, under the guardianship of Christian missionaries charged with their education and protection from satanic shamanism. This stereotype persisted beyond the French regime, throughout the British regime, and well into the Canadian national period. To accomplish the "elevation" of Amerindians—for that was what Turgot's Four States theory of human evolution indicated in the lectures delivered at the Sorbonne in 1749–1750 (Meek 1973:66, 89–90, 107)—the French introduced the reserve, the boarding school, the native catechist, the agricultural supervisor, and so on. These institutions survived the Conquest but accomplished little more after that turning point than had been accomplished prior to 1760.

Of course the French have often been portrayed as having a much more sympathetic approach, a much more open-minded attitude, and a more benevolent and humane policy toward native people than either the Iberians or the British displayed. This is part of the Parkman interpretation, perpetuated in Canadian historiography in some measure by Mason Wade and W. J. Eccles, and the French thesis of a *génie colonial* which sets them apart from all other colonizing people (Parkman 1899, 1:131; Wade 1969; Eccles 1972:39–40, 186; Boucher 1979). It is true that since the days of Montaigne there was a current of thought in France that accorded well with what would later be termed the "myth of the noble savage" (Frame 1963:89–117). There were many features of Amerindian life which were admired by the early traders, soldiers, and missionaries who lived with or in proximity of Amerindian villages and encampments. Their simplicity, hospitality, tolerance, and anti-authoritarianism appealed to Europeans who were so often repressed by the conventions of their sophisticated, disciplined, and authoritarian society. But it must be remembered that numerous positive testimonials to Amerindian social superiority may have been largely convenient and relatively safe ways to castigate the defects of European society, or indirect ways of criticizing both Church and State. Contrary to what has sometimes been said about Rousseau and his contemporaries, the *philosophes* had no great admiration for Amerindian society, were basically pessimistic about colonial ventures, and were more inclined to agree with De Pauw's thesis of colonial degeneration than with the hypothesis of the westward movement of genius (De Pauw 1770, 1:35, 121–23, 221; 2:102, 153–54, 164–65; De Premonval 1770:10–11, 78–104; De la Roche-Tilhac 1784:5, 433).

Just as there have been positive stereotypes of the French as colonizers, so there have been positive stereotypes of the Amerindians as the colonized, although, as a matter of fact, the French never colonized the Amerindians. They co-existed, so to speak, within their own areas, and while bound together by military pacts, trade, social communication, and often religion, they each maintained their own viable society under French sovereignty. Sometimes Amerindians have been depicted as pacific and permissive people who were goaded into cruel wars, encouraged to practice such cruel rites as scalping and platform torture, and incited into the barbarous delights of guerrilla warfare by the rapacious and power-hungry French and British (views that are criticized in Axtell 1981:16–35). Some writers have gone so far as to accuse the Europeans of introducing to North America the head-hunting practice of scalping one's enemy and promoting it through bounties. Warfare, seldom characterized as humane, existed in prehistoric times, and when the first permanent French settlers arrived they became entangled in the existing pattern of intertribal wars.

That Amerindian warfare could be intensive and have genocidal consequences did not have to await the French intrusion into Huronia to be demonstrated. Already in the sixteenth century, shortly after the visits of Jacques Cartier, the Laurentian Iroquois had been annihilated in an intertribal conflict which had not yet completely dissipated when Champlain arrived on the scene. Probably the reason the Huron have come down to us in many texts as docile and peaceful agriculturalists at the mercy of cruel, bloodthirsty Iroquois, is because they were allied to the French through the upper country trade and the Catholic missions.

On the other hand, Amerindians have also been portrayed as fighting solely for revenge or for personal glory. One writer said their cruelty and vindictiveness drove them even to crunch vermin with their teeth. While it is true that Amerindian and European motives for waging war sometimes differed, just as their conventional means of fighting and their conception of what constituted a "victory" differed, it should not be supposed that Amerindian motivations arose out of a baseness of nature, or of pure vindictiveness and malice. As we have said, warfare existed in North America long before the arrival of Europeans. Never-theless, European economic concerns, weapons, and trade all played a role in altering native patterns of warfare. The greatest change in intertribal conflict was probably the growing connection between war and trade. Amerindians began to wage war on each other for access to, or for control of, supplies of European wares. On the Western prairies, for example, horses and guns could be obtained only through war or trade. Conversely, possession of horses and guns helped assure a tribe's success in both war and trade. In other words, a closer analysis of native warfare seems to indicate more complexity than is found in traditional accounts.

Another stereotype which might be regarded as favorable to the Amerindians, at first glance, but which when considered more carefully does them little justice and less honor is the image of simple, unsophisticated people being exploited, defrauded, and ruthlessly taken advantage of first by unscrupulous fur traders, then by white settlers, and eventually by treaty negotiators. This image of the defenseless and vulnerable native, which some contemporary native leaders have exploited for propaganda purposes, scarcely does justice to the historic Amerindians who were resourceful, shrewd, and intelligent negotiators and traders. The native relationships with the French in the fur trade and in military alliances, and with the Hudson's Bay Company in the context of the fur trade, indicates how resourceful the Amerindians were in their dealing with foreigners. The fur trade was conducted in good measure to the satisfaction of the Amerindians, who prepared and supplied the furs in exchange for goods of the quality and the quantity they desired and at prices which were arrived at mutually through skillful negotiation. Amerindians were not exploited in the fur trade but knew how to reap the maximum benefits (Ray and Freeman 1978:125–62, 218–46). They were a dynamic and intelligent people in their negotiations with the French. Again, in evaluating the goods exchanged on each side, historians today need to take into consideration not only the prices prevalent at that time, but also the value (whether merely economic or also aesthetic and spiritual) the Amerindians placed on various items of trade. Trade, after all, was for natives more than a mere commercial exchange; it was a complex interaction among friends and allies that was hedged about by ceremonial and social considerations and which reaped non-commercial benefits as well as securing some material profit.

Similarly, the military alliances were operative only insofar as they satisfied their objectives and were conducted within the native framework of ceremonial and gift exchange. This was scarcely a case of gullible natives being cheated and defrauded by crafty Europeans. The French found satisfaction, too, in both their trade and military relations, to be sure, but they did not perceive the Amerindians as passive partners entombed in a static society.

In a different domain, the debate rages on about the exchange of contagious diseases, bacterial and viral, with which Amerindians and Europeans supposedly infected each other as a result of first contact. Syphilis probably traveled from America to Europe, and yellow fever and malaria probably came to America on European vessels from Africa in this transatlantic exchange. The greatest killers for the Amerindians were what Europeans called the childhood diseases: the respiratory infections, smallpox, and fevers. The early sources, whether French, English, Spanish, or oral Amerindian, seem to confirm a growing body of archeological and paleopathological evidence, that pre-contact Amerindians were generally quite healthy and that there was a marked decline in aboriginal population in the decades following initial contact. Howard Simpson has argued in *Invisible Armies* that the impact of epidemic disease was so great, not only in terms of depopulation but especially in undermining the traditional cultures and belief systems, that Europeans "conquered" America by waging "unpremeditated biological warfare" (1980:2, 8, 29).

I am not convinced from the sources we have that there was any special genetic susceptibility to imported disease of sufficient magnitude to account for the population declines claimed by James Mooney (1928), Sherburne Cook (1945), John Duffy (1953), and Wilbur Jacobs (1974). However, Alfred Crosby's thesis about "virgin soil epidemics" being deadly because none were immune and so none were left to care for the sick has much to commend it (1976). What seems to be equally important in accounting for the inordinate number of deaths was the inability to respond immediately with appropriate treatment and care, and the resort, all too often, to traditional practices, such as sweatbaths, which were in fact harmful in the case of smallpox. Panic set in as the fatalities mounted and the shamans were powerless to produce antidotes. Epidemics sometimes coincided with intensified warfare, as in the case of the Iroquois attack on the Hurons, or when Britain and France squared off in the New World and were caught in the tangled web of Amerindian alliances and confederacies. They also coincided, on occasion, with European encouragement of guerrilla warfare and scalping raids, through presents and bounties and the introduction of firearms to favored hunters and warriors. None of these factors would seem to have encouraged population growth. There is evidently a need to consider the demographic aspects of contact in a more comprehensive, even universal, context, as W. H. McNeill's *Plagues and Peoples* (1976) suggests. What occurred in North America in the seventeenth and eighteenth centuries was not without precedents nor counterparts.

In a similar vein, the question of the brandy traffic, alcoholism, and the alleged Amerindian intolerance to alcoholic beverages requires reexamination. Joy Leland's *Firewater Myths* (1976) questions the thesis that Mongoloid people, including Amerindians and Inuit, possess a peculiar genetic trait which makes them inordinately susceptible to alcohol, as witnessed by an extraordinary craving for the drug and exceptional changes for the worse in the imbiber's comportment. My own research in this domain supports the contention that the strong prohibitionist strain in French ordinances and in Catholic missionary pronouncements, all well reflected in the Abbé de Belmont's *Histoire de l'eau-de-vie en Canada* (1840), derive from missionary/trader conflicts in the field and from the revivalistic and mystical *dévot* Catholicism in Old France, which staffed and financed the foreign missions. The drive to impose total abstinence on the frontier, in other words, may have been impelled more directly by an Old World ideology than by a New World social situation.

Furthermore, our numerous primary sources do not indicate a condition now defined as alcohol addiction. The natives in contact with the French drank abundantly on specific occasions, as did many of the French. These occasions might be preludes to bartering sessions, the conclusion of a military alliance, the mounting of a military expedition, or a gift-giving ceremony. All of these occasions were ceremonial, social encounters conducted according to the general pattern of Amerindian traditional customs, and were neither extremely prolonged nor all that frequent. The brandy traffic, therefore, needs to be seen more in a social context than in a psycho-medical context.

The historical literature on this subject explains Amerindian drinking patterns—drinking rapidly, drinking in groups, and so on—as a desire to become "possessed" and acquire spiritual force, and in order to overcome cultural inhibitions and commit aggressive acts. The literature adds that drinking for inebriation was engaged in to inflate self-esteem and self-confidence. These traditional explanations indicate a parallel between drinking patterns and eating patterns, especially when one considers the "eat-all feasts." It is when we come to Donald Horton's thesis of insobriety being related to reduction of anxiety and stress (1943:223–70), and Nancy Lurie's (1971) depiction of drunkenness as a form of rebellion and protest on the part of individuals or groups who feel powerless, deprived, alienated, and dominated that we as historians must distinguish between contemporary manifestations and frequency of drunken behavior and the colonial experience of insobriety.

There is no compelling reason to believe that today's high suicide rates and high alcohol addiction rates of Canada's status and non-status Amerindians are the result of social, economic, and psychological conditions that were already present in colonial times. On the contrary, the situations prevailing in the urban ghettos, the reserves, and the northern ancestral hunting territories of native peoples today are vastly different from the relationships that existed between independent, self-sufficient, and dynamic tribes and bands and the largely dependent French traders, garrison troops, and missionaries in the eighteenth century.

The early sources do provide us with French interpretations of Amerindian behavior as motivated by desires to commit unconventional and culturally abhorrent acts, to engage in inverse or contrary behavior. If drunken comportment was a rite of reversal, it should be noted that it was directed in nearly all instances at fellow Amerindians and scarcely ever against the French. The primary sources also indicate other possible motives, which historians have not explicated to date. For example, one *mémoire*, written in 1730, contends that when the shamans lost power and prestige with the coming of the French missionaries and European technology, as evidenced by their inability to turn the tide of epidemic diseases, they turned to alcoholic bouts, or four-to-five-day "frolics" as the traders called them, in a last-ditch effort to regain their spiritual leadership (Public Archives of Canada 1730:14). Other sources suggest a much more practical and equally self-serving explanation: tribesmen who profited from the fur trade "tribute" and annual presents offered by the French Crown found it inconvenient to become burdened with material possessions. Instead, alcohol was a convenient commodity for both European trader and Amerindian fur supplier. Thus, as Arthur Ray has suggested, excessive drinking may have been rooted also in economic expediency (1977:14–16). Alcohol was simply a convenient means to absorb excess Amerindian purchasing power during periods of intensive competition between the French on the one hand and the Anglo-American and Hudson's Bay Company traders on the other hand.

Modern-day ecologists may find it very moving to consider the Amerindian respect for the plants, birds, and animals with whom they shared the bounties of nature. But this should not blind us to the fact that it would be historically unlikely that many Europeans would be so moved in the sixteenth or seventeenth century. There is a sensitization today to ecological issues because the stern facts of pollution, depletion of species, and the moral and physical toll of overcrowded urban living have forced themselves into our consciousness. Were this not so, the intellectual frameworks of our cultural heritage would not so soon be questioned.

Again, there is a danger of over-romanticizing the Amerindians as conservationists who never exhausted the natural resources of the lands they inhabited and never depleted the fish and game on which they depended. There is archeological and geological evidence that towards the end of the Ice Age the Amerindians in North America contributed to the extinction of over one hundred species of large animals. This overkilling of game was related in all probability to: an increasing human population, the specializing in the hunting of one kind of game once the technique of killing that particular animal had been mastered (e.g., elephant and bison in runs), and the destruction of the environment through such techniques as starting prairie and bush fires to drive game. In the historic period, the beaver was wiped out in large areas of eastern Canada to satisfy the demands of both Europeans and Amerindians. As a matter of fact, by the beginning of the eighteenth century the unrelenting pursuit of this animal was more immediately related to the Amerindian desire for certain European trade items than French demands for furs to be used in felting; indeed, there was a glut of beaver on the French market, but the French perceived that they were obliged to continue accepting North American peltries in order to maintain their alliances, their socio-economic relations, and their missions (Kip 1846:58; Normandin 1732:51–52). Similarly, buffalo were hunted in a wasteful manner, often only the tongues being taken for food, well into the nineteenth century, when the diminishing size of the herds was readily observable to all. The UNESCO World Heritage Committee, when it recently designated the Head-Smashed-In Bison Jump (the oldest and best preserved bison jump in America, near Fort MacLeod, Alberta) to be a World Heritage site, recognized a practice dating back at least five thousand years.

Finally, there is a tendency on the part of many native leaders and some of their academic defenders to overdo the spiritual aspects of Amerindian cultures to the detriment of their practical and materialistic contours. It has become somewhat fashionable in our time to emphasize the spiritual essence of the native way of life, and to assume that historical patterns corresponded to current trends. While it is true that in the past the spirituality of Amerindian cultures was neglected, the danger now is that the pendulum might swing too far in the other direction and result in a neglect of the practical and material aspects of Amerindian societies.

It was the materialistic and practical aspects of Amerindian life that the French adopted, not the spiritual values. Even the "renegade" *coureurs de bois*, the European who "went native," did so to enjoy the material and social arrangements of native life, without taking on the Amerindian cosmology. The early French colonists learned to use canoes, toboggans, and snowshoes; they dressed in moccasins and buckskins; they learned how to ice-fish and portage; they acquired new foods and ways of preserving and preparing them; they traveled along native water routes and forest trails, relying on native guides and maps. Most of the European captives who became the so-called "white Indians" retained their European religion. Among the Amerindians, on the other hand, the Micmacs, Abenakis, Hurons, and "mission Iroquois" soon developed their syncretic Catholicism, going so far as to transfer the traditional shamanistic role to the missionary. These colonial realities impose a certain balance in the evaluation of the overall weight of native spirituality.

My greatest plea, in conclusion, is for an historical perspective and sensitivity in native studies. Just as ethnologists argue that each culture must be judged by its own values and norms, so historians contend that each epoch, each event, must be understood in its own evolutionary context. Amerindian societies were no less dynamic than European ones, to be sure, and each must be appreciated in its own time and space. Whether we look at theological and philosophical perceptions, trade, warfare, colonization theories, epidemics, conservation, alcohol consumption, or spiritual values, to name but those issues we have touched upon briefly, the danger is that we should mistake current trends and patterns for historical ones.

In an effort to arrive at some satisfactory historical evaluation of the French contact with Amerindian cultures, while taking into account the anthropological and ethnological insights, I have discovered our historiography to be as burdened with myths and stereotypes on the European side of the equation as on the Amerindian side. There is no merit in revisionism for its own sake, any more than in the malicious debunking of accepted interpretations, yet history must constantly renew itself if research and reflection are to have any purposeful end.

5

Demographics of
Native American History

HENRY F. DOBYNS

Pueblo peoples regularly perform ritual dance-dramas. They tolerate visitors who watch the public portions of these fascinating rituals. The cadenced dramatization by colorfully garbed participants, the monotonous music, and intense sunlight can generate intense emotional responses in spectators.

Some years ago a Hopi communal dance-drama deeply affected a psychologist fairly well-known for publishing long analyses of Native American ethnopsychiatry. Leaving the public performance, the psychologist verbalized his response to a university student who also had watched the ceremony. Untying his horse's reins in preparation for departure, the psychologist exclaimed something like, "Oh, it was just too wonderful for words," while lifting his face and hands to the evening sky. Showing how overwhelmed he was, the man let his arms fall dramatically across his horse's rump. Not being imbued with the metaphysics of the dance-drama, the horse perceived the slap as a slap. The startled mount galloped off, leaving the psychologist sprawled on the ground. The automobile that brought the student to the scene carried the fellow to his quarters.

Calvin Martin's enchantment with "the Indian thoughtworld" (1979; reprinted as Chapter 1) reminds me very strongly of the "Ah, the wonder of it!" approach to cross-cultural experiences. In my own cross-cultural research, which began thirty-five years ago, I have never found that the "Ah, the wonder of it!" approach led anywhere except down analytical dead-end streets. It signifies an individual's retreat into introspection when faced with significant stimulation. In historical analysis

all that such a retreat into one's self achieves is to return the level of
interpretation of events to the zero-sum of each individual's consciousness.

If the history of Native American interactions with invaders is to be
anything more than mere chronicle written by authors with literary
pretensions, it must become a social science. To do so, historical analysis must accumulate understandings that accord with interpretive theories of anthropology, sociology, economics, and demography. Scientific
history cannot, like literary history, collapse into individual, atomistic
introspection when confronted with data. Nor can history become a
social science as long as useful analytical concepts collapse every time a
writer pens another passage of precious prose. All too many historians
pay homage to their literary tradition by striving for elegance of expression at the price of accuracy in both analysis and communication to
others. Frequently, the cost of the felicitous phrase is the loss of
replicability of analysis—a requirement in a science.

One basic social scientific perspective on what Martin mislabels
"Indian-white history" is that it treats only one segment of intergroup
interaction during the process of Christian Europe's worldwide demographic, economic, political, and religious expansion. The accompanying chart may help the reader visualize the niche occupied by Native
American experience in the United States in the broad course of post-
fifteenth-century world transformation. The scientific historian of the
peoples of the New World can productively compare Native American
experience during European expansion to Oriental, South Asian, Middle Eastern, and/or African experiences during the European explosion
overseas. As Woodrow Borah has pointed out (1964), the contrast
between the fates of Orientals and Native Americans emphasizes the
fundamental importance of Eurasian immunities and consequent population stability, and population collapse in the New World.

Not every study need be comparative to be instructive. Yet few studies
that ignore this spatial-temporal framework will contribute significant
new understanding of the Native American role in the hemispheric or
even narrower national past. Extant publications abundantly attest to
the pride historians take in ferreting out documentary sources of information. The texts of those same publications also demonstrate that
their authors are dreadfully deficient in knowledge of social scientific
techniques and concepts for analyzing such information.

European expansion affected peoples outside Europe differently, not
because of cosmological differences, but depending upon the degree to

Chart of the Position of Native American History in the
United States in the General History of European Expansion

A	B	C	D	E	F	G	H	I	J
Europe	Mass	Polynesia	Columbian Exchange Causing Native Population Collapse	Permanent European Colonization	Uruguay	100%	Extinct	Calusa	Vacant Florida, West Texas
		Australia			Venezuela Brazil Chile Argentina	95% Euro-American and Afro-American		Timucua	
		Native America			Canada			Coahuiltecs	
					United States				
					Bolivia Peru Ecuador Guatemala	Indo-American Highland	Forcibly Removed from Ethnic Holy Lands	Cherokee Creek Choctaw Chickasaw	Concentration of Removed Ethnic Enclaves in Oklahoma
	Emigration			Slavery	Mexico Paraguay	Mestizo			
		Africa			El Salvador Costa Rica Honduras Nicaragua Colombia Panama	Afro-American Coast		Quapaw Oneida Osage	
	Selective	Middle East	Native Population Stability	Transient Colonialism	Cuba Dominican Republic Guyana Barbados Haiti Jamaica Belize	European-African Amalgam	Reservations Within Ethnic Holy Lands	Mohawk Onondaga Seneca Penobscot Zuñi Hopi Pima	Continued Identification with Ethnic Sacred Shrines
		South Asia							
		Orient							

which the expanders altered non-European disease environments. Europeans carried many pathogens that evolved in Old World populations. Those pathogens had little demographic effect on other Eurasians, because they were as resistant as Europeans to diseases to which their forefathers had been repeatedly exposed. Long isolated from the Old World, the natives of the Americas, the Pacific Islands, New Zealand, and Australia lacked such immunity. As a result, accurate history of Native Americans must relate other events to a major demographic collapse under repeated onslaughts by Old World pathogens. There are three biological cases of collapse, as indicated in the chart: (a) Polynesians, including New Zealand's Maoris, (b) Australian Aborigines, and (c) Native Americans. In "The Fatal Confrontation" (1971), Wilbur R. Jacobs recognized that disease played a basic role in interethnic interaction on the European-native frontiers of Australia, New Guinea, and the United States. More such comparisons that identify crucial factors are sorely needed, to develop a scientific history.

Innumerable primary documents describe incidents in the demographic catastrophe that struck Native Americans. Many historians who interpreted these sources perceived a "Vanishing Indian." Yet, none accurately reconstructed the true scale and course of Native American demographic collapse. This reconstruction is, therefore, the single most important task for contemporary scientific historians who would increase our collective comprehension of Native American interactions with invaders.

During its expansionist period, Europe exported millions of people. Differences in mortality caused by Eurasian diseases spread overseas largely determined the areas where the majority of the emigrants could colonize. Some migrants colonized by armed force, subjugating many native populations outside Europe. Where native populations remained dense, however, relatively small numbers of European elites gained only an impermanent military, political, and social dominance. The general demise of European colonialism in the Middle East, South Asia, the Orient, and Africa emphasizes the fundamental importance of the relative numbers of dominant and subordinate groups (see lower columns C, D, E). Population numbers do equal power, other factors being equal.

The demographic collapse of Polynesians, Aborigines, and Native Americans opened land on a larger scale than anywhere else on earth to mass European immigration (see columns B, C, D, E, top). So many Europeans migrated to the Americas, Australia, and Polynesia that their progeny became not only the socio-political elite but also the majority of the population. Native Americans declined to a minority within most of their homelands. Australia, New Zealand, Canada, and the United States became English-style democratic nations because people accustomed to such governance colonized their territories in overwhelming numbers. The relative functional efficiency or moral value of English or Native American or Polynesian social structure had very little to do with the outcome, although many a nationalistic historian has claimed that it did.

The demographic collapse was not equal throughout the Americas. The tropics were densely populated by civilized peoples when the Columbian Exchange began (Crosby 1972). Several Old World pathogens—malaria, yellow and dengue fevers, for example—depend on lowland vectors. Some, such as hookworm, cannot live at high altitudes. These diseases, combined with those that spread to peoples living at all altitudes, virtually exterminated tropical lowland natives.

Voluntary European and involuntary African immigrants to the depopulated tropical lowlands of the Americas brought different immunological defenses. Proportionally more Africans than Europeans survived fevers; thus the population of tropical American coasts became Afro-American. That historic reality again emphasizes the fundamental importance of demography in the history of the New World. Native Americans interacted not only with Europeans, but also with Africans, even in the United States.

An expanding world market kept Europeans traveling across Afro-American populated zones, and upland-dwelling Euro-American elites maintained political control over littoral populations. Post-colonial Colombia, Panama, Costa Rica, Nicaragua, Honduras, and Belize divide the coastal Afro-Americans (bottom, columns F, G). Only Costa Rica lacks Native Americans interacting with Afro-Americans.

Although thinned by geographically mobile diseases, numerous natives survived at higher elevations in the Andes and southern New Spain. The mountains remained Indo-American. Sufficient farming and grazing land did not become vacant by Native American deaths to attract many European immigrants. So Europeans who colonized the highlands achieved colonial dominance but remained a minority (Dobyns and Doughty 1976). Euro-American domination of Bolivian, Peruvian, Ecuadorian, and Guatemalan Native American masses is incomplete because altitude demographically differentiates the highlands and the rest of the Americas (center, columns F, G). Natives at high altitudes are genetically adapted to living on less oxygen than are low altitude populations. The history of Native American interaction with other ethnic groups in these nations, and Paraguay and Mexico, simply cannot be understood without taking ethnic demography into account.

When the Columbian Exchange began, the temperate zones of the Americas supported fewer people than the tropics did. Eurasian pathogens reduced the indigenes by more than 95 percent. So these zones attracted most of the Europeans who came to the Americas seeking to exploit land. Some European colonists tried utilizing Native American labor. Most preferred to remove surviving natives from areas which invading diseases had not entirely depopulated. Native American minorities constitute less than 5 percent of the present population of nations in the temperate zones (top, columns F, G).

In the United States, some aboriginal populations are extinct (top, columns H, I, J). To illustrate the importance of the population collapse, the disappearance of Coahuiltec speakers left large portions of Texas depopulated—vacant for Euro-American colonization.

Not content with the rate of Native American depopulation, Euro-American policy-makers forcibly removed numerous eastern Native American ethnic groups from their aboriginal Holy Lands (center, columns H, I, J). Migration, voluntary or forced, is a demographic phenomenon. It has had basic effects on Native American historic behavior and current attitudes quite independent of aboriginal ethnic thoughtworlds.

By the mid-nineteenth century, westward movement by citizen traders, miners, and would-be farmers made Native American removal impractical. Then policy-makers reserved reduced areas for declining native ethnic groups within aboriginal Holy Lands (bottom, columns H, I, J). Thus, surviving Native American enclaves in this country can be divided into two broad groups depending on whether they still live within the territories where they believe their ethnic gods placed them or not. I deliberately write *ethnic group* and *enclave* and emphasize that living within or having been forced out of one's aboriginal Holy Land strongly influences interactions between Native Americans and invaders. Southern Paiute funeral songs recount supernatural placement of ancestors where Southern Paiutes now reside, strongly linking past and present. Oklahoma Cherokee Baptists, in contrast, cannot see their ancestral sacred places of the Appalachian mountains.

One of the fatal fallacies of thinking about "the Indian thought-world" is the perpetuation, in spite of disclaimers, of the initial European error that perceived all Native Americans as one people. To paraphrase Martin, writing the history of Native American interactions with invaders is profoundly vitiated by continuing to think about Native Americans as "a people." There was and there is no single "native phenomenology, epistemology, and ontology."

There are several thousand different Native American distinctive enclave phenomenologies, epistemologies, and ontologies. There are more than five thousand indigenous communities—little religious groups with independent thoughtworlds—in modern Peru alone (Dobyns 1964). Even where surviving Native Americans constitute less than five percent of the national population, there are still hundreds of such independent ethnic cosmological systems. Column I of the chart only hints at the diversity of more than three hundred such ethnic thought-worlds in the United States. The cosmology of Onondagas who follow the code of Handsome Lake differs from that of traditional Hopis, which is not like that of Seminoles.

History of Native American interactions with invaders that rings true to members of Native American enclaves must be truly ethnic history. It has to be microhistory of each enclave with its originally distinctive cosmology and not macrohistory of national policies, because each enclave has been defined by a distinctive sequence of events. Members of every enclave have interacted with Europeans, Euro-Americans, and Afro-Americans somewhat differently from members of any other enclave. This is not an abstract assertion, but the voice of experience. Papago reservation librarians have pled for help in obtaining copies of their microhistory (Dobyns 1972). At last report, demand for the book among the Desert People themselves is so great that shelf copies have nearly disappeared.

Quite diverse Native American thoughtworlds interpreted distinctively European or Euro-American historic Indian policies. Initial cosmological diversity helped differentiate each group from every other Native American ethnic group. Even so general a policy as reserving lands for Native American populations has produced very diverse consequences under dissimilar circumstances. Different peoples have chosen distinctive major forms of economic activity as a result of varying combinations of natural resources, traditional technologies, and what they learned from intruders.

Even when contemporary ethnic groups engage in similar economic activities, they have not necessarily learned them under parallel historic circumstances. Navajos, Papagos, and Walapais all husband domestic animals on reserved lands. Navajos acquired sheep and learned to herd them from colonial Spaniards. They have differed from all other Native North Americans ever since. Mutton apparently fueled Navajo population growth to the largest Native American group in the United States, and encouraged pastoralists' invasion of Hopi and Southern Paiute ancestral territories. Papagos and Walapais herd range cattle. The former first acquired cattle from colonial missionaries before the end of the seventeenth century. In 1914, the Bureau of Indian Affairs initiated a planned change program that established Walapais in the cattle business. By 1930, all Walapai reservation-dwelling families owned some cattle. Then population recovery began, and by 1945 veterans returning from World War II could not enter the cattle business because no range land was available (Dobyns and Euler 1976). A similar demographic transition characterized nearly all United States reservations. It has virtually nothing to do with ethnic cosmologies, but a great deal to do with sanitation, immunization, and nutrition. To understand Native American interaction with invaders, scientific historians must reconstruct demographic trends first, and then relate other events to them. Navajo-specific historic experience has brought the Native American Church the most Navajo adherents of any denomination. Papago-specific experience converted most Desert People to Catholic participants in the Magdalena, Mexico, regional St. Francis Xavier pilgrimage. Walapai-specific experience generated Pilgrim Holiness Church and Mormon congregations.

Research in the social sciences indicates that few if any human behaviors stem from single causes. The style of historical writing that focuses on thesis and antithesis significantly inhibits, therefore, the development of a truly scientific history. If we are to understand human events that have multiple causes, we must analyze all of those causes, beginning with demographic trends, and not neglect specific ethnic group cosmologies, general national policies, and other such influences as may be pertinent.

6

Pagans, Converts, and Backsliders, All: A Secular View of the Metaphysics of Indian–White Relations

MARY YOUNG

My intention in this essay is to complicate the issues Calvin Martin raises in his thoughtful exploration of the "metaphysics" of Indian-white relations. As I translate that essay, Martin is appealing for a more empathetic understanding of the world view of those Indians who were, or are, animists and polytheists. Certainly, informed empathy is an important professional tool for historians, and a useful attitude for human beings generally. But I think it equally important for the historian who deals with contacts between Indians and whites to reconstruct empathetically the world view of the whites. Neither task is simple.

Whites produced most of the written documents we have from the sixteenth, seventeenth, eighteenth, and nineteenth centuries, including those records of Indian mythology and commentary from which we try to reconstruct the "Indian" point of view. Even so, entering into the outlook of a person who hopefully anticipates the triumphant return of Jesus Christ and the inauguration of His thousand-year reign within his or her own lifetime may prove as difficult for a modern secular historian as acquiring a true understanding of persons who believe that beavers hold councils and hatch plots. Since beavers engage in impressive collective action, some careful students of animal behavior—whether pagan, Christian, or secular—may, in fact, find the latter view more nearly plausible than the former. Such a student may even regard the beaver as "sacred," though that belief probably affects the post-

MARY YOUNG

modern biologist's outlook and behavior differently than it affected the
world view and activities of the average seventeenth-century Micmac.

I would further suggest that any approach to reconstructing the
metaphysical beliefs of either whites or Indians should be concretely
historical and should begin by acknowledging that beliefs among whites
and among Indians probably varied a lot even during the early contact
periods. One consequence of several centuries of contact has been to
increase and multiply the variations.

Variations over time within the groups we may call simply "Indian"
or "white" have made even the language we use anachronistic, oversimplified, and suspect. During the April 1982 meetings of the Organization of American Historians, Francis Jennings, an eminent analyst of
the "Invasion of America," argued that using color terms like "white" is
racist, and that we should refer to the invaders as "Anglo-American," or
"Euro-American." Those terms may indeed more accurately describe
the Indians' immigrant antagonists of the sixteenth and seventeenth
centuries than does the word "white." When we refer to encounters of
the nineteenth and twentieth centuries, however, we must acknowledge
that both "Indians" and "whites" might be described more accurately as
"Native Americans"—but then, how to mark the distinction?

It is difficult to designate distinctions between "Indians" and "whites"
as social and cultural groups without using terms that refer either to
color or to ancestry. After several generations of contact and intermar-
riage, references to ancestry are likely to prove as inaccurate as references to color. Both John Ross, Principal Chief of the Cherokee from
1828 to 1866, and his antagonist, Andrew Jackson, were native-born
Americans. The ancestors of both were predominantly emigrants from
Scotland. Ross's skin tones included olive, white, and red. So did
President Jackson's, except when Ross provoked him to turn pale with
anger. Ross called himself an Indian, and sometimes referred to the
group to which he belonged as "red," though more chromatically
sensitive contemporaries referred to the Cherokees' skin color as
"olive." Ross called Jackson and members of Jackson's social group
"whites." I see no reason to regard John Ross as a racist; nor do I
believe that an historian who uses a chromatically oversimplified designation such as "red," "white," or "black," is any more racist than one
who employs oversimplified designations with respect to the probable
geographic locations of people's remote ancestors. "White" and
"Anglo-American," like "Indian" and "Native American," are oversimplified terms in common usage by people who are not bigots. For

practical purposes, these terms may be taken as useful pairs of synonyms. The most ambiguous term referring to color is probably "red." A. Mitchell Palmer, J. Edgar Hoover, and other patriots have long since contaminated its connotations by using it to denote Communists. Yet Vine Deloria still contends that God is Red. Our language cannot escape history.

Let us return to the varieties of Indian-white "relations." Some themes of that story appear and reappear with the wearisome consistency of a repetition compulsion: the devastating impact of communicable disease; whites' "land hunger" and their overriding conviction that they can make more productive use of natural resources than natives can; mutual ethnocentricity; and the dilemma both whites and Indians have faced as to whether segregation or assimilation should be the proximate strategy or ultimate fate of the Native American.

Even these reliable variables, however, have had radically different import at different times and places. The Yamasee have vanished; the Mandan were literally decimated; the Navajo have increased and multiplied. The land hunger of the ninteenth-century intruders on the Sac and Fox and the Cherokee reflected the aspirations of sons and daughters of farmers whose families had increased at a rate which made the replication of the parents' yeoman lifestyle wholly dependent upon the rapid expansion of the agricultural frontier. Now the standard of living to be sustained, if possible, depends more acutely on coal, gas, and uranium than on arable land; the agents of imperialism are multinational corporations; and questions of ownership have practical consequence mainly as they affect methods of conservation and the distribution of income—though these questions too have substantial import for the maintenance of Indian communities. The question whether tribal Indians should have special legal status and the problem of what constitutes an "Indian" identity remain. But most contemporary Native Americans—like some of their ancestors—have opted both for "assimilation" in work, language, and perhaps residence and religious affiliation, and for segregation at those points in their life-cycle or annual calendar when joining kin in a common territory offers refuge, or the opportunity for renewing community and "Indian" identity.

Changes in Native American world views within this dynamic environment represent particularly salient examples of highly complex and varied transformations. Missionaries since the seventeenth century have quite correctly apprehended critical differences between the Christian view of man's place in the universe, and the traditional native view of

the human predicament. In every case, they have encountered difficulties that are both cognitive and affective.

Christian conversion required the native to accept both intellectual
abstractions and psychological distancing alien to the Indian's sense of
himself in relation to others. For many spirits—friends, enemies, grandmothers, grandfathers, mothers, sisters, and brothers—substitute a single, exclusive, distant, perpetually invisible, patriarchal God; for animal
friends, enemies, and relatives, substitute animals as distinct and subordinate species; for a common afterlife to which most relatives' spirits
might make the final journey, substitute a final segregation between
converted kin who go to heaven, and the unconverted who go to hell.
For visible violations of correct standards of conduct, remediable by
ceremonies that restore the individual's proper relations with his community and its guardian spirits—here and now—substitute innate sin-
fulness and perhaps irremediable depravity.

Given the cognitive and affective developments essential to such
attitudinal transformations, one can only agree with the missionaries
that radical changes in work life, kinship behavior, perhaps even language, would be required to achieve them. Some Indians mastered
those tasks. Faced, for example, with the loss of kin, territory, or
traditional occupation, and the choice between regression into apathy,
random fury, and alcoholism, or a progressive reintegration of their
sense of the world's meaning, some moral athletes were able to make
the leap into a more abstract and universal perspective. Their earlier
experience of an integrated and supportive world of close kin and
communicative spirits may indeed have strengthened them for the
journey.

At the same time, however, popular Christianity contained many of
the magical and ceremonial elements—and metaphysical assumptions—common to Native American religions. One could, for example,
petition God, Jesus, perhaps Mary, or a pantheon of saints; and proper
petitions, rituals, sacrifices, might bring health, fish, or good hunting,
even as a proper petition to the Guardian Spirits might bring out the
beaver for a happy hunting trip.

Missionaries differed widely among themselves with respect to the
relative emphasis they placed upon similarities with and differences
between their world view and ceremonial practice, and the natives'.
Those who emphasized similarities best encouraged conversion—or
perhaps more accurately, an acceptable syncretism. One instructive
example might be found among the Aleuts, who were assimilated into

the Russian Orthodox fold in the early nineteenth century. No professed missionaries converted them; simple fishermen and laborers who were not theologians, but neighbors and fellow workers, welcomed them into communion.[1]

Indian people have shown great creativity in adapting Christian themes to fit native spiritual needs in a variety of settings, from the revelations of the Delaware Prophet and the missionary work of native converts like Samson Occom to the invention of new denominations such as the Indian Shakers and the Native American Church. Other Native American spiritual leaders have modified native ceremony and ideology to fit changed conditions—as, for example, in the revival of the Sun Dance. Still others have maintained or revived more ancient traditions.

Missionaries were among the first of an army of teachers to combat "pagan superstition" with mathematics, astronomy, and geography. Among Indians, as well as whites, such teachers have facilitated "conversion" to a secular, scientific world view which some do, and some do not find compatible with a traditional religious outlook.

In the face of this vast, complex, and creative history of innovation, adaptation, and inevitable loss, it seems not only unhistorical but ungenerous to treat a single metaphysical outlook as "Indian," even though some features of that outlook remain an essential source of strength to many Indian persons and communities.

The historian who examines the history of a single tribe, during a brief period of time, may even in such restricted compass find it difficult to discern the character and distribution of beliefs within the native community. In part, this difficulty arises because most of our documents reflect the views of white authors. Even in those cases where Indians have spoken and written eloquently from their own points of view, they have sometimes found it strategic to ignore the persistence of a "traditional" persuasion, or of substantial diversities of outlook, within their own communities. A case in point, "well-documented" from both sides but still perplexing, is the story of the Cherokee, regarded in the nineteenth century as the most "civilized" of the civilized tribes.

The nineteenth-century Cherokee represent an unusually fortunate group of Native Americans. Unlike most of their tribal neighbors—the Yamasee, for example—they had survived the exchange of goods, germs, and hostilities with seventeenth- and eighteenth-century colonists; and at the time of the passage of the Indian Removal Act (May

1830) they were growing in numbers and wealth. In part, their flourish-ing condition may be attributed to their having adopted stock-raising and fairly intensive methods of agriculture in imitation of white resi-dents of the Cherokee Nation. Significant numbers of Cherokee for several generations had married white men and women, and métis offspring had married whites, Cherokees, and one another. Substantial numbers of Cherokee of mixed ancestry, and some of unmixed Chero-kee heritage, had acquired black slaves, and successfully exploited their labor. Scores of Cherokees, mainly but not exclusively the wealthier, could read and write English and keep track of money. Hundreds were literate in their own syllabary, developed after "white" models by the métis, George Guess, or Sequoyah, during the decade following the Creek War—a conflict wherein the Cherokee prudently sided with the United States.

The tribe's political unity was reinforced by a written constitution, a document non-traditional in many respects, and suspect among some Cherokee traditionalists, yet one designed to enable the tribe to pre-serve ancestral lands and cultural and political autonomy.

Most Cherokee of the 1830s believed their land to be inhabited by a rich variety of spirits—some helpful, some playful, some malevolent and easier to provoke than to escape. Several hundred members of the tribe had professed to believe in Jesus Christ and accepted some variety of Christian discipline. Converts periodically distressed their mission-ary friends by praying to the spirits of the four directions for rain and other benefits. Some Methodist and Presbyterian missionaries, unlike the Cherokee, and unlike other Presbyterians, regarded theology and medicine as separate realms. They accepted the Cherokee prayers to their spirits as sound enough medical practice.[2]

Andrew Jackson believed that moving the southern Appalachian Cherokee to what is now northeastern Oklahoma would preserve their lives, their wealth, and their national existence. He also believed that such a removal would get the enterprising frontier citizens of Georgia off the backs of both the Cherokee and the President. Jackson thought the Cherokee pagan, on the whole, but he proved far less interested in changing their outlook than in changing their residence. Missionaries—including two who went to jail in Georgia in defense of Cherokee rights—believed it far more important that Cherokee souls go to heaven than that Cherokee bodies remain in Georgia.

The elected Cherokee government launched a massive legal defense of their homeland on grounds that various efforts to secure their removal violated their rights under the United States Constitution. John Marshall, Chief Justice of the Supreme Court, agreed with the Cherokee. Andrew Jackson treated the Chief Justice's decision with disdain. He could not understand why the Cherokee preferred to live in the neighborhood of whites who unrepentantly abused them, when the President was willing to offer them millions to take up good farm land in a remote and protected area. Jackson did not even believe that the "real" Cherokee—as distinct from their "aristocratic" government— really wanted to stay in North Carolina and Georgia.

Cherokee delegations did not even try to explain to Andrew Jackson that the Thunderers might inhabit particular mountains, and the water spirits, particular streams. They decried the lack of water in Oklahoma, but did not try to explain how essential it was for every family (of traditionalists) to "go to water" for medicinal and ceremonial purposes each day. Even if the Methodist Principal Chief and the Presbyterian Assistant Chief of the tribe had believed in the spirit people—a matter on which we have little evidence—they would hardly have expected the President to understand. They spoke of progress, and of rights.

Except for a remote enclave in the Appalachian summit region of North Carolina, the Cherokee lost their eastern lands in 1838. Forcibly removed in keeping with a "pretended treaty," they found other lands— and spirit people—in Oklahoma. Though the Cherokee Nation West in Oklahoma lost its national domain and jurisdiction two generations after the death of Andrew Jackson, Cherokee people today still have a tribal identity, a living language, and at least two governmental bodies—the Cherokee Nation East and the Cherokee Nation West. That's more than one can say of the Yamasee.

Microbes, intertribal and interracial war, and removals account for the historical decimation of Indian people less fortunate than the Cherokee, and for substantial loss of life on the part of the most fortunate tribes. White "land hunger" (whose motivations and variations in particular regions and at particular stages of capitalist development scholars have more often ignored or taken for granted, than explored) accounts for the dispossession of most Indian people in the United States.

Stereotyping and other kinds of misunderstanding derived from differences in metaphysical assumptions have enhanced the cumulative tragedy, but they do not, primarily, account for it. Certainly ethnocentrism and cultural misunderstanding of Indians by whites contributed significantly to the misdirected goodwill reflected in such "reforms" as allotment and the forcible re-education of children apart from their parents. At some times and places, one might regard well-intentioned practices of forced acculturation as a kind of cultural genocide. But even in such instances, the Indians' relative lack of resources and automony, rather than the whites' cultural blindness per se, is at issue. One might well find instances—among the nineteenth-century Seneca, Nez Perce, and Cherokee, for example—where missionary efforts, however ethnocentric and even divisive, contributed to the physical and spiritual revitalization, even the survival, of significant numbers of Native Americans.

Where Native Americans have survived, they have managed that feat through a variety of strategies. At one pole, more people of Indian ancestry than anyone now can count have simply "disappeared"—but survived by assimilation into the "mainstream" society and culture. Precisely because they have ceased to be visible as members of separate Indian communities, and have not called attention to their uniqueness, these persons have not served as objects of study. For that reason, scholars have probably much underestimated the success (by ethnocentric standards) of assimilationist policies.

At the opposite pole, some Indian communities have managed by physical isolation, institutional innovation, or both, to preserve the boundaries of a traditional culture whose development they have been able to control quite well for themselves.

Probably most Indians who have survived and retained or renewed their "Indian" identity have managed through accommodation—spiritual, legal, economic, geographic, genetic. They remain Indians, but would probably not agree fully among themselves on what characteristics define the "essentially Indian."

If there is a moral to this story, beyond a kind of Faulknerian appreciation of endurance under duress, I would formulate it in the terms of a twentieth-century moral relativist. "Do not do unto others as you would have them do unto you. Their tastes may be different." For the more normatively inclined, this injunction might read, "Our Father's house has many mansions."

Notes

1. On the Aleuts, see Lydia T. Black (1981). My characterization of Indian ideological development draws heavily on Howard Gardner (1981), Robert F. Berkhofer, Jr.

(1965), and Henry Warner Bowden (1981). My interpretation is also inspired by the autobiography of the Santee Sioux and sometime Christian missionary, Charles Eastman, especially, *From the Deep Woods to Civilization* (1977).

2. What I have to say here about the Cherokee has benefited immensely from the work of several generations of authors who have dealt with that tribe, notably James Mooney, Marion Starkey, Morris Wardell, Thurman Wilkins, Henry T. Malone, Robert Berkhofer, Rennard Strickland, Raymond Fogelson, Jack and Anna Gritts Kilpatrick, Murray Wax, William C. McLoughlin, Theda Perdue, and Duane King. I think my interpretations not inconsistent with their findings. For specific documentation of my own interpretation, see Young (1961, 1975, 1981a). My characterization of the behavior of Cherokee converts and the attitudes of missionaries toward them is based on the extensive Cherokee files of the American Board of Commissioners for Foreign Missions in the Houghton Library, Harvard University.

7

Revision and Reversion

VINE DELORIA, JR.

During the trial of Robert Butler and Dino Robideaux for the killing of two FBI agents on the Pine Ridge Reservation in South Dakota in June 1975, a confidential Justice Department memo came into the possession of the defense team at Cedar Rapids, Iowa. This document purported to explain why the Justice Department had lost so many cases involving Wounded Knee defendants. The memo argued that individual United States Attorneys were the victims of a "roving band" of liberal attorneys and two leftist, revisionist historians, Dee Brown and Vine Deloria, Jr., who overpowered and outmanned district office attorneys. Not surprisingly, the memo did not discuss the misconduct of federal agencies which had produced a dismissal of the Means-Banks trial for government pollution of the waters of justice.

The only time that Dee Brown and I were together, with the "roving band" at any rate, was the Means-Banks trial in Minneapolis, where we gave testimony on the circumstances surrounding the signing of the Treaty of 1868. Our testimony can be obtained from the federal courthouse there and it will show no effort to revise what is already recorded in numerous government documents. Thus we were "revisionists" in the sense that we introduced into the record materials that had not previously been used to understand that period of history. By contrast it is worth noting that the government's witness in the Lincoln, Nebraska, hearings on the same treaty, Dr. Joseph Cash of the University of South Dakota, testified that he was an expert on several books, which were wholly fictional titles satirically devised at breakfast to see whether Cash was familiar with the subject area. When pressed by the defense Cash admitted that the Indian version of the circumstances of the treaty was essentially correct. Cash, to my knowledge, is not regarded as a revisionist historian.

The identification of scholars working in the field of Indian-white relations has this strange quality to it: proponents of the Indian version of things become "revisionists," while advocates of the traditional white interpretation of events retain a measure of prestige and reputation. Often the controversy revolves about beliefs held so tenaciously that questioning the orthodox point of view becomes a personal offense. Some years ago I was working with Elliot Arnold on a TV scenario for Marlon Brando. I favorably mentioned Thomas Marquis's fine book, *Keep the Last Bullet for Yourself* (1976), in which Marquis suggested that Custer's green troops, fearful they might fall into the hands of the Sioux and be tortured, fired a few shots and then killed themselves. When I began to talk about Marquis's evidence, Elliot's hands began to shake. He screamed that he would not discuss Marquis under any circumstances. The idea that American soldiers might consider this measure was beyond the scope of his emotional conception of Western history.

So Indian-white relations have many more pitfalls than we would suspect and most of these obstacles have little to do with historical facts or data. They are remnants of beliefs derived from other areas of experience—patriotism, the movies, older books advocating manifest destiny, personal preferences derived from participation in Westerner Clubs. Whether we can clean out the emotional swamp of white America and recount Indian-white relations more objectively or whether we must continue to struggle with old beliefs and shibboleths when we could be doing more important work remains to be seen. There are hardly any subjects we might mention that do not have this heavy investment of emotions on the part of white writers and historians.

"Revisionist" seems to be the label applied indiscriminately to people taking the Indian side of the story. This classification is merely an effort to influence the manner in which we consider historical fact, not a true statement of the writer's intent. In many respects the writing that most needs revision is that which seems to favor Indians. It is not inaccurate, it is simply too generalized and tends to mislead Indians into adopting liberal myths instead of conservative myths. A true revisionist would seek more precise interpretation of data regardless of the orientation of the writer, and there are very few of these people writing Indian-white history. Let me give some examples of generalizations that seem favorably inclined toward Indians but actually have negative implications when they are seen within the context of contemporary Indian life.

The General Allotment Act, passed in 1887, gave the President the authority to negotiate with Indian tribes for the cession of lands the government felt were "surplus" to the reservations. As a result of this statute, which was actually a detailed policy directive, United States Indian Inspectors were sent to the various tribes to negotiate allotments and reduced reservations. A number of special commissions were authorized by Congress also, for example, the Crook Commission to the Sioux, and the Dawes Commission to the Five Civilized Tribes, and these commissions forced these larger tribes to agree to allotments and reduced land holdings. The government finally stopped these negotiations in 1914, when the agreement with the Ute Mountain Utes of Colorado was made. Some tribes agreed to reduced reservations but not to allotments: the Red Lake Chippewa and the Hopi saved their reservations from allotment, the Sioux reservations adopted allotment in later agreements after they had agreed to a reduced number of smaller reservations in 1889.

When writers deal with this topic, they seem to neglect the history of Indians over the thirty-year period following the General Allotment Act and give to this statute a power and effect that it certainly did not have at the time it was passed. Nearly all Indian writers adopt the interpretation that *the act itself* allotted the reservations. All the white writers I have read have accepted this interpretation without a hint that it might be too general an interpretation to be valid. Within this general interpretation of the General Allotment Act we find two basic themes. Some writers take a very sympathetic view and recite the series of disasters that befell Indian culture following the act. Other writers sternly see in allotment an inevitable process which helped to settle and civilize the western states.

A good deal of important history is overlooked when this interpretation of allotment is uncritically accepted. Almost all of the tribes who made agreements with the United States secured some additional legal rights, generally unique to their own situation, in these negotiations. Contemporary Indians, bureaucrats, and attorneys pursuing remedies for federal intrusions against the tribe are prone to overlook or denigrate the agreements because they do not seem to be a part of the general historical flow that they find in books describing the treatment of Indians by the federal government. Thus interpretations of *policy* are mistaken for statements about *history*.

Breaking treaties is another subject that lends itself to misinterpretation when inadequately researched or understood. The general theme of writers dealing with Indian-white relations when dealing with treaties is to adopt the interpretation that the United States "broke" every treaty it signed with the Indians. So deeply entrenched is this belief that a writer hazards his reputation by suggesting otherwise. Yet this phrase has many unfortunate connotations which make it a difficult and misleading characterization of the situation. First, not all treaties that were made with the Indians were treaties that provided legal rights or demanded federal responsibilities toward Indians. A good many of the treaties were simple recitations of friendship and goodwill which each party agreed to display toward the other. Apart from a resolution by Congress stating that it did not want to remain friendly with a tribe, it is difficult to see how such a document could be breached.

There is a question whether a treaty can be legally breached apart from a straightforward abrogation by one of the parties. Federal courts have traditionally used a device called "severability" to interpret treaties. To find severability in a treaty one separates the article that is the subject of controversy from the remainder of the document and comments on its validity or relevance in law. Some articles of treaties have been abrogated, others have become void with the passage of time or the fulfilment of conditions, and still others have been included in subsequent amendments. Nullification of one article does not void a treaty as a legal document; the single article under consideration becomes void, the remainder of the treaty holds.

The belief that all treaties have been broken has many by-products. Conservatives find their mustaches bristling as if this idea had breached the wall of sensibility and patriotism, also. Indians harbor deep resentment against a society which so blithely breaks its word. Liberals wring their hands in anguish and find further evidence of a monstrous conspiracy to trample a helpless people. The simple fact is that the statement that all treaties have been broken is a moral rather than an historical judgment. Yet when it appears in historical writing without some explanatory comment it takes on wholly different connotations and triggers a set of responses, predictable to the last ounce of emotion, which are unwarranted. Tribes still enforce their treaty rights even though few people believe that the treaties have any efficacy at all.

People writing on the Indian Reorganization Act generally characterize this statute as the first opportunity Indians had for self-government in this century. Since the Indian Reorganization Act is the major policy shift that counteracts the effects of allotment, it is usually discussed as the reversal of allotment, and self-government is seen as an innovation devised by John Collier and Felix Cohen. Indians are generally described as greeting the opportunity to govern themselves with unrestrained enthusiasm. A great deal of this optimistic aura surrounding the Indian Reorganization Act comes from Collier's own writings, which describe in anecdotal form some of the successes that tribes enjoyed after operating under the provisions of the act for several years.

The fact is that tribes maintained some identifiable form of government long before the Indian Reorganization Act. The Five Civilized Tribes, for example, continued to hold meetings even though their governments had been reduced to presidentially appointed chiefs with little to do except appear at Fourth of July celebrations. The Sioux continued traditional forms of government in the Black Hills Treaty Council, the Chippewas continued to operate under traditional chiefs as did the Umatillas and other tribes. The Klamaths and Nooksacks had already adopted constitutions and by-laws decades before the Indian Reorganization Act. The effect of the act, when all is said and done, was to recognize the tribal governments as federal corporations and to require them to adopt new constitutions and by-laws approved by the Department of the Interior. Existing political powers of the tribes were clarified in law.

Indians and others reading descriptions of the Indian Reorganization Act come to believe that prior to its passage the people on the reservation had no institutions that could represent them, and did not know how to go about forming such groups. When traditional Indians raise complaints about the high-handed tactics of the Bureau of Indian Affairs in getting the tribes to adopt the IRA, or accuse the existing tribal government of being a white man's government, they have a great deal of historical fact behind their arguments, but these data are completely obscured by the mass of writing which suggests otherwise.

These examples could be multiplied many times with other specific topics. The cumulative weight of evidence would seem to suggest that when we speak of revisionists we are really speaking of people working with more data and seeking more precise articulations of the historical incidents and developments under consideration. If we return to Marquis's theory concerning the Little Big Horn, we would note painstakingly precise counts of the expended cartridges found at the sites where the soldiers' bodies were located and a comparison of these sites with other known battles in which no survivors were able to tell the white man's side of the story. Indications, according to Marquis, based on more precise use of evidence that had never before been considered, show that the soldiers fired a few times and then killed themselves. Where large piles of cartridges were found, there were also found the bodies of experienced Indian fighters and impressions where a number of Indians fell. This conclusion is simply more precise; emotional response to it calls it revisionist, as if Marquis were attempting to change history for his own purposes.

We should probably classify people who write on Indian-white relations as revisionists and reversionists: those who bring more data into their schemes of interpretation and thereby gain additional precision in describing the situation, and those who revert to older, more accepted ways of describing historical events without bothering to check the data to see if they really support the orthodox rendering of the situation. If this classification were accepted we would have a giant crowd of reversionists and a few isolated revisionists, and within the large crowd of reversionists we would have two camps, liberals and conservatives. Such a classification would cut across the whole spectrum of writing on Indian-white relations and include most Indian writers in the reversionist camp.

A great need exists, and will continue to exist, for more revisionist writers. When the cumulative impact of continuous misinterpretation of historical events is surveyed and appraised we will find that much of what passes for history dealing with Indians and whites is a mythological treatment of the development of policy disguised as history. We can grant that the General Allotment Act established an intellectual milieu within which a number of readily definable things happened to Indians and Indian properties, without negating the historical period that followed and the events of that era which have influenced the subsequent course of events, and continue to be influential today.

Political history is but one aspect of the much larger task of writing more precise treatments of developments, events, and personalities. The treatment of Indian religion begs to have a complete overhaul. Publications in that field today have such an aura of the exotic and mystical it is difficult to distinguish fact from fiction. Pre-Columbian history is another subject that begs further study. Orthodoxy insists on the preservation of certain themes and much evidence is collected to support those themes without a thought for alternative explanations.

The origin of our problem in writing more accurate and precise books and articles on Indian-white relations lies in the educational system itself. Throughout our academic careers we are fed summaries and generalizations which are acceptable because they require little imagination and less thought. By the time we recognize that the comfortable and uniform version of human experiences we have learned is not accurate, we have already taken much misinformation and misinterpretation into ourselves and have great difficulty in separating fact from mythology. Our academic institutions, from primary school through graduate study, all assume that at some later date we will adopt the posture of the cultivated, educated man, don our smoking jackets, and sit comfortably in our easy chairs filling in the gaps in our education. Unfortunately, the pace of modern life precludes almost all of us from even contemplating this luxury, and we know only that bit of history that we have managed to remember from what we have heard or have had the opportunity to read.

Bringing this confusion regarding Indian-white relations into some new and, one hopes, better orthodoxy by which we can become enlightened seems a forlorn hope at best. The qualifications for writing in the field of Indian-white relations now seem to be only sincerity and the confession that the writer has "always been interested in Indians." Exactly what that phrase means is never made clear. Presumably the attractiveness of the subject matter and the lack of clarity make it a field that appears to have many hidden and exotic secrets which need to be unfolded. The great mass of material in the field, much of which has not been brought into the arena of popular consumption, suggests that all of us could labor the remainder of our natural lives without acquiring a more precise knowledge of our subject.

We should, perhaps, popularize the idea of reversionism because it may act as a motivating force to encourage the next generation to undertake more precise renderings of this theme of Indian-white relations without lapsing into a recitation of the ideas that have been already articulated. Each generation should build on the accomplishments of its predecessors, yet writers in the area of Indian-white relations have not benefited from this expectation that knowledge eventually will be cumulative. Let us hope that more acquaintance with the source materials will produce some better writing in the future.

8

Distinguishing History from Moral Philosophy and Public Advocacy

WILCOMB E. WASHBURN

When I began to write the history of the American Indian, the subject
was a minor subset of conventional history. Anthropology existed in a
separate disciplinary territory, and the numerous ethnographies dealing
with the American Indian were objects of curiosity to most historians,
as was the craft of history to anthropologists. My efforts to integrate
the two in my Ph.D. work at Harvard in the History of American
Civilization (I entered the graduate school in 1948) were rebuffed even
by a department which encouraged consideration of every aspect of the
American experience. I had to take my anthropology on the sly by
auditing the Harvard anthropology greats such as Hooton, Kluckhohn,
and Kidder.

The distance separating anthropologists and historians has since that
time been largely erased. The Harvard American Civilization Program
allows candidates for the Ph.D. to include anthropology along with
fields such as history, fine arts, English, or philosophy among their
fields of study, while the Harvard Anthropology Department trains
anthropologists in historical archeology and other historically based
subjects. Historians have moved into a greater familiarity with anthropologists, and anthropologists, with historians. Organizations such as
the American Society for Ethnohistory, which publishes the journal
Ethnohistory, have provided a meeting ground for those from either
discipline interested in the rounded study of the American Indian. Since
the Indian was never fully available for study by outsiders in the pristine
pre-contact form in which anthropologists formerly sought to portray
him (termed "the ethnographic present"), all historical study of the

American Indian, I would assert, is contact history. Those who decry the intrusion of the white presence in Indian history are often simply unwilling to recognize that Indian history is, for good or ill, shaped by the white presence, whether physically, in terms of European immigrants, or intellectually, in terms of Western historical or anthropological theories. Consideration *by Indians* of the Indian past *prior* to white contact must, of course, be excluded from this generalization, but *since* contact such consideration must be included in it, however much one may argue about the uniqueness of the Indians' view of their history.

I am sure that others in this volume will recount the joys and sorrows of writing Indian history from the uncertain and unstable position of a combined anthropological-historical perspective. However skilled many of the new practitioners, they still resemble the circus performer who rides two horses abreast while standing with a foot on the back of each; the performance is exhilarating but dangerous. Rather than talking of my early work with anthropologists (work that resulted in election to the presidency of the American Society for Ethnohistory in 1958), I would prefer to talk about my more recent experiences in writing Indian history, which involve combat with radical theorists on the ideological front.

Recent Indian history, in particular, is shrouded, or clouded, by the fog of war, the smoke of deliberate deception, and the coloring of special interest. Historical facts, to the extent they are used at all, are filtered through the ideological perspective of the writer. Since the elaboration of an ideological position is more a mental exercise than a search for factual knowledge, and since it requires assumptions about motives and purposes, Indian history has increasingly become a matter of assumptions and assertions rather than a catalog or analysis of factual truths.

Because most Indian history is written within the university, and because most university campuses are centers for left-of-center beliefs, most recent Indian history has emerged packaged in what anthropologist Edward Bruner of the University of Illinois has called an "ethnic resurgence" model (1986). From earlier models of acculturation and assimilation, the new Indian history views the present as a "resistance movement," the past as "exploitation," and the future as "ethnic resurgence." Terms like exploitation, oppression, colonialism, resistance, liberation, independence, nationalism, tribalism, identity, tradition, and ethnicity, Bruner notes, are the "code words of the 1970s." Examples of this literature are not hard to find. The morning mail brought

Jack D. Forbes's *Native Americans and Nixon: Presidential Politics and Minority Self-Determination, 1969-1972* (1981). Where Professor Forbes (of the University of California at Davis), a redoubtable warrior of the radical left, concedes, "if Nixon people score low marks it must also be noted that their scores were *no lower* than those of the Kennedy, Johnson, Ford and Carter Indian Affairs staffs" (1981:122), Roxanne Dunbar Ortiz (of California State University at Hayward) feels no such residual sympathy for a disgraced President. She asserts in her fore-word to the Forbes volume, "The Nixon Administration's neocolonial strategy, whether designed to destroy Indian 'militancy' or as a counter-force to Black militancy or an attempt to build a model of successful capitalist development among the poor, had the effect of lending credi-bility to the Indian governments that the administration planned to manipulate" (1981:21).

Because I frequently travel abroad, the significance of Indian history in foreigners' perceptions of the United States has always interested me. But I little expected to find myself traveling in the footsteps of Ameri-can Indian Movement radical spokesmen who seemed to have unlim-ited funds to travel abroad, and no difficulty in finding willing univer-sity audiences for their explanation of American "colonialism," "imperialism," and "exploitation" at home as merely one aspect of a unified policy of exploiting native people throughout the world. Much as I tried to convince the true believers among European students that American policy was not to sterilize Indian women or to carry out a policy of genocide toward the Native American, I found that the facts usually ran a poor second to the emotional and ideological assumptions upon which Indian history was perceived overseas.

What particularly annoyed me was that the version of Indian history gaining greatest currency abroad was that purveyed by self-appointed Indian spokesmen (i.e., individual Indians claiming to speak for their tribes or for all Indians and often anointed as "Indian leaders" by the white media) who had no claim to be the legitimate representatives of their tribes. Indeed, their very recognition of this fact led these radical Indians to denigrate tribal leaders who had won the mandate of leader-ship through a majority vote of their tribes. Hence, much of the ideological fire in the radical movement was devoted to ridiculing and invalidating the claim to legitimacy of elected tribal leaders. "Puppet" was perhaps the kindest word a radical Indian historian could use for an elected leader. Journals like *Akwesasne Notes* would publish historical accounts purporting to be scholarly to show that the elective process was a trick foisted upon unwilling and unknowing tribal societies to prevent the true leaders from emerging. Such articles would be published even when the authors were aware of their falsity. Such is the account of Hopi history published in *Akwesasne Notes* in serial form, in the issues of Spring, Summer, and Winter 1979, that had been produced by Tim Coulter's Indian Law Resource Center in Washington, D. C. (Indian Law Resource Center 1979). When I personally pointed out to Mr. Coulter prior to publication that his facts were all wrong about the numbers voting in Hopi elections in the 1930s, and gave him a copy of my article, "On the Trail of the Activist Anthropologist" (1979), Coulter nevertheless allowed the article produced by his staff to run without even calling attention to my article, let alone refuting it. When I chided Mr. Coulter for this omission, during a March 1983 conference in Florence, Italy, in which we both participated, he responded that he had no time to read my writings, but had assigned that task to others on his staff. It is this sort of casual ignoring of the historian's responsibility to truth that I find all too common today among those propagandists—I will not call them historians—who struggle to convince readers of their particular views of Indian history.

Because of the impact of this radical view abroad I have found myself in various foreign nations attempting to justify United States policy on the one hand, and history as a scholarly discipline on the other. It is possible to spike assertions of genocide by pointing out that the American Indian birth-rate is twice that of the non-Indian population and the growth rate is three times that of the non-Indian population, but it is more difficult to disprove the assertion that, say, multinational corporations control the United States Government and seek to exploit the resources of all native peoples against their will.

Many Americans have never heard of the Fourth Russell Tribunal held at Rotterdam between November 24 and 30, 1980, at which United States Indian policy was condemned by a tribunal consisting of leftist anthropologists such as Robert Jaulin of the University of Paris and Karl Schlesier of Wichita State University, Kansas. The tribunal heard presentations by various groups and condemned the United States for various crimes of omission and commission against the Indians. While the tribunal was conducted more like a theatre of the absurd than an historical seminar, its form provided an ideal basis for weighing evidence and drawing conclusions. But, because none of the dozen or so representatives of various Indian groups had been elected by tribal members to represent them, and none had any official standing, as I pointed out in an article, "The Russell Tribunal—Who Speaks for Indian Tribes?" (1981c), the statements of the issues made by these representatives were as flawed as the judgments.

The Sandinista repression of the Miskito and other Indians of Nicaragua after assuming power in 1979 has put many left-oriented scholars in an embarrassing dilemma. That dilemma has been evident in the pages of *Akwesasne Notes,* as the writers represented in that journal wrestle with the question of whether to support the Indians of Nicaragua in their opposition to their Sandinista rulers. Some scholars, like Roxanne Dunbar Ortiz, have unhesitatingly opted to support the Sandinistas against the Indians, as is evident in the pages of the journal she edits, *Indigenous World/El Mundo Indígena*, published by the Capp Street Foundation, San Francisco. Other scholars, like Robert Jaulin, have unhesitatingly supported the Indians against what they perceive as ethnocide if not genocide against Nicaragua's Indians. In the process of watching this interesting debate, I have published several op-ed pieces in the *Washington Times*, specifically "Leftist Academics and Ethnic Minorities" (1982), and "A Rollback of Left in Nicaragua Too?" (1983; see also 1984b, 1985a, b).

Historians as activists march to a different tune and hear a different piper than historians as scholars. It is a commentary on the state of historical scholarship in the United States that a distinguished professor at an Ivy League University, Lee Benson, could deliver a keynote address at a plenary session of the Organization of American Historians convention, calling upon historians to form alliances with non-scholarly groups organized for action to solve specified societal problems, with the expectation that historians could function "both as moral philosophers and public advocates" (1981). In the process of using history to promote non-historical causes, the enterprise of history is inevitably lost or cheapened. Ideological concepts replace specific facts. Action replaces thought. I am not one to decry activism. I enjoy a fight. I relish debate and advocacy. But the individual as advocate has different standards and obligations than the individual as historian. If the obligation to truth is not the first and most overriding obligation of the historian, then he is not a historian. If he cannot put his argument in a form in which his facts can be checked and his assertions documented, then he is merely using his profession for ulterior purposes.

A word about ethnic purity. Indians are coming into the field of scholarship, more often in anthropology than in history, and writing their "own" history. While they are writing in English and in the scholarly form prescribed by the traditions of Western scholarship, Indian practitioners occasionally conclude that their ethnic identity gives them a special authority or right. In certain cases this authority may exist, but in other cases the assertions of an ethnic claim to ethnic history is spurious. In its extreme form it can reach the level expressed in the volume produced by Allen P. Slickpoo, Sr., and Deward E. Walker, Jr., *Noon nee-me-poo* (*We, the Nez Perces*), in explaining the absence of footnotes: "It is our culture and history and we do not have to prove it to anyone by footnoting" (1973:viii). History is not owned by anyone or any group.

Finally, the Indian as a symbol requires comment. Robert Berkhofer has explored in depth this vast subject in his *White Man's Indian: Images of the American Indian from Columbus to the Present* (1978). Symbols have power, particularly in this media-conscious and image-filled world. As a result, activists and those with a practical interest to serve wish to control the images of the Indian, either to present a favorable image in the media, or to ban an unfavorable image that is thought to be hostile or belittling to an ethnic group. Indian activists, led by Russell Means, started a campaign against the Indian symbols used to represent many sports teams, symbols they found demeaning or insulting in many cases. There followed a campaign waged on many university campuses to eliminate the symbol, even if it was a positive, heroic one. Dartmouth College was perhaps the most famous of the colleges at which the Native American students acted to eliminate the Indian symbol. Here again, those who ventured into the fray seemed to me to be almost entirely oblivious to the meaning of symbols and to their significance, as well as to how their use related to the rights of free speech. I published a couple of articles in the *Dartmouth Review* on the subject (1981a, b), and one in the *Washington Times* (1984a), and have persistently but unsuccessfully hoped for the opportunity to discuss the issue in terms of reason instead of emotion in the pages of the *Dartmouth Alumni Magazine*. Needless to say, the Indian symbol issue continues to fester at Dartmouth College, where murals depicting Dartmouth's founding as an Indian school have been covered over.

The editor of this volume has sought to illuminate our understanding of the "different views of humanity and humaneness" represented by the Indian and non-Indian points of view (Martin 1982:1). I have some qualms about a book that concerns itself with "the metaphysics of writing Indian-white history," having some sympathy for the skeptical point of view of metaphysics espoused by Voltaire (as I hope accurately quoted by my father), that "we know about metaphysics what we have known throughout the ages, which is to say, very little indeed." Nevertheless I am in full agreement with the editor in recognizing the vast differences in underlying theory, method, and form of expression of Indian and white history, as well as in the necessity to attempt to resolve those differences with a new synthetic approach. Moreover, I am in agreement with the editor in personally considering the Indian view of humanity and humaneness "the wiser and, ultimately, the more practical" approach (Martin 1982:2). Some will recognize my lifelong and quixotic pursuit of the reality of the Indian as "noble" in the face of the received wisdom of anthropologists, literary scholars, and historians (Washburn 1957, 1973, 1976).

But all my efforts are guided by, and subject to, the limitations of historical truth rather than guided by myth or ideology. As an historian, I will accept nothing on religious faith, on ethnic tradition, or because of personal belief in the justice of a particular point of view. There is no place in the scholarly profession of history for such distorting lenses. History to me means a commitment to truth, however difficult to achieve, however contradictory it may be to our inherited beliefs or acquired convictions about how the world should be.

Indian-white history, pursued by the rigorous canons of such a belief, can be liberating, because the clash of values and perceptions requires a deeper and more careful sifting of the evidence regarding the actions and motives of both groups. Neither Indian history by itself—least of all that parody of history that asserts ideologically the rightness of an Indian point of view merely because it is Indian—nor white history in its now discredited "settlement of the West" form, in which the Indian is merely a surrogate for nature, can stand the test of a bicultural history grounded in the commitment to a non-ethnic, non-religious, non-ideological truth.

9

Indians on the Shelf
MICHAEL DORRIS

While on my way to do fieldwork in New Zealand several years ago, I stopped in Avarua, capital of the Cook Islands. To my tourist's eye it was a tropical paradise right out of Michener: palm trees, breadfruit and pineapples, crashing surf, and a profusion of flowers. Most people spoke Maori, and traditional Polynesian music and dance were much in evidence; there was no television, one movie theatre, one radio station, and few private telephones.

There were, of course, gift shops, aimed primarily at people like myself who wanted to take with them some memento of days spent sitting in the sun, eating arrowroot pudding and smelling frangipani in every breeze. And so I browsed, past the Fijian tapa cloth, past the puka shell necklaces, past the coconut oil perfume, and came face to face with an all-too-familiar sight: perched in a prominent position on a shelf behind the cash register was an army of stuffed monkeys, each wearing a turkey-feather imitation of a Sioux war bonnet and clasping in right paw a plywood tomahawk. "The Indians" had beaten *this* Indian to Rarotonga.

The salesperson replied to my startled question that, yes, indeed, these simian braves were a hot item, popular with tourist and native alike. She herself, she added with a broad smile, had played cowboys and Indians as a child.

More recently, I entertained in my home a young man from Zaire who was spending the summer at Dartmouth College in order to teach Swahili to students who would travel the next winter in Kenya on a foreign study program. My guest spoke very little English, a good deal more French, and three East African languages.

He was homesick for his tiny village on the west shore of Lake

Tanganyika, and the Santa Clara pueblo chili I served reminded him of the spicy stews he ate as a child. We compared tribes, his and mine, and he listened with rare appreciation to recordings of southwestern Indian music. He had never met "real" Indians before, he reported, and was interested and curious about every detail. But it was not until I brought out an old eagle-feather headdress, a family treasure, that his eyes lit up with true recognition. Sweeping it out of my hand, and with an innocent and ingenuous laugh, he plopped it on his head, assumed a fierce expression and, patting his hand over his mouth, said "woo woo woo." He, too, in his radioless, roadless, remote village, had played cowboys and Indians; it was part of his culture, and he knew how to behave.

Generations of Germans have learned to read with Karl May's romanticized Indian novels; Hungarian intellectuals dressed in cultural drag cavort in imitation buckskin each summer, playing Indians for a week on a Danube island; and an unpleasant, right-wing student newspaper at the college where I teach tries to make some symbolic "conservative" point by peddling "Indian-head" doormats for fifteen dollars each. Far from vanishing, as some once forecast, the First American seems if anything to be gaining ground as a cultural icon.

As folklore, Indians seem infinitely flexible; they can be tough and savage, as in the Washington Redskins football team, or, starring in environmental commercials, turn maudlin and weepy at the sight of litter. In advertising they are inextricably linked with those products (corn oil, tobacco) the general public acknowledges as indigenous to the Americas. Ersatz Indians have inspired hippies, Ralph Lauren designs, and boy scouts. But flesh and blood Native Americans have rarely participated in or benefited from the creation of these imaginary Indians, whose recognition factor, as they say on Madison Avenue, outranks, on a world scale, that of Santa Claus, Mickey Mouse, and Coca Cola combined.

For most people, the myth has become real and a preferred substitute for ethnographic reality. The Indian mystique was designed for mass consumption by a European audience, the fulfillment of old and deep-seated expectations for "the Other." It is little wonder, then, that many non-Indians literally would not know a real Native American if they fell over one, for they have been prepared for a well-defined, carefully honed legend. Ordinary human beings, with widely variable phenotypes and personalities, fall short of the mold. Unless they talk "Indian" (a kind of metaphoric mumbo jumbo pidgin of English), ooze nostalgia for bygone days, and come bedecked with metallic or beaded jewelry, many native people who hold positions of respect and authority within their own communities are disappointments to non-Indians whose standards of ethnic validity are based on Pocahontas, Squanto, or Tonto.

In a certain sense, for five hundred years Indian people have been measured and have competed against a fantasy over which they have had no control. They are compared with beings who never really *were*, yet the stereotype is taken for truth. Lask week my local mail carrier knocked at my door and announced that he was taking a group of little boys into the woods where they intended to live "like real Iroquois" for two days; did I have any advice, he wondered? In reply I suggested simply that they bring along their mommies, pointing out that in a matrilineal society children of that age would be entirely bound by the dictates of their assorted clan mothers. This was not what he wanted to hear; it ran counter to his assumption of a macho, male-bonded Indian culture where men were dominant and women were "squaws," retiring and ineffectual unless there was a travois to pull. He and his group did not want to live like "real" Iroquois, and he was chagrined that the Six Nations did not conform to his version of proper savage behavior.

Such attitudes are difficult to rebut successfully, grounded as they are in long traditions of unilateral definitions. In the centuries since Columbus got lost in 1492, a plethora of European social philosophers have attempted to "place" Indians within the context of a Western intellectual tradition that never expected a Western Hemisphere, much less an inhabited one, to exist. It has been the vogue for hundreds of years for Europeans to describe Native Americans not in terms of themselves, but only in terms of who they are (or are not) vis-à-vis non-Indians. Hardly a possible explanation, from Lost Tribes of Israel to outer space or Atlantis refugees, has been eschewed in the quest for a properly rationalized explanation. Puritans viewed Indians as temptations from the devil; Frederick Jackson Turner, when he noticed them at all, saw them as obstacles to be overcome on the frontier; and expansionists, from President Andrew Jackson to Interior Secretary James Watt, have regarded them as simply and annoyingly in the way.

Popular American history, as taught in the schools, omits mention of the large precontact Indian population and its rapid decline due to the spread of European diseases. Instead, students are given the erroneous impression that the few indigenous people who did live in the Americas were dispatched to the Happy Hunting Ground due to conflict with stalwart pioneers and cavalrymen. Such a view of history, clearly at odds with well-documented facts, only serves to reinforce the myth of Indian aggressiveness and bellicosity and further suggests that they got what they deserved. In addition, by picturing Indians as a warlike and dangerous foe, Euro-American ancestors reap honor by having been victorious.

The pattern of Indian-European negotiation for land title in the seventeenth, eighteenth, and nineteenth centuries is also misrepresented; though students learn about the fifty states, they remain unaware of the existence of close to two hundred "domestic, dependent nations" within the country, and regard reservations, if they are conscious of them at all, as transitory poverty pockets "given" to the Indians by philanthropic bureaucrats. In many respects living Native Americans remain as mysterious, exotic, and unfathomable to their contemporaries in the 1980s as Powhatan appeared to John Smith over three hundred fifty years ago. Native rights, motives, customs, languages, and aspirations are misunderstood out of an ignorance that is both self-serving and self-righteous.

Part of the problem may well stem from the long-standing tendency of European or Euro-American thinkers to regard Indians as so "Other," so fundamentally and profoundly different, that they fail to extend to native peoples certain traits commonly regarded as human. A survey of literature dealing with Indians over the past two or three hundred years would seem to imply that Indians are motivated more often by mysticism than by ambition, are charged more by unfathomable visions than by intelligence or introspection, and in effect derive their understandings of the world more from an appeal to the irrational than to empiricism. Since the whys and wherefores of Native American society are not easily accessible to those culture-bound by Western traditional values, there is a tendency to assume that Indians are creatures either of instinct or whimsy.

This idea is certainly not new; Rousseau's noble savages wandered, pure of heart, through a preconcupiscent world, never having had so much as a bite of the fruit from the "tree of the knowledge of good and evil" (Genesis 2:17). Romantics, most of whom had never seen a living specimen, patronized Indians by eulogizing them, and thus denied them a common bond of humanity with other men and women. Since native people were assumed a priori to be incomprehensible, they were seldom comprehended; their societies were simply beheld, often through cloudy glasses, and rarely penetrated by the tools of logic and deductive analysis automatically reserved for cultures prejudged to be "civilized."

And on those occasions when Europeans did attempt to relate themselves to native societies, it was not, ordinarily, on a human being to human being basis, but rather through an ancestor-descendant model. Indians, though obviously contemporary with their observers, were somehow regarded as ancient, as examples of what Stone Age Europeans were like. In the paradigm of European confusion, Indians have been objects of mystery and speculation, not people.

It makes a great story, a real international crowd-pleaser that spans historical ages and generations, but there is a difficulty: Indians were, and are, *Homo sapiens sapiens*. Unless the presence of a shovel-shaped incisor, an epicanthic fold or an extra molar cusp (or the absence of Type B blood) affords one an extra toe in the metaphysical door, native people have had to cope, for the last 40,000 or so years, just like everyone else. Their cultures have had to make internal sense, their medicines have had to work consistently and practically, their philosophical explanations have had to be reasonably satisfying and dependable, or else the ancestors of those we call Indians really would have vanished long ago.

In other words, Native American societies rested upon intelligence. They developed and maintained usable, pragmatic views of the world. Those of their systems that had survived long enough to have been observed by fifteenth-century Europeans were certainly dynamic but clearly had worked for millennia.

The difficulty in accepting this almost tautological fact comes from the Eurocentric conviction that the West holds a virtual monopoly on "science," logic, and clear-thinking. To admit that other, culturally divergent viewpoints are equally plausible is to cast doubt on the monolithic center of Judeo-Christian belief: that there is but *one* of everything—God, right way, truth—and Europeans alone knew what that was. If Indian cultures were admitted to be possibly viable, then European societies were not the exclusive club they had always maintained they were.

It is little wonder, therefore, that Indian peoples were perceived not as they were but as they *had* to be, from a European point of view. They were whisked out of the realm of the real and into the land of make-believe. Indians became variably super and subhuman, never ordinary. They dealt in magic, not judgment. They were imagined to be stuck in their past, not guided by its precedents.

Such a situation argues strongly for the development and dissemination of a more accurate, more objective historical account of native people, but this is easier said than done. Inasmuch as the Indian peoples of North America were, before and during much of their contact period with Europe, non-literate, the requirements for recounting an emic native history are particularly demanding and, by the standards of most traditional methodology, unorthodox. There do not exist the familiar and reassuring kinds of written documentation that one finds in European societies of equivalent chronological periods, and the forms of tribal record preservation that are available—oral history, tales, mnemonic devices, and religious rituals—strike the average, university-trained academic as inexact, unreliable, and suspect. Culture-bound by their own approach to knowledge, they are apt to throw up their hands in despair and exclaim that *nothing* can be known of Indian history. By this logic, an absolute void is more acceptable than a reasonable, educated guess, and "evidence" is defined in only the most narrow sense.

Furthermore, it is naive to assume that most historians can view their subject without certain impediments to objectivity. Every professor in the last three hundred years, whether he or she was enculturated in Rarotonga or Zaire, in Hanover, New Hampshire or Vienna, was exposed at an early age to one or another form of folklore about Indians. For some it may well be that the very ideas about Native American cultures that initially attracted them to the field of American history are the items most firmly rooted in myth. They may have come to first "like" Indians because they believed them to be more honest, stoic, and brave than other people, and forever after have to strive against this bias in presenting their subjects as real, complicated people. Or they may discover to their disillusionment that all Indians are not pure of heart and have to suppress, consciously or unconsciously, their abiding resentment and disenchantment.

For most people, serious learning about Native American culture and history is different from acquiring knowledge in other fields, for it requires an initial, abrupt, and wrenching demythologizing. One does not start from point zero, but from minus ten, and is often required to abandon cherished childhood fantasies of super-heroes and larger-than-life villains.

There would seem to be a certain starting advantage here for historians or anthropologists who also happen to be ethnically Native American, especially if they grew up in the context of tribal society. For them, at least, Indians have always been and are real, and they may have less difficulty in establishing links of continuity between contemporary and historical populations. They may have access to traditionally-kept records and escape some of the prejudice against non-Western methods. They may be more comfortable with taking analytical risks in hypothesizing explanations for traditional practices, basing their assumptions upon subtle but persuasive clues surviving in their own cultural experience.

Native scholars, of course, have their own special problems. For one thing, few of them have avoided exposure to the media blitz on folkloric or fantasy Indians. Indian children are as often tempted to "play Indian" as are their non-native contemporaries. They may be expected to live up to their mythic counterparts and feel like failures when they cry at pain or make noise in the woods. American Indians who deal as scholars with Indian materials are assumed by some non-natives to be hopelessly subjective and biased, and as such their work is dismissed as self-serving. Certainly it is true that most Native American scholarship could be termed "revisionist," but that in itself does not prove illegitimacy. Europeans and Euro-Americans have not felt shy in writing about their respective ancestors and are not automatically accused of aggrandizing them; why should native scholars be less capable of relatively impartial retrospection?

Whoever attempts to write Native American history must admit in advance to fallibility. There is not and never will be any proof, no possibility of "hard evidence" to support a conjecture based on deduction. David Bradley, in *The Chaneysville Incident*, writes wistfully of a firmly fixed chamber in Historian's Heaven in which all things are clear. "And we believe," he says, "if we have been good little historians, just before they do whatever it is they finally do with us, they'll take us in there and show us what was *really* going on. It's not that we want so much to know we were right. We *know* we're not right (although it would be nice to see exactly how close we came). It's just that we want to, really, truly, utterly, absolutely, completely, finally *know*" (1982: 277).

Indian history hardly even offers purgatory. It depends on the imperfect evidence of archeology; the barely-disguised, self-focused testimony of traders, missionaries, and soldiers, all of whom had their own axes to grind and viewed native peoples through a narrow scope; and, last and most suspect of all, common sense. The making of cross-cultural, cross-temporal assumptions is enough to send every well-trained Western academic into catatonia, but there is no avoiding it. If we stipulate only a few givens—that Indian societies were composed of people of the normal range of intelligence; that human beings *qua* human beings, where and whenever they may live, share some traits; that Indians were and are human beings—then we have at least a start. We can dare, having amassed and digested all the hard data we can lay our hands on, to leap into the void and attempt to see the world through the eyes of our historical subjects. We can try to make sense out of practices and beliefs and reactions that do not conform to a Western model but must, within the configurations of their own cultures, have an explanation. We can stop treating Indians like sacred, one-dimensional European myths and begin the hard, terribly difficult and unpredictable quest of regarding them as human beings.

10

The Metaphysics of Dancing Tribes

RICHARD DRINNON

> Their worship is dance.
> They are tribes of dancers.
> SUSANNE K. LANGER

"It is the season of Indian tribal dances," warned the breathless *National News Extra* on December 15, 1974, "and every man, woman, and child in the nation is in danger of being kidnapped and used in the barbaric rituals." Meanwhile, *Indian Trails*, a mission newspaper in Arizona, asked readers to "pray for Mishongnovi, a Hopi village steeped in witchcraft. . . . If you are ever near one of these dances, you can feel the very presence of evil forces as they actually worship the devil. This is in the United States!" It is, indeed, and the current frozen Fundamentalists are not the only heirs of centuries of fearful clichés about the barbaric madness of Indian dances.

In *Facing West* I tried to account for this perennial revulsion, and incautiously concluded the book by drawing on the wisdom of Lame Deer, the Sioux holy man: with Native American help, "Americans of all colors might just conceivably dance into being a really new period in their history" (1980:467). That was "an inappropriate ending," reproved a friendly critic: "Drinnon's own work is testimony to the importance of less dancing and more analysis" (LaFeber 1980:26). But was it? And a moderately hostile reader disliked my "dark, dancing tribesmen" and undertook to teach me the realities of tribal life: "[O]ne cannot look to Native American societies, past or present, for models of life without

repression, projection, sadism, ethnocentrism (God is Red?), and violence. The Noble Savage is also a racist stereotype" (Young 1981b:413).
But "savages," noble or ignoble, had entered my pages only as inner
demons of the white invaders, so why this defensiveness and misdirected admonition? Finally, a thoroughly disgusted reviewer lamented
my want of propriety:

> When [Thomas L.] McKenney reveals the sexual limitations of his Quaker
> upbringing after oberving an Indian dance, Drinnon makes some revela-
> tions of his own. If McKenney had let go, surmises Drinnon, "a dancing
> counterpart might have leaped out of him, joined the circle, chanted,
> copulated, and run off into the free and boundless forest." McKenney may
> well have entertained such infantile fantasies, but at least he had the good
> sense to repress them (Sheehan 1981:434).

But had the first head of our Indian service acted out the fantasy—
including that hair-raising copulation—would that have been so awful?
Should we admire his good sense in repressing his impulses and in
throwing his adult energies instead into pulling his wards out of the
circle, cutting their ties to the forest, stripping them of their languages,
and breaking up their cultures? Anyhow, this offended historian brings
us back around to the very presence of evil forces—or at least unseemly
fantasies—and to the missionary attitude toward the body's rhythms.

Yes, on this Turtle Continent God may indeed be Red, for all we non-
Indians know. Our arrogant refusal to treat the lands and indigenous
peoples with friendly respect has long since become a fixed national
tradition. In his "Presidential Address" of December 1981, for instance,
Bernard Bailyn informed the assembled members of the American
Historical Association of his current, large-scale project, "an effort to
describe as a single story the recruitment, settlement patterns, and
developing character of the American population in the preindustrial
era. It covers a long period of time—the two hundred years from the
early seventeenth century to the advent of industrialism" (1982:1). *A
long period of time*! And when we are not leaving the original in-
dwellers out of our stories of "peopling" the continent and developing
"the" American population, we have been misdiscovering, misnaming,
and misunderstanding them. As the quinquecentennial of the archetypal misdiscovery draws near, that collective incomprehension is surely
one of our most revealing and least endearing characteristics. Why have
we been stone-blind so long? Let us return to 1492 for clues.

With first landfall on October 12 came Columbus's very first thought of enslaving the gentle islanders, who had "very handsome bodies and very fine faces. . . . [T]hey are of the color of the Canary Islanders, neither black nor white." From then on the entries in his *Diario* made plain that he had jumped at the chance to make himself and his men masters of those who were "very poor in everything" and who went about "naked as their mothers bore them." For openers he determined to carry off by force six of these cultureless nudes "to Your Highnesses, that they may learn to speak." All through the West Indies the admiral left copious evidence in his wake that he had spontaneously implemented a cardinal principle of Western "civilization." In his unsettling volume, *La paix blanche*, the French anthropolgist Robert Jaulin called that principle "the negation of the other," and contrasted it with the principle of affirmation characteristic of tribal cultures, wherein you affirm "the other who affirms you" (1970:11, 203-8, 294-95).[1]

In those relatively innocent first days of the invasion, that tribal affirmation reached out to Columbus and his sailors: "They remained so much our [friends] that it was a marvel, later they came swimming to the ships' boats in which we were, and brought us parrots and cotton thread in skeins and darts and many other things. . . ." In his famous "Letter to the Sovereigns" (1493) he reported that he had been everywhere so received: "[T]hey are so artless and so free with all they possess, that no one would believe it without having seen it. Of anything they have, if you ask them for it, they never say no; rather they invite the person to share it, and show as much love as if they were giving their hearts." Without having seen it, I believe it.

I also confess to having been long baffled by this "first contact" and all the others that followed. Why were tribal peoples almost invariably welcoming, generous, so filled with that "marvelous love" the admiral experienced? Robert Jaulin's abstract formulations neatly dovetailed with all the evidence of their hospitality, and explained how those who affirmed themselves by negating the Other so easily victimized these people who lived by affirming the Other (who reciprocally affirmed them), but left relatively unexplained the origin and particulars of their life-cherishing affirmation. Columbus himself explained that his misnamed *Indios* located the source of all power and goodness in the sky and believed that was where he had come from, greeting him everywhere with cries of "Come! Come! See the people from the sky!"[2] But with only an Arabic interpreter along, he had to gather his ethnographic data through signs and gestures, and his reading of those may have simply revealed that he liked feeling like a Judeo-Christian god, a being above or out of the nature in which his hosts so obviously reveled. Still, as in the Aztec myth of Quetzalcoatl, maybe the islanders really did see him as a bearded white god. Or so I puzzled over this first meeting and made the monumental error, I now believe, of not seeing that for tribal peoples even invaders from the sky were still *in* nature, not above or out of it, just as in their metaphysics the sky and the sea and the land were inextricably connected in the web of life. *Supernatural* beings were strictly creatures of Columbus's white world and of mine.

Throughout the Americas tribal people extended their hands in friendship because they affirmed the invaders as parts of the creation they worshiped all the days of their lives. I had failed to see that their principle of affirmation always carried with it the possibility of extension outward beyond family and clan and tribe to all other beings and things, in a universal embrace which reflected humankind's unconscious yearnings for the unity of all people and lands. Native Americans did not need Charles Darwin to tell them that they were parts of the animal world, Sigmund Freud to tell them that dreams were prime pathways to the animals within and to other two-legged and four-legged animals without, or Albert Einstein to tell them that their dancing bodies were akin to the dancing particles of dust from which we all came—their "animism" and stones that they believed held life were their benign counterparts of Einstein's atoms and his fateful discovery of the tremendous latent energy in inert mass. With their keen sense of the relatedness of everything, they did not need the modern biologist Lewis Thomas to tell them that the earth is like a cell and warn them of the mystery of "the enormous, imponderable system of life in which we are embedded as working parts" (Schell 1982a:97). In every season they venerated that mystery in ceremonies made splendid by their humility and intimate communion with what the Hopi people call the "Mighty Something" (Whorf 1956:60). And at the spiritual center of their great affirmation was the dance, the moving means of interweaving life, culture, land. As in the Ojibwa song/dance of thanksgiving, the pulsating feet of their bronze bodies caressed and communed with the body of the earth (Evans-Wentz 1981:111):

> Behold! Our Mother Earth is lying here;
> Behold! She giveth of her fruitfulness.
> Truly, her power she giveth unto us;
> Give thanks to Mother Earth who lieth here!

In *Problems of Art*, Susanne K. Langer had the insight that tribal
peoples have been dancing worshipers, credited them with having developed the dance as the first "high art," and defined this precursor form as
the "outward showing of inward nature, an objective presentation of
subjective reality." Admirably lucid on the evolution and meaning of
the dance in Western experience, this able philosopher still inadvertently illustrated the ethnocentric folly intrinsic to her presumption that
she was using objective and hence universal terms. Tribal people have
no "high art," or indeed any "low," for that matter, since in their
metaphysics the aesthetic, religious, intellectual, social, political, and
economic realms form a seamless whole. More importantly, they have
never made our alienating disjunction between subjective inner life and
objective outer reality — they would be truly mystified, I venture, by
Langer's summary of the dance as "an *objectification* [her emphasis] of
subjective life" (1957:9). For the tribal mind, their dancing bodies are in
nature and nature is in their bodies.

I do not use *bodies* here as a code word for bouncy genitalia, those
"evil forces" of the Arizona missionary and my disgusted reviewer. I do
not mean the whited sepulchres of their predecessor St. John Chrysos-
tom, the early Christian Father who reviled bodies as tombs with inner
parts full of filth (Rogers 1966:18). Rather I mean *whole persons*, as the
Wintu people are said to render our word.

Whole persons were Columbus's real discoveries at Guanahaní, the
island he renamed after the Christian Lord and Savior. Coming out of
two thousand years and more of negations, he could not see that in his
discoveries he had caught up with his own feared body out there on the
shining coral sand. Those "very handsome bodies with very fine faces"
were stand-ins for the whole persons, for the soul *and* body persons
buried in him and his crew under their armor of repressions. His first
impulse was to enchain those bodies, just as he sought to subjugate the
rest of nature—conquest of nature was always synonymous with conquest of the unconscious. He was stone-blind to the truth that his hosts
were whole persons with their own culture and language, in fine,
because they represented what he was negating in himself. To have
grasped their hands and entered their world, he would have had to
become a child of nature. He would have had to see that the Other we
negate is ourselves. He would have had to stop his negations.

White history has been the history of such negations. Admiral Samuel Eliot Morison proved himself no less blind to tribal realities—or in
his words, to the "guilelessness and generosity of the simple savage"—

than his hero, Admiral Christopher Columbus (1942, 1:303). Like Morison and his Harvard successor, Bernard Bailyn, American historians have sung hallelujahs in chorus for the conquerors of the so-called New World. Like Columbus they have tried to leave the growth-and-decay cycles of their own bodies behind by serving as guardians of a linear, continuous, irreversible Time of perpetual progress. With rare exceptions, they have been the secular heirs of Judeo-Christian teleology with its reified Time—as Vine Deloria, Jr., pointed out in *God Is Red*, "Christian religion and the Western idea of history are inseparable and mutually self-supporting" (1973:127). Believing with Francis Bacon that knowledge is power, many have sought to make their discipline scientific in order to predict and control history itself. Even some of the more perceptive champion the repressive domination of reason over feeling and, like my friendly critic, call for "less dancing and more analysis."

With our objectified Time, we historians have hidden the cyclical world of myth under our linear writings and have thereby robbed tribal people of their reality. I am not sure that a marriage of history and anthropology will produce kinder offspring. With rare exceptions again, anthropologists have also marched in step with Western "civilization," coming in after the soldier and the missionary to round off the conquest. In their reports back to the metropolis, tribal people are not subjects but "objects of study." Anthropologists have furthered the despiritualization of tribal worlds by thrusting their way into underground sacred traditions. With reason, as Claude Duret reported in 1607, some "Indians, fearing that their secrets would be recorded and revealed, would not approach certain trees whose leaves the Spanish used for paper" (Greenblatt 1976, 2:568). With reason the Taos Pueblo people have always kept whites from witnessing their secret ceremonies at Blue Lake. Some secrets should stay secret. But we non-Indians carry along our old patterns of thought and feeling even in the present surge of interest in tribal worlds. "The white man's attitude is positive and dominating," recently observed Emory Sekaquaptewa, the Hopi teacher, "and he is employing this attitude even now in seeking to understand the Indian" (Sekaquaptewa 1976:113). In such positivistic hands ethnohistory will be merely another way of negating the native.

The Dream of Reason has bred monsters but conceivably we could change. As everybody knows, we are sliding swiftly down our linear history to extinction. The history that has swallowed up so much already will shortly swallow up itself. For that not to happen, for us not to blow up our world and with it all the other worlds that were never ours to destroy, Jonathan Schell suggests that we begin with three basic principles of life: "respect for human beings, born and unborn"; "respect for the earth"; "respect for God or nature, or whatever one chooses to call the universal dust that made, or became us." Our power to "stop the future generations from entering into life compels us to ask basic new questions about our existence," Schell rightly notes, and then wrongly adds that "no one has ever thought to ask this question before our time, because no generation before ours has ever held the life and death of the species in its hands" (1982b:59, 108-9). No tribal people have ever held such apocalyptic power, of course, but some have been profoundly concerned for the unborn and have judged decisions precisely in the light of that old question. The distinguished Onondaga spokesman, Oren Lyons, has said that one of the first mandates given to him and other Iroquois chiefs was "to make every decision . . . relate to the welfare and well-being of the seventh generation to come, and that is the basis by which we make decisions in council. We consider: will this be to the benefit of the seventh generation?" (1980:173). Schell's principles of life have always been basic to tribal metaphysics. That realization and the very extremity of our predicament might help swing us away from our history and toward life.

Nothing less than a full turnabout will do. It will never be accomplished with one foot in ethnography and one foot in history, as we have known those disciplines. It will call forth from within these fiefdoms charges of romanticism, primitivism, of "going native," and will elicit impatient reminders that "the Noble Savage is also a racist stereotype." It will make timely Herman Melville's discovery a century and more ago that it was impossible to be simultaneously a patriotic United States citizen and a committed opponent of Indian-hating. It will require *seeing* the existence of other metaphysics that call into question the universality and beneficence of all our cherished binary oppositions: time/matter, spirit/flesh, reason/passion, sacred/profane, animate/inanimate, subjective/objective, supernatural/natural, imagination/understanding—the lot. Above all, it will demand humility before the "Mighty Something." We shall have to stop our negations, become children of nature, and lift ourselves to the Sioux truth: "We are all related!"[3]

I grant that this is a tall order, but then so is survival. We shall have to learn to speak a new language, the secret language of the body, as Martha Graham called the dance. Or rather, we shall have to relearn an old language, as Lame Deer knew we would: Human beings "have forgotten the secret knowledge of their bodies, their senses . . . their dreams" (Fire and Erdoes 1972:157). We have some way to go and the hour is late.

Notes

1. See also the interview with Jaulin by Françoise Morin and Jacques Mousseau (1971).

2. For the quotations from Columbus's *Diario* and his "Letter to the Sovereigns," see Morison (1963:64–66, 183–84).

3. I am indebted to Joseph Epes Brown for his insightful essay, "The Roots of Renewal" (1976).

11

On the Revision of Monuments

FREDERICK TURNER

At the 1982 convention of the Western Writers of America, held in Santa Fe, a local historian amused his audience with an anecdote about the historical monument that dominates the plaza in the city's center. Three sides of that 1868 monument are innocuous enough (unless you happen to harbor unreconstructed secessionist sympathies), for they pay a bland tribute to the bravery of the Union troops in Civil War engagements. But, as the historian observed, the fourth side has caused trouble in recent years. It used to read: "TO THE HEROES WHO HAVE FALLEN IN THE VARIOUS BATTLES WITH SAVAGE INDIANS IN THE TERRITORY OF NEW MEXICO."

The offending word was "savage," and the historian told how a blue-ribbon state commission had been created to address what he clearly perceived was a pseudo-problem. The result was the placement of a kind of appendix to the monument, a small, carefully-worded sign at its base, reminding visitors that monuments reflect their times and that the use of the word "savage" in 1868 was not then offensive. "Attitudes," the sign claimed, "change, and prejudices hopefully dissolve." The historian considered the appendix unnecessary, a "painful belaboring of the obvious," but, as he said, the whole matter has become even more absurd since subsequently the offending word was neatly, mysteriously, chiseled out. So now the appendix referred to nothing visible.

Across the street from the monument, under the long portal of the Palace of the Governors, where in Spanish colonial days they used to exhibit Apache scalps, Pueblo artisans sit in shadow, selling their wares to a ceaseless wave of tourists. For generations before it became offensive, "savage" stared both Indian and tourist straight in the face.

It is the nature of monuments to represent a kind of permanence. They are things the generations live by, standing for grand events and personalities, values mutually understood, a past concretized. But durable as they seem, they are not immune from the revising hand of subsequent times. At Compiègne, the French raised a monument commemorating the armistice they forced on the Germans in 1918. The Germans defaced that and erected a monument of their own, to celebrate the capitulation of the French on that same spot in 1940. And, after 1945, the French defaced the German monument and put up still another, celebrating the defeat of the Nazis. On Boston's Common, Saint-Gaudens's tribute to Colonel Shaw and his black regiment of the Civil War has been successively decorated with civil rights banners and anti-busing slogans.

If stone and bronze, as large in size as in reference, are subject to such treatment, what kinder fate may we expect for those countless, more perishable monuments of books? And, among books, surely the most perishable of the genus are books of history. Here no work, however monumental, has been safe from the revisionists. Gibbon, Macaulay, Henry Charles Lea—all have been subjected to the improvements of later writers—and in American historiography a whole industry and entire careers have been built on tinkering with Frederick Jackson Turner's essay, "The Significance of the Frontier in American History" (1893 [1963]). Emerson regarded it as the positive duty of each age to write its own histories, and American historians like Beard and Becker have said it was impossible for it to be otherwise—that the tenor of the times inevitably influences our selection and interpretation of data.

But whether duty or inescapable necessity, I know of nothing so trivial and dated as a certain sort of revisionist history. I mean the sort that, masquerading as new light or the redress of old errors, is actually a sub-species of generational revenge, sons rising up against dead fathers. Such revisionist writing generally takes the form of substitution: of one cause for another; of effect for cause; of the procrustean application of some newly-available principle (like psychoanalysis) to explain everything; or of simple transpositions in which, for instance, black is now made to equal good, and white, bad.

In too much of the revisionist writing on Indians and whites in America something like this last has been the case. In the years since Peter Farb called attention to the need for a fresh look at the Indians, in *Man's Rise to Civilization* (1968 [1978]), a great many shallowly-conceived works have seen print. These have at least the merit of being more generous toward Indians than earlier works are, but it is an open question as to whether they have significantly deepened our understanding of the Indians and of the complexities of Indian-white history. In recent years we have been creating a red Ecological Wise Man, who is in some ways as inhuman and fictive as the cunning savage in the bad old books of Simms, Parkman, and Roosevelt, so that at last we have fully earned the hard-edged liberalism of the Santa Fe historian who spoke so scornfully of the revisionist sign. Perhaps we really have been "belaboring the painfully obvious." But I would dispute the claim that the sign is unnecessary, that everyone knows that "savage" is an outmoded word having no place in the grammar of our time. Quite the opposite, I think, is the case; for though "savage" is no longer either serviceable or polite, the *idea* of the savage is still with us, and as a civilization we remain in need of revisionistic appendices to our monuments.

This kind of activity is, however, cumbersome, and a landscape of defaced or amended monuments may not be the best way to go about the task of changing attitudes and dissolving prejudices. Hence the unique virtue of those less conspicuous monuments of books. But here I think we need to revise in a different spirit. We need to ask more of ourselves as writers, and more of our readers. We need to raise the terms of the challenge to something approaching the level of Comte, who said it ought to be the duty of the revisionist historian to create out of the old, worn materials a more meaningful sequence, one which would not only illuminate the past of which it speaks but would also point toward a future it would influence.

To revise in this spirit might be to create monuments that would outlast the occasion of their making. Such monuments would have a chance for durability, I think, because in order to point to the past and be available to the future they would have to have their roots in both; and the only way they could achieve such transhistorical harmony would be by adopting a view of existence so broad and so fundamental to the species that it would be literally timeless, and even in a sense ahistorical. Here is a paradox (which, as we should remember, is a *seeming* contradiction containing a truth): the way the revising of Indian-white history may become truly significant is by a conscious abandonment of our Western view of life and human history. In order to begin to understand the Indians and the complexities of our mutual history, we shall have to attempt the strategic adoption of an aboriginal view of life.

Broadly speaking, that aboriginal view sees that our necessary human condition is to be a part of the total living universe, that we cannot be anything other than part of this gigantic organism, and that spiritual health is to be had only by accepting this condition and by attempting to live in accordance with it. If there is one theme that unites the hundreds of aboriginal cultures of North America, it is this one, and a serious contemplation of it would eventually force upon us authentic revisions of many of those events we thought we knew, from Columbus's landfall to the American Indian Movement to those Pueblo artisans under the portal in Santa Fe. This is the stunning implication of Calvin Martin's essay, "The Metaphysics of Writing Indian-White History" (1979; reprinted as Chapter 1). To take seriously the native view of life would be to see Indian-white history from the *inside* of the lodges, from which vantage everything would look different and from which new narrative sequences would *have* to emerge. William Carlos Williams was thinking along these very lines years ago, in his *In the American Grain*, and so was moved to write, "However hopeless it may seem, we have no other choice: we must go back to the beginning; it must all be done over. . . ." (1925:215)

Attempting to adopt such a view is no easy matter of fashion or of a moment, for what is required is the surrender of what we take to be our humanity to the magic and mystery of a universe no less alive in any of its phenomena—earth, stones, water, stars—than we ourselves are alive. Such a surrender is freighted with the threat of loss, of radical disorientation, of intellectual chaos. Surrendering to magic, to mystery, to a universe pulsating with vitality would seem to be to give up the long history of our own "rise to civilization," and in some sense this really would be the case. To most, including most professional historians, this surrender is neither necessary nor desirable. Yet I do not see how anything less than this can allow us to create the new and durable sequences we should be seeking.

Our resistance to this aboriginal life-view is both deep and long standing, for that life-view is in fact as much the meaning of the recently-offensive word "savage" as torture, scalping, and other real and imaginary Indian practices. But the Indians have not been the only victims, in letters and in life, of our resistance: we have also thus victimized ourselves as well. Here is that fundamental, more obdurate problem addressed by Richard Drinnon in "The Metaphysics of Dancing Tribes" (in this volume, Chapter 10). For more than a thousand years in the West, whites have been walling themselves off from an acknowledgment of the interconnectedness of all things, from an acceptance of the fact that there neither is nor ever can be any such entity as "human nature" considered apart from the rest of creation. And to the extent that we believe in spiritual health at all, we believe it is to be had through the vigorous exercise of those faculties that have allowed us to dominate the earth and the space around it. Immured thus in a prison of our own devising, we have almost forgotten who and what we are, and so have recourse to terms like "pagan," "primitive," and "animistic" to label those who have believed themselves part of a cosmos that nurtured many forms of life. We have used the term "romantic" to disparage those among us who have attempted to explain such a life-view or have felt its strange, compelling power.

Compared to this aboriginal life-view, ours is a shockingly dead view of creation. We ourselves are the only things in the universe to which we grant an authentic vitality, and because of this we are not fully alive. Surely we are not as alive to the wonder of existence as the natives once were. Even space, the new world, seems empty to us, and the moon is a dead satellite. In Thomas Berger's *Little Big Man*, a profound re-vision of the Western, the Cheyenne chief, Old Lodge Skins, explains that the essential difference between Indians and whites is that Indians believe everything is alive. "But white men believe everything is dead: stones, earth, animals, and people. And if, in spite of that, things persist in trying to live, white men will rub them out" (1964:214).

These words, admittedly fictional but grounded in solid ethnohistorical truth, direct our attention to the large consequences of our Western vision of the way things are, consequences that, as Drinnon suggests, stretch beyond the writing and revising of history to affect the future of the human species and the planet on which it lives. To have created a weapon in the name of saving some American lives but which is capable of annihilating *all* life and polluting the reaches of space—this, Drinnon makes us see, is the ultimate consequence of a life-view that could not make sense of the Native American.

Under the brooding specter of this cloud, the composing of such revisionist monuments as I have in mind might seem a paltry and even nugatory exercise, about the equivalent of worrying over the nutritional balance of foods stored for use during a nuclear war. Not so. All efforts to express our radical, essential humanity and the inseparability of that humanity from the universe are necessary efforts. All such efforts work toward the goal of fostering a genuine, religious respect for life in all its forms, a respect for human cultures in all their diversities.

So, to those of us who are engaged in the revising of Indian-white history I would say, let us not fear to take the necessary risk, to attempt the crucial surrender, as in their own time our ancestors in coming to these shores feared to do, and so lost their chance to revise their own history. Physically insignificant, perishable as paper, these small monuments may yet help us and indeed future generations to recover a lost and larger world that is our common birthright—as Americans, as human beings.

12

Envision Ourselves Darkly, Imagine Ourselves Richly
CHRISTOPHER VECSEY

We want to know ourselves. All people do. Each of us questions to some extent the value and purpose of our actions and arrangements; some of us even make a profession of self-examination. We study a body of knowledge and train our senses, placing our individual, social, and species lives in the perspectives of our learned disciplines. For instance, biologists situate human life in the great chain of animate existence, geologists in the layers of the planetary epochs, chemists in the combinations of material elements, and so on. All of the academic disciplines, like all human musings, aim for us to know ourselves better.

I am an historian with a special interest in American Indians and their religions. In writing this essay about what I have learned from my research, I do not imply that my learning should, or can, serve as a model for others. Like a father who can explain his fatherly enrichment only by virtue of having experienced fatherhood, I can only say what I have gained, and I do not offer my program of study for others to follow, expecting that they will find what I have found.

In retrospect, my grandest hope in becoming an historian was to examine the whole of human life, of which I represent a unit, by immersing myself—as all historians do—in my subject matter, my humanity, and at the same time engaging my critical faculties—as all historians do—to judge the merits of recorded, past human events. I wanted simultaneously to appreciate and criticize human life as a phenomenon and in all its parts.

Like any historian, I came to my craft in a milieu that shaped my academic interests and posed for me the queries that I made of life around me. In a broad sense my milieu was my American culture, and I made it my goal to understand—appreciating and criticizing—American nationality in all its diversity and continuity, wishing that my work might help Americans to examine themselves and their identity as a people.

More specifically, I was influenced by the political events of my 1960s schooldays—the civil rights movement and the Vietnam War—which raised unsettling issues concerning American habits and policies. As a result, I started as a muckraking American historian who hoped that his uncoverings would help produce ameliorative change in America. Not that I did so much of the raking myself, but rather I sought out the historians who had discovered the hidden, forbidden records of American life, the repressed underside of our national experience.

And like any historian, I chose for myself an area of concentration, the focus of which would serve as a symbol for American (and, by extension, all human) experience. I selected American Indian history, for reasons that I shall attempt to make clear in the following pages.

First, I was eager to encounter and tell what I thought were the untold stories about American oppression of Indians. In this exercise I was to emphasize my critical skills. By studying the invading and conquering white Americans in contact with American Indians, I found for myself the stained world of racism, venality, and brutality rarely discussed then in textbooks (although already well know to Indians and the specialists who studied them), a world whose image reflected my dark vision of America. American Indian history dredged up America at its worst (as the "Pogo" cartoon strip put it, "We have met the enemy and he is us") in order that we might see ourselves more completely and offer possibilities for our reformation.

More than a decade later, many of my colleagues say that the muckraking impulse (the "unAmerican Studies" approach) is naïve and repetitious. The verdict is in, they say, and America has been found guilty; now let us move on to some other topic. Academic wisdom these days notes that everyone knows America has acted badly toward Indians, so what else can we say about massacres and deceptions a century and more old?

I maintain, however, that a moral examination of our American policies regarding Indians is anything but outdated. On the contrary, vigilance is essential. In an age when a President can concoct fictional public accounts of American policy in Vietnam, when books are published that charge war protesters rather than war criminals with immorality, we historians must not cease to tell the stories, no matter how lurid, of our American-Indian relations. I must admit that teaching the history of Indian-white contact sometimes makes me cringe for the carnage; nevertheless, I realize that stories die when we stop telling them. Our task is to keep them alive. Otherwise the stories will disappear from public consciousness; they will submerge to the dim shelves of our neglected libraries and to our dimmer memories. We will forget the grisly truth about ourselves and our past.

Of course we must take into account the historical contexts in which American Indian history has taken place, being careful not to impose contemporary or Indian standards on the actions of past white Americans; however, even according to the standards of white America, past and present, we have acted badly, often hideously, and the truth must be told and retold.

Moreover, American Indian policy is not a dead issue, although it may be a deadly one. Indians are the fastest growing ethnic population within the borders of the United States, a population that presently feels besieged by America's addiction to high-tech energy, high-waste pollution, and high-and-mighty claims to sovereignty. In the southwest, Navajos face removals and uranium poisoning; Mohawks in the northeast face police and military harassment; Dakotas on the Plains face judicial abandonment of their treaties; and Alaskan natives face vigilante attempts to skin them of their fishing rights. If we care about the future of Indian peoples, we must persist in telling the truth, as we see it, about their past and present conditions. Cynicism and sophistication must not cause our moral outrage to falter. The stories of Indian-white contact reveal to us the stain on our national wealth, spirit, and character, and help us as well to envision ourselves darkly, and thus more fully.

So, I started out as an historian looking for the stories about our mistreatment of Indians, in order to understand the darkness of our American heritage. Reading classics like Helen Hunt Jackson's *Century of Dishonor* (1881), and the more recent *Fathers and Children* (1975), by Michael Paul Rogin, fed and whetted my appetite for such fare. In the process, however, I realized that my studies were focused upon white Americans, not the Indians themselves. I was engaged in American, not American Indian, historiography. *Century of Dishonor* was not a book about Indians, but rather about us and our dishonor. Rogin was writing about Andrew Jackson and the white American mentality.

Neither these authors nor I were sufficiently concerned about the Indians' sides of things.

I at first believed that primary Indian documents were lacking (an irony that has led us to see more clearly our own sins, having documented them so thoroughly, whereas non-literate Indians left fewer traces of their darkness), but I would soon learn that Indian texts are not unavailable. In graduate school I turned to these primary Indian texts in order to understand Indians themselves. In particular, I turned to their religious documents, especially their mythic narratives. As a teacher I have become engrossed in their kinship organization and in the processes of their material lives, their hunting, gathering, farming, house-building, and other survival skills. I have turned from our stories about ourselves in relation to Indians, and turned to Indian documentation about themselves.

By studying Indian texts about themselves, I have found, we can go beyond the necessary, but limiting, "victim" syndrome that epitomizes the muckraking history. The ways Indians have lived their lives, and the ways they have examined their lives—their action-wisdom and their thought-wisdom—transcend the terrible lessons of Indian-white history. Their existence transcends our contact with them, stretching as it does into deep prehistory, into the glacial past. I have learned that Indians in their material, societal, and spiritual lives offer us texts to ponder and to learn from and, perhaps in a limited way, to emulate. For this reason I have concentrated my study on Indian environmental adaptations, social formations, and spiritual relations.

I have learned about Indian people who gained their livelihood through centuries of modifications in their immediate and changing ecosystems: their careful observation and pragmatic use of local minerals, plants, and animals, and their creative development of numerous plant forms for human benefit, set in an explicit (and frequently observed) ideology of respect for non-human beings. I have learned about totemic groups of people who have existed for millennia in societal orders that are based on an enduring trust for kinship relations. Indian social life, for all its diversity from tribe to tribe, has held the family bond as a supreme ideal, valuing highly the necessity of face-to-face contact with people of a shared lineage, with a common mode of production, grounded in familial reciprocity and tribal tradition. And I have learned about Indian spirituality: undogmatic, experiential, integrated into a whole way of life, including environmental and kinship relations, with goals not only to worship suprahuman powers but also to protect, repair, and improve the life of the individual and the tribe. In short, Indian materiality, sociality, and religiosity all have structures with a long, interconnected history from which I (and others) can learn.

In addition to the manner of Indian lives, I have focused my attention on the means by which Indians have traditionally examined their lives—their own stories. In their stories American Indians have examined their lives in a way at least as valid as the discursive methods of academics. We often repeat Socrates' dictum that the unexamined life is not worth living, as though it meant that we Westerners (or, more exactly, we academics) are the only people who examine our lives and try to know ourselves. This is a false and degrading misconception. American Indians have examined their lives, both discursively and narratively. They have been willing to enter metaphysical disputations (we have records of such encounters), but in the main they have relied on their storytelling for self-knowledge. And if we believe that an *unexamined* life is not worth living, their stories indicate that examining life's possibilities and problems accomplishes nothing if it takes place apart from the life-sustaining web of human, environmental, and spiritual relations. In Indian stories, I have found, it is the *rootless* life that is not only worthless but impossible.

In the winter of 1979 I visited the Grassy Narrows Reserve in western Ontario to gather information from the Ojibwa Indians there for their legal claims regarding a mercury despoliation case. I interviewed an old man, John Beaver, who answered many of my questions with seasoned Ojibwa stories. When I asked him what distinguished an Indian hunter from a white hunter, he replied that the difference lay in their differing attitudes toward the animals they hunt. He proceeded to narrate a lengthy story about a bear who adopts a boy. Taking the child into his den and calling him his grandson, the bear shows what happens when bears allow themselves to be killed by hunters. If the hunters perform the proper thanksgiving rituals for the fallen animal, the bear comes back to life and can give himself to another hunter. After having demonstrated also that bears live in societies similar to those of humans, with similar motives and emotions of sexuality, protectiveness, and belonging, and with laughable foolishness similar to that of humans, the bear gives himself up to another hunter, who turns out to be the boy's father. The man and his son are reunited. John Beaver taught me that to Indians (at least the Ojibwa), human life depends upon other-than-human persons who give up their lives so humans can live, and who deserve and demand human respect.

The following year at Hopiland I heard from Eugene Sekaquaptewa a shortened version of the famous story of Hopi origins. At the invitation of the god, Masau'u, the ancestors of the Hopis emerge from the earth, trek across the body of the land, and establish what is now their homeland, becoming a people in the course of their journey and settlement. Through this story the Hopis define their human essence in terms of human community. Their story demonstrates that community networks are a matter of life and death; that human life depends on community cooperation; that disruptions, jealousy, and factionalism make human persistence impossible and, indeed, are pivotal factors in bringing death into the world. At its core the story is a declaration of dependence on community cooperation, just as the Ojibwa story is a declaration of dependence on the earth and its creatures.

Both stories indicate also that the spiritual world cares deeply about human life and promises to nurture it, if humans can live harmoniously with themselves and their fellow beings. These two stories epitomize for me the grand corpus of Indian stories that espouse a triplefold declaration of dependence on the surrounding world: of the individual on the community, of the community on nature, and of nature on the ultimately powerful world of spirit. It seems to me that the crucial matters of Indian stories—their thought-about-world—are crucial to us, too, just as our knowledge of their lived-in-world is important.

As an American historian I began with the stories about our relations with Indians, our stories about us in relation to them. In time I concentrated on stories about them and their existence both in relation to us, and in relation to their environmental, community, and spiritual worlds. And, finally, I have focused on their stories about themselves and their surrounding worlds. What have I found to be the purpose of my program?

At its best, historical scholarship grants us the opportunity of an imaginative double vision. We set our sights on people of another time, place, or habit, and we see them, to the best of our abilities, as they have seen themselves. At the same time, we see them as they have *not* seen themselves, in short, as *we* see them. Simultaneously, we employ our empathy to envision their motives, feelings, social relations, and material existence as they might have experienced them, and we employ our hindsight to survey their situations and thoughts from our objectifying distance, with the advantage of an outsider's perspective. So, our attitude toward our subjects is twofold: we associate with them and disassociate from them, and then we combine our loving and scrutinizing viewpoints to achieve historical vision.

Add to this the fact that in studying Indian-white history we must try to understand both Indian and white viewpoints (with many variations within each culture), and we multiply our visionary possibilities. I have found that the study of Indian-white contact—of two cultures not only interacting but conflicting with one another—provides us with clues to the historical differences that are important in the largest sense, differences that have truly set us apart as we have questioned and threatened each other's lifeways. We can see, for example, how our material values are so deeply embedded that our missionaries have aimed to teach Indians selfishness—to put them into "trousers with a pocket that aches to be filled with dollars" (Gates 1897:11)—and that our laws have tried to prevent Indian dances that have included the ritual sharing of wealth. A contrast of such Indian and white cultural traits can be revelatory to us. What we learn about ourselves is that we white Americans are more deeply and tragically human than we tell ourselves in our political and congratulatory rhetoric. Our national pride must be tempered with critical self-knowledge. Our faith in ourselves must incorporate doubt into itself if it is to be a lasting, effective faith. The study of our contact with Indians, the envisioning of our dark American selves, can instill such a strengthening doubt.

Furthermore, the study of Indian life that transcends Indian-white contact can help us expand our concept of who we are. Too readily we think of ourselves as white Western moderns, belonging to a Judeo-Christian religion and a Greco-Roman polity. However, by seeing our humanity reflected and revealed in the lives of those who have suffered under the tread of our national progress, we can see that we are more than white Americans. Historians like myself can teach us to say, "We have met the Indians and they are us." In this way history can serve as cultural therapy, releasing for us and our students the repressed images of our full humanity. By retelling the stories of Indian lives, stories which are, I contend, our own stories, and by imagining ourselves as humans (and I admit that it takes a strong imagination) instead of contemporary, white Americans, we can make manifest some crucial latencies of our human nature. Indian traditions have something to offer us non-Indians: values we have repressed or never known regarding environment, society, and the spiritual world. Their texts offer us insights concerning the possibility of human systems that we might recover or attain. The study of American Indians, I have found, challenges us in our Americanness and enriches us in our humanness, permitting us—as N. Scott Momaday has recommended (1980)—to "imagine ourselves richly," to know ourselves well.

13

Fox and Chickadee
ROBIN RIDINGTON

I grew up in Maryland, Pennsylvania, and New Jersey. Until I left this eastern enclave I had no opportunity to make contact with "real live Indians." I never experienced a natural landform or a climax community of plants and animals. Everywhere, the land and its life were transformed by farming and industry. History was written in the stones that settlers sweated and skidded from forest floors, and heaped at the boundaries of their property lines. History was a resource to be mined from lodes of artifacts and documents. History was dead and gone from the breath of experience. It was about a past that would not return to life. Beyond history lay myth and legend. Beyond history lay the land as it was before being shaped to our purposes. Beyond history lay the world of Indians, to me as yet a dreamworld.

My first contact with the Indian world began in 1959 when I spent a summer with friends who were homesteading land north of the Peace River in British Columbia, Canada. The land on which they built their cabin was in traditional hunting and trapping territory of Athapaskan-speaking Beaver Indians. According to the government of Canada, the land my friends had chosen belonged to the Crown. According to the Indians, native people belonged to the land because they knew it in ways the government could not even imagine. As I came to know the Indians I began to widen my own ways of thinking. I saw a connection between people and environment that could not be represented by legal documents alone.

When I returned to school in the East, I studied anthropology. In 1964 I began the anthropological rite of passage known as fieldwork. I wanted to understand the cultural psychology of people who lived by hunting. I headed back to the Peace River country.

In August 1964, I had been doing fieldwork with the Beaver Indians of the Prophet River reserve for about six weeks. I was camped with a small band of about two dozen people just off the Alaska Highway between Fort St. John and Fort Nelson, British Columbia. A large oil drilling camp run by the Majestic Construction Company was less than two miles from our fires, but the distance between us could also have been measured in thousands of years. Our camp was an irregular cluster of wall tents, a tipi, and brush-sided double lean-tos set on either side of a seismic oil exploration line cut through the brush by huge D 8 "Cats." The Indians called these tractors "kettles walking" in their language. The Indians were there to make drymeat. I was there to administer projective tests and collect data for a Ph.D. thesis.

In my research proposal I had said I would use the test results to examine the hypothesis that low accumulation hunting economies are associated with high levels of a personality variable called Need for Achievement, or "N Ach," as it was referred to in psychologese. The Indians were doing very well in their hunting, but my testing was not going well at all. The Indians were reluctant to take the tests. When they did take pity on my desperate need to accumulate "data," their responses were minimal. Preliminary analysis indicated they were severely withdrawn if not virtually autistic, but they did not act that way outside of the test situation. My questions, on the other hand, clearly revealed my own high level of performance anxiety. In order to elicit responses from them, I generally had to ask questions that were longer and more revealing than their answers. From time to time they suggested that they knew "Indian stories," much more interesting than the ones I wanted them to make up in response to the set of standardized pictures I had brought with me. For a long time I rejected their suggestions. These stories were not the scientific data I required.

One day a tiny, frail old man was led into our camp by his grandson. I had met him earlier in the Fort Nelson hospital, and later at the reserve where people lived during the winter. He had been in and out of the hospital for several months, suffering from a series of heart attacks. Despite pressure from white doctors and the local school teacher to return to the hospital as the attacks became more frequent and more severe, he wished to be in the bush with his people. He needed moosemeat, wind, stars, his language, and his relatives, rather than the narrow white bed on which I had seen him perched cross-legged, like a tiny bird. His name was Japasa—"Chickadee."

On the evening of his arrival the old man suffered another attack. As he struggled and moaned two of his grandchildren and two old men held him, rubbed his arms and chest. A young daughter also came in to touch him. Outside the tent a circle of people watched in silence. Rainwater, collected as it ran down the trunk of a living spruce tree, was sprinkled on the fire. Gradually he became quiet and passed into a normal sleep. A few people remained to watch over him through the night and to keep a large fire burning.

The next evening people gathered around the old man's fire, after the day's work of hunting and preparing meat and hides. His son told a story about how he and the old man survived the terrible flu of 1918–19 that had killed many people. Then Japasa began speaking softly, apparently to himself, as if he were looking back into a dream to find the words. His son whispered a simultaneous translation into English for my benefit. It must have been important to him that I share this event. He wanted me to understand enough of what was going on at the time that I could discover its meaning later in my life. This is the essence of Japasa's revelation as related to me by his son. I have told it in my own words from notes I made later that evening.

My dad said that when he was a boy, about nine years old, he went into the bush alone. He was lost from his people. In the night it rained. He was cold and wet from the rain, but in the morning he found himself warm and dry. A pair of silver foxes had come and protected him. After that, the foxes kept him and looked after him. He stayed with them and they protected him. Those foxes had three pups. The male and female foxes brought food for the pups. They brought food for my dad, too. They looked after him as if they were all the same. Those foxes wore clothes like people. My dad said he could understand their language. He said they taught him a song.

At this point in the narrative the old man sang the boy's song. He sang his medicine song. I did not know then that this song could be heard only when death was near to the singer or to the listener. I did not know he was giving up the power the foxes gave to him in a time out of time, alone in the bush in the 1890s.

My dad said he stayed out in the bush for twenty days. Ever since that time foxes have been his friends. Anytime he wanted to he could set a trap and get foxes. When he lived with the foxes that time he saw rabbits, too. The rabbits were wearing clothes like people. They were packing things on their backs.

The first night out in the bush he was cold and wet from the rain. In the morning when he woke up warm and dry the wind came to him, too. The wind came to him in the form of a person. That person said, "See, you're dry now. I'm your friend." The wind has been his friend ever since. He can call the wind. He can call the rain. He can also make them go away. One time when I was twelve, I was with my dad and some other people when we got trapped by a forest fire. One of our horses got burned and we put the others in a creek. My dad told all the people to look for clouds even though it hadn't rained for a long time. They found a little black cloud and my dad called it to help us. In just about ten minutes there was thunder and lightning and heavy rain that put out the fire. We were really wet but we were glad to be saved from that fire.

My dad sang for the rain to come a couple of days ago. He sang for it to come and make him well. That rain came right away. This morning he called the wind and rain. They came and then he told them to go away. He told them he was too old and he didn't need their help any more. He wanted to tell them he was too old and didn't need them. He said it was time to die. He told them they could leave him now.

After he had been in the bush twenty days he almost forgot about his people. Then he heard a song. It was coming from his people. He remembered them and he went toward the song. Every time he got to where the song had been it moved farther away. Finally, by following that song he was led back to his people.

After Japasa had told the story of his medicines the normal life of a hunting camp resumed. Men continued their hunting. They were very successful. Women were busy making drymeat and scraping hides. The old man stayed near his fire. From time to time we could hear the sound of his voice rising and falling in song like a distant wind. He had no more attacks. On the seventh day after giving away his medicines he remained well throughout the day. In the evening I returned to camp with some older men and boys after riding all day out to where a large moose had been killed. It took four pack horses to bring back the meat. The hunter's wife received it and then distributed meat to the other women of our camp.

Suddenly, it felt as if a wind were sweeping across the camp. It was a wind of alarm, of emotion, of change. I saw people flying toward Japasa's camp as if they were leaves in a wind. Their words were snatched away like cries in a storm. My fatigue and saddle sores from the day's ride vanished as I joined the flow of people. For the first time in my life I heard the rattle of death wrack a human body. People rubbed the old man as they had done before, but it was clear his breath would not return this time. A stillness came over us, then a gentle rain of tears. The tent was rolled back to make a kind of backdrop. The body was turned around to lie open to the sky. A friend and I dressed the old man's body in good clothes he had brought to be buried in. On his feet we placed a new pair of beaded moccasins made for him by a young woman who had died the year before. The moccasins may have helped him follow her song on what I learned later was called "the trail to heaven." Wearing these new moccasins the boy who knew foxes would be able to follow a trail of song to another camp.

After Japasa's death the tests seemed less important to me. I cared less about data relevant to the language of personality theory and more about data relevant to understanding the stories the old man had made known to me seven days before I heard his death rattle. In the seventeen years that have passed since I heard Japasa give away his songs I have never again been close enough to death to hear a person sing the songs of his or her medicine. I have, however, listened to a wealth of Indian stories. I have studied them, dreamed them, told them, taught them, and made them my own.

The stories are windows into the thoughtworld of Indian people. Their time is different from ours. The old man and the boy circle around to touch one another, just as the hunter circles around to touch his game and the sun circles around to touch a different place on the horizon with every passing day. During the year it circles from northern to southern points of rising and setting. It circles like the grouse in their mating dance. It circles like the swans who fly south to a land of flowing water when winter takes the northern forest in its teeth of ice. The sun circles like the mind of a dreamer whose body lies pressed to earth, head to the east, in anticipation of its return. The sun and the dreamer's mind shine on one another.

On the evening when Japasa gave up his medicines he gave me two stories, as well. One was about how Indian people from far and wide used to gather in the prairie country near the Peace River to dry saskatoon berries. They came down the rivers in canoes full of drymeat, bear tallow, and berries. They sang and danced and played the hand game in which teams of men bet against one another in guessing which hand conceals a small stone or bone. The other story was about frogs who play-gamble, just like people. He said he knew frogs because he once lived with them on the bottom of a lake.

The old man's stories recalled times that we would think of as being very different from one another. One we would call history; the other, myth. Written documents going back as far as the late eighteenth century describe Indians coming together to sing, dance, and gamble in the Peace River prairie country. We can use the traditions of historical scholarship to substantiate that what Japasa described really happened. There is no documentary or scientific evidence to indicate that frogs really sing and dance and gamble beneath the waters of a pond, but the old man said he experienced this, too. Because we lack documentary evidence we are compelled to class his second story as myth. In our thoughtworld myth and reality are opposites. Unless we can find some way to understand the reality of mythic thinking we remain prisoners of our own language, our own thoughtworld. In this world one story is real, the other, fantasy. In the Indian way of thinking both stories are true because they describe personal experience. Their truths are complementary.

Both of Japasa's stories were true to his experience. When he was a boy Japasa knew frogs and foxes and wind. He knew their songs. He entered the myths that are told about them. He obtained power by joining his own life force to theirs. He knew them in the bush away from the society of other humans. He knew them in the searing transformation of his vision quest. He became their child, one of their kind. He saw them clothed in a culture like his own. He carried them through to the end of his life, and then he let them go.

Japasa also knew the social power created by his people when they came together in good times. At the time of his death both forms of power were strong all around him. Hunters were making contact with their game. Women passed the meat from camp to camp, making the people strong together. On the morning after he told us the stories of his medicines we saw a moose cross the seismic line within sight of camp. Never before or since have I known game animals to come that close to where hunters are camped. People said the animals were coming around the old man to say goodbye to him. They said they knew from the tracks that foxes came to his camp in the night. For seven days after Japasa let go of his powers the people were all around him. He became like the child he was before his vision quest. He was within the strength of his people when he left on the trail of a different song.

Historical events happen once and are gone forever. Mythic events return like the swans of spring. The events of history are unique and particular to their time and place. They cannot be experienced directly by people of different times and places. I can know about Napoleon, but I cannot be Napoleon if I wish to be regarded as sane. Mythic events are different. They are essential truths, not contingent ones. I can be a frog or a fox and still be a person. I can know them as I know myself. If I am Indian I can be led toward a place where this knowledge will come naturally. The foxes that came to Japasa before he died were the same as the foxes he knew as a boy. The wind came to him as a person, the foxes wore clothes and spoke in a language he could understand, the frogs gathered to drum and gamble. They gave this boy their songs as guides to the powers he would have as a man. Throughout his life he returned in his dreams to that visionary time-out-of-time. His powers were forces within him as well as forces of nature. His experience was always within nature. Even in times of hardship he did not move against it. At the end of his life people and animals came together around him. When he died he returned to the mythic time, like the swans who fly south in the fall. As long as mythic time remains we can expect his return.

For northern hunting people, knowledge and power are one. To be in possession of knowledge is more important than to be in possession of an artifact. Their technology depends upon artifice rather than on artifact. They live by knowing how to integrate their own activities with those of the sentient beings around them. The most effective technology for nomadic people is one that can be carried around in their minds. Hunting people are able to create a way of life by applying knowledge to local resources. Their dreaming provides access to a wealth of information. Their vision quests and their myths integrate the qualities of autonomy and community that are necessary for successful adaptation to the northern forest environment. The truths of the hunting way of life are essential, and unchanging from generation to generation. In spirit, they may very well reflect paleolithic traditions of our own distant ancestors.

The mythic thinking of northern native people combines the individual intelligence we all have as members of a common species with a cultural intelligence embedded in the wealth of knowledge they carry around in their minds. Their stories tell them how to make sense of themselves in relation to a natural world of sentient beings. Their dreams and visions give direct access to this wealth of information. Individual intelligence and the intelligence of cultural tradition work together. Both are dedicated to making sense of human life in relation to the life of nature. These hunters act on the basis of knowledge and understanding rather than from orders passed down through a social hierarchy.

Our own traditions strongly stress obedience to duly constituted authority. This authority is frequently intellectual as well as social and political. We are more often taught answers than how to solve questions that come to mind. We are literal-minded in interpreting the meaning of experience in a hunting culture. We misunderstand myth by interpreting it as flawed history. For hunters, it is appropriate to place human life within nature. For historians, human life is inevitably placed within the stream of history. For hunters, dreams and visions validate and explain the past in terms of present experience. For historians, the past is validated by documents rather than by personal experience. When historians attempt to write the history of hunting people they must find ways of recognizing the validity of personal experience without violating their own scholarly traditions of obtaining valid information about the past. Historians must be wary of dreaming up other cultures, but they can, perhaps, dream into the rich store of information that hunters have given us about themselves. The true history of these people will have to be written in a mythic language. Like the stories of Japasa, it will have to combine stories of people coming together with other people, and those that tell of people coming together with animals.

When I heard old man Japasa speak in 1964 about his medicine animals, I knew with absolute certainty this man was neither lying nor deluding himself. It was I who indulged in self-delusion when I persisted in asking for data in a form that could not accommodate Beaver Indian reality. In his last days on earth, the old man gave me his vision of that reality. I hope that the trust he placed in me has been justified in some small measure by the work I have chosen to do in my life.

14

I May Connect Time
PETER IVERSON

When my grandfather, Paul Schmitt, and my grandmother, Veronica Koppes, were married at the turn of the century, the Marysville, Kansas, newspaper suggested that these two young people came from two of the best families in Marshall County. They were the children of immigrants, farmers and shoemakers from Luxemburg, who spoke German. Their parents had come to Kansas, as did so many in nineteenth-century America, to work the land or to have their own businesses and thus regenerate their fortunes.

Paul Schmitt had attended St. Benedict's at Atchison, where he studied Latin and Greek and considered becoming a priest. Instead, he became a school teacher. He gradually rose through the ranks in the county, eventually becoming superintendent of schools. With the outbreak of the First World War, as I have been told, he lost his job. A victim of the anti-German feelings rampant at the time, he faced an uncertain future. He had four daughters and was no longer a young man.

After working in various family concerns for some time, Paul Schmitt went back to school at the University of Kansas. He earned his baccalaureate and gained a position teaching in the junior high division of Haskell Indian School. From Lawrence, Kansas, he moved to Mount Pleasant, Michigan, to become principal of a school for Ojibwa and other Indian students. It was a promotion, and his superiors in the Indian Service reminded him that his daughters could attend the little teachers' college in town.

His daughters proceeded to do just that, but in the early 1930s the Indian school was closed and Paul and Veronica Schmitt moved once again. They went this time to Fort Wingate, New Mexico, at the edge of

Navajo country, where he served as principal of the high school. After three years, he was transferred somewhat involuntarily to the boarding school at Keams Canyon on the Hopi reservation. I have heard that the previous principal was having an affair, and the Bureau of Indian Affairs officials knew that in my grandfather there would not be the slightest chance that such scandalous behavior would be repeated. Fort Wingate had been near Gallup; Keams was a long way from Holbrook, and my grandmother thought she was close to the end of the world. In two years, Paul Schmitt concluded his work in the Indian Service with a post at Toadlena, New Mexico. There he was principal, with additional responsibilities for other schools on each side of the Lukachukai mountains. In the heart of the Two Grey Hills weaving country, he bought, alas, but one rug, a magnificent one purchased for fifty dollars from Newcomb's trading post.

Paul Schmitt retired to California and he lived to be an old man. He would carve apples with an ancient pocket-knife that I now treasure, and would tell stories about his years as a teacher for the Bureau. It was always the stories from Navajo country that especially fascinated me. I could see him driving his Oldsmobile purchased from Rico Motors in Gallup over the Lukachukais. I imagined people such as Father Berard Haile, the Franciscan priest from St. Michael's, who gained so much knowledge about Navajo history, language, and culture, or Navajo political leaders such as Chee Dodge, Jacob Morgan, and Howard Gorman. I pictured places: Canyon de Chelly, Teec Nos Pos, Ganado, Wide Ruins.

And thus in my childhood, Indians in general and Navajos in particular became real to me. I knew that Indians were not people with only a past. Rather they were continuing, indeed enduring. Just as others did, they had problems to deal with; and just as others did, they had successes. They had fears and dreams, hopes and ideals. Indians had a present and they had a future, too.

Years later, I went to college and then began graduate school in American history at the University of Wisconsin. I learned of a new college being started by the Navajos and I wrote to learn more about it. It was called Navajo Community College, I discovered; it was heralded as the first college established by Indians on a reservation. The new institution shared facilities with a recently constructed boarding high school in Many Farms, not too far from Chinle and Canyon de Chelly. I realized that being at such a place could be a wonderful opportunity. But I was just finishing my M. A. and did not think that there was much of a chance I could take part in this fledgling educational experiment.

In the spring of 1969, college officials called to offer me an interview. The catch proved to be that I would have to pay my own way down to Many Farms from Madison, and I did not feel I could afford such a venture. So, reluctantly, I declined. A person with a Ph.D. obtained the job and I prepared to continue in graduate school. Then in late summer the new employee backed out. Needing a replacement at the last possible minute, a Navajo Community College administrator tracked me down, offered me the job, and gave me two days to decide. I think I needed less time.

I taught at the college for three years. In that time much happened that will always affect me. In a personal and a professional sense, it was my immigration to a new land and it regenerated my life and my career. It altered how I taught, how I wrote, and what I wanted to write about. And it reaffirmed what I had learned from my grandfather: Indians had a present and a future, as well as a recent past that indicated they could change, adapt, go on. Indians did not cease to exist in the snows of Wounded Knee in 1890. Their languages did not halt; their traditions had not been erased entirely.

Over Thanksgiving vacation in 1969 I drove to California to see my grandparents. It was good that I did, for the following summer my grandfather would die. But that weekend was filled with memories and new impressions and it marked a very special connecting of time between my grandparents and me. Both the continuity and the change in Navajo life impressed us. That young upstart, Howard Gorman, was now a distinguished senior member of the Tribal Council and a member of the Navajo Community College Board of Regents. Where there had been generally unpaved roads, one could now drive on good highways in a circle from Window Rock to Ganado to Chinle to Round Rock to Fort Defiance, but the road over the Lukachukais seemed about the same; I gained new respect for Oldsmobiles from the 1930s. Two Grey Hills rugs were more valuable than ever, but the price had escalated impressively. And some of my grandfather's students at Fort Wingate, it emerged, were now colleagues of mine.

I returned to Many Farms armed with the old Wingate yearbooks. The master silversmith, Kenneth Begay, drew himself up to his most dignified posture when accosted with a photograph of himself in his high school football uniform: "*Where* did you get that?" He and his wife remembered my grandparents fondly, but the linguist, William Mor-

gan, who was having very mixed success in teaching me Navajo, recalled more unhappily that my grandfather had tried to make him
into a blacksmith. Lee Kanaswood, father of anthropologist Priscilla
Kanaswood, spoke volumes with his silence, as Navajos often do. When
Percy told her dad about my tie with an earlier era, he was quiet for a
long time. Then he said slowly, "So your grandfather was Paul
Schmitt?" That was all he said.

I learned about silence and many other things, I believe, during those
years. Many of the deepest impressions had nothing to do directly with
the research that I ultimately would undertake. Yet in one way or
another they influenced clearly what I wanted to say, for they mirrored
far-ranging aspects of contemporary life in the Navajo Nation. And
they often made a connection with places I had already been to in my
imagination.

I remember watching at sunset the birds fly off the edge of Canyon de
Chelly near Three Turkey Ruins. There was no sound save the wind.
The beauty and the power of the scene overwhelmed me.

I remember driving seventy miles to play basketball in the tiny gym of
Teec Nos Pos boarding school. It was, after all, the seventh annual
Sheep Herders Classic. For the first and last time in my life, I had
become a center. There were to be no twenty-foot jump shots: Clifford
Beck (now a well-known artist), Jack Jackson (a prominent member of
the Native American Church), and others would cheerfully advise me to
rebound and pass the ball.

I remember the chill of the early morning air, watching the bluebird
song being chanted by the white-painted yei-bi-chai masked figures.
The air smelled richly of smoke and the red cliffs of the Lukachukais
loomed in the distance.

I remember driving sixty miles through open range in the middle of
the night to the old Presbyterian mission hospital at Ganado. Nearby a
sign once had read, "Tradition Is the Enemy of Progress." Project Hope
now operated the hospital where my daughter came into the world.
There were horses grazing outside the hospital window and in the joy
and excitement of the day I walked over to the old Hubbell trading post
and bought two rugs, one from Wide Ruins and one from Two Grey
Hills. My daughter soon would receive her social security number,
enclosed in a letter addressed to "Dear Indian Parents."

Despite that title, I learned one of the most important lessons early
on—that I was not a Navajo and I never would be one. "Were you
accepted?" I was often asked in the years that followed; and the answer

quickly became, "Yes, for what I was, and what I was not." The ethnic boundary described by Fredrik Barth and other observers definitely applied to the Diné (Navajo); no honorary memberships would be bestowed to some visiting political dignitary by this tribe. However, one could be appreciated as a friend, a colleague, one who recognized the values and traditions inherent in Navajo culture.

At the same time, one had to be absolutely blind not to notice the very real and pressing difficulties within Navajo society. Generally, the Navajos I knew wanted one to see those considered as well. They had grown weary of the well-intentioned reporters for a liberal magazine or a big newspaper who had been dispatched to the reservation for a quick view of "Lo, the Poor Indian." They had tired of reading about or hearing reports that emphasized exclusively alcoholism, unemployment, poor housing. They did not deny that these problems existed—far from it. What they wanted was an evaluation of Navajo life that encompassed both the richness of it as well as the problems that beset it.

That approach was essential, I realized, for those of us who wanted to write about Indians and their history. We who are non-Indians do no one a favor by presenting either an entirely romantic view or a perspective that is entirely pessimistic. What we need to do is to learn about Indian life and then present that sense in a straightforward fashion, though there can be silences in our writing, too. My years living in Many Farms, built from the foundation allowed by the stories of my childhood, afforded me the opportunity few historians seek, let alone have. My writing always will be affected by the sight of the yei-bi-chai dancers. But it also will be influenced by the tragedy of a teen-aged boy who died from wood alcohol poisoning. He was found in the sand five feet from my door.

For historians, the reality of Indian life is difficult to perceive. We are trained to rely on the written record and the printed word. We burrow into archives. We troop diligently from one library to the next. Surely that work is important, but our evaluation of works in Indian history cannot be based exclusively on that standard. We cannot judge books based on the length of the bibliography or whether the author has neglected an archival source we have found helpful in writing our books.

What I am suggesting that students of Indian history must do is rely on more than the written record and the printed word. Even if we choose to write about the distant past, we need to travel to the land where the people lived. If the people still live there, then we must listen to them and think about what they have to say. We must be able to think about different ways of seeing a historical event or person. And, as N. Scott Momaday has written, we must learn about the land:

> Once in his life a man ought to concentrate his mind upon the remembered earth, I believe. He ought to give himself up to a particular landscape in his experience, to look at it from as many angles as he can, to wonder about it, to dwell upon it. He ought to imagine that he touches it with his hands at every season and listens to the sounds that are made upon it. He ought to imagine the creatures that are there and all the faintest motions in the wind. He ought to recollect the glare of noon and all the colors of the dawn and dusk (1981:164–65).

It is in the writing of twentieth-century Indian history that we have a special opportunity. For we can speak to Indian people who have lived through these times and we can employ tribal records. We can, in sum, provide a kind of history that does not read primarily as an account of the whites as actors and the Indians as the acted-upon. It is an exciting prospect to watch such history being written, but it is not without its dangers.

These are dangers that colonial historians, for example, need not encounter. Several years ago, Michael Green invited me to give a paper on the administration of Navajo chairman Peter MacDonald, at the annual Native American Studies conference at Dartmouth. Ready for a respite from Laramie's eight-month-long winter and naturally flattered by an invitation to appear at Dartmouth, I accepted after a proper, deliberate pause of, say, four seconds. Then Green pounced: "By the way, we've also invited MacDonald to give a major address and be on hand to comment on your paper." He encouraged me to send a draft of my paper to MacDonald ahead of time. The chairman was a busy man, he somewhat needlessly informed me, but he might grab a minute beforehand to glance at my paper.

Indeed he did. About a week before departure for Hanover I received a call from MacDonald's public relations man, an Irishman who had recently arrived in the Navajo Nation, who was unswervingly loyal to his boss, and who figured I was simply uninformed on a couple of points. A mountain of photocopied press clippings soon came in the mail. Then one of the attorneys for the Navajo Nation, from whom I had not heard in years, called to renew an old friendship and incidentally fill me in on a few points discussed in my paper. I did not change the talk, and after my forty-minute presentation, MacDonald responded for well over an hour, neatly exhausting our allotted time. In essence he thought the things I had praised in his administration represented genuine insight and perception on my part. As for the shortcomings I had observed, well, I just needed a little more information.

While I can look back upon the event in relatively light-hearted fashion, I am sympathetic to the problems naturally posed by interpretation of the recent past. One can annoy people who are important. One can close down potential sources who do not like what we say. One will meet continually people who fulfil that old adage that people who ask for criticism really expect praise. But one can write with a kind of scrupulousness and care born of the knowledge that one is writing about people and feelings that are very much alive. That will encourage, more than anything, fairness and responsibility on our part. The final result can be only better history.

I thought about that responsibility and that promise last week as I drove down through the majestic San Juan mountains of southwestern Colorado and on to Navajo land. It had been ten years since I had been a resident in the Navajo Nation. Much had changed in my life during that decade and much had changed in Navajo life, too. Yet I was struck primarily, as I am on each return to my former home, by how much had remained the same. There were changes, to be sure. A new Bashas' supermarket had opened in Chinle, while Burnsides Corner no longer sold Shell gasoline and Valley Store had closed. But the land and the sky remained constant. And the Navajo broadcaster on the radio still hurled long Athapaskan sentences at a mile a minute, interspersed with untranslatable English phrases such as Colonel Sanders' Kentucky-Fried Chicken.

My work will continue to focus on Indians in the twentieth-century West, and on a merging of past, present, and future. As I write of these people and their histories, I hope to remember the poem of a young Navajo woman (Nakai 1980:91):

    i must be like a bridge
       for my people
    i may connect time; yesterday

today   and tomorrow—for my people
   who are in transition, also.
i must be enough in tomorrow, to give warning—
   if i should,
i must be enough in yesterday, to hold a cherished secret.
Does it seem like we are walking as one?

15

Present Memories, Past History

PETER NABOKOV

How often on reservations and in libraries the realization came to me: my look at Indian and white relations was amounting to a chronicle of little victories of spirit and meaning over space and time.

I am in a tarpaper cabana on Indian Island, Maine, talking with a tipsy old Penobscot herbalist who has just penned a "wind letter" to his lady love, a scrawled plea that she visit soon. He puts a match to it and steps outside to pulverize the ashes into the breeze. Back on his cot he describes how his "great-great-grandmother" saved her son from red-coated soldiers. With the child on her back she swam this river over there. It was the time of the assault on the Catholic priest's stronghold at Norridgewock. As she clambered up the bank the soldiers shot her dead. The boy escaped into the woods, surviving on berries and leaves. He was rescued by a grinning Frenchman who gave him his own name. It sounded like yesterday.

Later I became aware that in his cups he'd combined the generations of The Whaler's wife and Père Sébastien Rale, but in those moments of his talking, two and a half centuries just slipped away. In my awareness the tumult of a nation's birth became immediate, personal, and credible for the first time. Not the Mutual Life statue with the flintlock nor the bloodied piccolo player nor wigged generals nor smoke puffs on the green. The intimate, colloquial event of this telling had salvaged flesh and blood from advertising-copy, depersonalized history. Through a mother's flight to save her babe the past was thrust into my face in that storyteller's voice, which broke at the memory. He paused after his story, demanding recognition and relationship. The feeling was not unlike being in a jury box. As a friend who is ninety-five commented,

144

when we were discussing the First World War, "You have history, I have memories."

The paradox of memorized history that is spoken and heard is that while it can preserve intimacy and locality over astonishing time depths, it seems to be only one generation away from extinction. It is a fragile linkage of spider strands across time. For it to endure someone somewhere must continue to bear witness, must intuitively resist the demands of media and archive in favor of the interactive, oral narrative. For this sort of history to preserve the economy and actuality of memory, it roots its actions in place, not dates. It neglects time to inject energy instead into the human and supernatural neighborhoods of its tales. It is called into being during and for interpersonal situations. It nurtures the family and community and cosmic continuities of which it speaks. In our day there is almost something fugitive and conspiratorial about such vernacular history—it is not for all to know. This history also looks at life realistically: if I am needed someone will harbor me and find a language for me and speak me when there is a reason. Unless I have a purpose now or for tomorrow, what good am I? Let me die.

I am peering into the Crow Fair dance arena from the encircling arbor. The Montana afternoon is hot. I hear cheers from the rodeo grounds, but in this orbit there are only silent, waiting Indians. A massive giveaway is imminent, to be followed by a rare, modern-day coup-counting. A shirtless man dashes into the piles of quilts and Pendletons, holding for dear life to the halter of a bareback stallion. Around and around they yank each other in tightening circles, kicking up the earth. It is a royal gift for some guest. In their wake boys dive for flung dimes which glitter in the ochre dust like mica. The goods distributed, respectful clapping and names of donors and guests declaimed, punctuation of drum rolls over—out stride four men in eagle-tail bonnets and face paint. Through the hoarse mike one recalls a footrace won barefoot at Haskell Indian School fifty years ago. Their voices rise and fall, blurting in staccato Crow the facts of deeds done.

The last man stands forward and I ask an onlooker to translate. The orator and I have laughed and drunk together, yet this afternoon he is transformed. I would think twice about approaching him. He proclaims to all: "I am crawling toward the officer's camp. It is night. I see horses. I cut a rope and mount." An enraptured smile expands on my translator's face. In the dust motes and dappled light we are all in Germany as he steals the enemy herd back through the woods.

In that year I was winding up a book on the making of a Crow warrior. Until that moment, however, I had not experienced the warrior ethos. I had not believed it. This recitation was neither entertainment nor nostalgia. It took that ethos for granted. As the drums thumped in praise when he was done, a queer feeling of vulnerability came over me, as if time and space had cracked open and I was no longer a spectator.

Although diluted, something of the potency of oral narrative might survive conversion into print. Researching Indian points of view for an anthology on Indian and white relations some time later, I stumbled upon the life of a Northern Cheyenne woman named Iron Teeth. Her ninety-five years touched upon virtually every stage of Indian and white interaction, yet were encapsulated in twenty-two pages. It was an epic in a nutshell, unhurried but precise, unembellished yet uncannily vivid in image and detail.

She was born around 1834. Her grandmother actually remembered life before the horse, when dogs had dragged their lodge poles. At the age of six, Iron Teeth used her prehistoric-style digging stick to plant corn in the Black Hills. She remembered running for her life when Pawnees attacked her village. For weeks afterward she wept for her doll stuffed with buffalo hair, with beads for eyes, imagining the Pawnees torturing its body. She watched as Jim Bridger handed the first government presents to her parents: brass finger rings, metal awls, and green coffee which they thought were beans but tasted awful when boiled. On a river bank deep with soft sand she broke wild horses she had lassoed herself. She caught beaver and skunk with her bare hands. She once saved a four-year-old white child and cared for her, a girl who grew to womanhood, married a Cheyenne, and stained her skin so she would not be recaptured by her own people. Iron Teeth married Red Pipe when she was twenty-one. She bore three daughters and two sons of her own.

She watched as her husband fell from white soldier bullets on the upper Powder River. With the rebels who hated their Oklahoma reservation she fled for Tongue River. She was among the ninety-seven men, women, and children who were kept without food, water, or heat for eleven days in a thirty-foot-square brig at Fort Robinson in the dead of winter. She hid a pistol beneath her rags for the breakout, saw four women friends shot to death in the snow, and was recaptured. She learned from others how her oldest son was killed decoying cavalry troops away from his little sister. The only possession she never parted with was the yellowed elk-horn handle of her buffalo hidescraper. On it were notches marking every year that each of her children had survived.

She endured numerous refugee camps before ending her days as a woodcutter near Lame Deer, Montana. She stopped smoking at ninety because it was not good for her health. She confessed that once she had hated white people. Now, she said, when she saw around her the descendants of that white child captive she had saved, "it seems like I am living in another world. My thoughts go back eighty years to the time when I as a big girl fled through rain and darkness while carrying on my back a sleeping little white girl who afterward became a woman, then an old woman, and then died, and who was their great-grandmother" (Marquis 1973:15).

I'd read Mari Sandoz's *Cheyenne Autumn* (1953) (and by now Father Peter Powell's masterful *People of the Sacred Mountain* [1979]), telling of the hegira of the Northern Cheyenne. Somehow neither contained for me the authenticity and intimacy of this deceptively simple reminiscence. Iron Teeth was devoid of self-pity and self-consciousness, yet point-of-view gave life to every descriptive detail, building a wondrous tension between her modesty and one's response. Her testimony seemed to exemplify how a lifetime of taking spoken words as seriously as breaking horses or scraping hides might economize the memory toward some transcendent narrative clarity. Born of the cleanly-observed and long-distilled personal experience, it managed to communicate things universal and essential. The writer in me marvelled; the human being closed the pages with a pounding heart.

Researching that anthology on Indian-white relations overwhelmed me with other personal testimonies, prophecy myths, formal folklore well smoothened with retelling, and the localized story fragments which anthropologist Paul Radin valued and dubbed "ethnological chit-chat." In some of the folklore I began to sense a covert design. I came to wonder if they were not so much entertainments as interpretations. The plots involving Indian and white interaction seemed to possess ironic power, as if they were secretly helping their listeners to identify and contextualize these aggressive newcomers, and functioned as a manual in their defense against them. This hunch was reinforced by folklorist Madronna Holden's provocative essay, "Making All the Crooked Ways Straight." Examining traditional tales of the Coast Salish of the Olympic Peninsula of Washington, Holden suggested that old plot motifs had been retooled to add veiled commentary that underscored how whites

violated the moral order. With satirical deftness, whites were impli-
cated, in but one example, in the recasting of the Raven's making of a
human fishtrap. He bosses people into a line, and soon they are tied
together at their waists, standing knee-deep in the icy water. It takes
Moon to admonish Ravin, " 'Never do this again.' . . . 'These people
here are human beings' " (1976:283). Related for home consumption
only, this was folklore as sedition. Its in-jokes and ethical lessons
enabled listeners to recover some measure of cultural pride and order;
through such story-lessons they compensated spiritually and morally
for the political power they had lost.

According to P. Joseph Cahill, the tales of Trickster, or Wisakechak,
told by the Canadian Cree of Alberta, which often treated Indian and
white relations, served a more public, equalizing function. When the
two peoples met for council, Cree elders would insist on retelling
Wisakechak's prophecy of the white man's arrival and character. With
the solemnity of a benediction, all were reminded of those original
warnings about drink, currency, and Christianity so the imminent
negotiation might follow the proper path. This establishment of an
"evident sacral atmosphere" helped restore a separate but equal foundation for realistic discussion across cultural boundaries (Cahill
1977:211).

I could imagine prairie diplomats twitching their feet, sensing they
were one-upped as the old men droned and stopped, droned and
stopped, allowing the silent intervals to do their work at conjuring up
the prescience of Wisakechak so he might protect his people as he had
always done. It helped me to understand why President Taft had
interrupted the Hopi traditionalist Yukeoma, when the old man came to
the White House in 1911 and opened his argument on why Hopi boys
and girls shouldn't attend white schools. A diehard pacifist and objector
to the white man's ways, Yukeoma had been repeatedly jailed for
resisting efforts of assimilation. Decked in his Antelope Priest's ceremonial attire, Yukeoma tried to explain why the Hopi were meant to
"roam free without the white man always there to tell us what we must
do and what we cannot do." He tried making his case the best way he
could, by explaining how the Hopi believed the world truly began and
should forever be, speaking within the framework of the Hopi origin
saga and its prophecies. But he was cut short by Taft, who insisted that
the Hopi had to accept education and the white man's authority, and
Yukeoma was hustled over to the Bureau of Indian Affairs to recite the
lengthy Hopi myths that backed up the Hopi claim of divine right (K.

Turner 1951:200–6). The White House was not the place for evoking anybody else's sacral atmosphere.

Just as Norman Mailer once argued, that there could be no fact without its nuance, those encounters among Indians and in the printed middens of their ways suggested to me that there was no historical incident without its ahistorical emotional legacy. My world gave lip service to Santayana's "those who cannot remember the past are condemned to repeat it," but the task of discovering how to revitalize primordial wisdom was usually sidestepped in favor of the safer goals of objective scholarship. Here, however, I had tasted histories premised upon n̶ ̶ ̶ A sense of coiled intentionality underlay these recollec- ̶ ̶ ̶ ̶d prophecies which I was amassing from the archives. ̶ ̶ ̶ed as actions, not pieces of evidence. Pertinence re- ̶ ̶ ̶eir index of utility. Their past was not prologue but ̶ ̶ ̶ent. Their moral program was not eviscerated by the ̶ ̶ ̶ ̶t; it was safeguarded and coded for interpersonal netwo̶ ̶ ̶ and users. My collection of Indian accounts took on the imp̶ ̶ ̶ of captured enemy documents. As I hunted in the library stacks I ̶ ̶ ̶d to be moving through shelves of rifled medicine bundles, their vo̶ ̶ ̶ and motives released only by beliefs and imperatives my society d̶ ̶ ̶t share.

Victories of spir̶ ̶ ̶d meaning over space and time—it is sobering how noble realizatio̶ ̶ ̶an turn a man into a common scold. When the poet William Carlos̶ ̶ liams excoriated American Puritanism and the self-righteous intolera̶ ̶ it stood for, the French historian Valéry Larbaud was amused by t̶ ̶ ̶oung man's fury. "This interests me greatly," reflected Larbaud, "bec̶ ̶ ̶e I see you brimming—you, yourself—with those three things of wl̶ ̶ ̶ you speak: a puritanical sense of order, a practical mysticism as o̶ ̶ ̶e Jesuits, and the sum all those qualities defeated in the savage me̶ ̶ your country by the first two. These three things I see still battling i̶ ̶ ̶ur heart" (Williams 1925:116).

Undertaking this antholo̶ ̶ had placed me in another conflict. I had to accept that I was not assembling it for closed tribal audiences. The cultural specifics that began to fall on my cutting room floor too often reflected the very internal, local contexts which tribal storytellers cherished most and were trying to preserve. Yet I had to sacrifice much of that in favor of historically visible moments in which Indians and whites took part. As I struggled with these issues, my classes and personal journal expressed a related discontent. My exposure to the personalized impact of oral tradition, to Indian modes of spiritual persistence, was arousing some unpleasant symptoms of religious conversion: loss of humor and irony, a cold heart toward my cultural past, a suspicion of impartial study. Guilty about white America's rationalist and imperialist record at home and abroad, I repudiated its communities and history and began to exhibit that profile of the true believer, which religious scholars label "the chastised self." Like the textbook convert, I caught myself haranguing for nothing less than cultural exorcism and redemption. I came close to lumping Indians into one blinding, guiding light, and grew sympathetic to simplistic calls that my people shed their over-civilized skins and reunite with the animals and the stars.

In my way I was reflecting the waves of expiatory history and exotic primitivism which informed a number of ethnic awareness programs during those years. To be sure, scholarly muckraking and personal reevaluations were necessary to move beyond colonial habits, demeaning texts, and institutional racism. But corrective history and "cultural appreciation" proved weak premises on which to build durable curriculae. Besides, in the final analysis they insulted the deeper riches of the heritages they sought to serve. They did not follow the lessons of oral history. They looked backward.

As I was getting stale and stuck in these postures, I noticed an associated barrenness in my anthology research dealing with the twentieth-century Indian experience. Instead of accounts that drew their force from objective testimony, I found polemical overkill, editorial hysteria, and flailing calls to conscience. Venting made Indian speakers feel good, too, but as an editor I saw how unconvincing it made my book selections. They sometimes worked if one was already familiar with the specific Bureau of Indian Affairs conditions Carlos Montezuma was railing against, or the Navajo Reservation during the days John Collier was making the Navajos reduce their sheep, or the Byzantine politics of Pine Ridge before Wounded Knee II. Without this background, however, there was rarely a graphic, non-editorialized account to grasp. Fury compromised testimony. It evidenced a sad corruption of modern times, as print and television seemed to usurp oral tradition in form and content. Editing was painful because when I cut away the name-calling and bitterness, little story line, meaning, or mystery remained.

On the national scene some Indian leaders also seemed to succumb to rage, yet their shrillness lost power as it became tailored for the media, which cooly consumed it and passed on. In those same years, through books or campus tours, self-appointed seers attracted other yearning primitivists back to sacred paths. The elusive "traditional" became some alluring point just before most of us were born. Anyone who claimed access to it through dream, age, or birthright had a ready following.

One who swims between cultures can get stranded from either shore. On the reservation my Indian hosts would look bewildered when I used Indian existence to pick at the scab of my own resentments. They would hear me scorn family, custom, and government, and they would seem to be thinking: This is a strange bird that defecates in his own nest. Where can he go when he gets broke or sick or wants a meal? Before long I realized I was falling into the trap of violating the Indian ways I had found so vital, by sentimentalizing and fossilizing them. Like many others I was in danger of idealizing the trappings of Indian culture and contorting my research to conform to that ideal. I began to wonder, Was there no end to this search for a pure home base? It was as if were there not Indians we would have somehow come around to inventing them, as a utopian antithesis to so much that alienated us. I seemed to be floundering in the dilemma mercilessly described by Vine Deloria, Jr.: "Underneath all the conflicting images of the Indian one fundamental truth emerges—the white man *knows* that he is an alien and he *knows* that North America is Indian—and he will never let go of the Indian image because he thinks that by some clever manipulation he can achieve an authenticity that cannot ever be his" (1980:xvi).

Around this period a friend asked bluntly: What does *Indian* mean to you? I don't know if that was what triggered the return of an old memory. I was six and being taken from the east coast to live with my grandparents in Minnesota for I knew not how long. Our train was crossing the Wisconsin Dells, when out of the window I saw a hamlet of domed wigwams. The scene came back with utter clarity. I felt such relief at recovering it. I could not imagine how it had been submerged so long. I see them today, something secret and trustworthy about their closeness to the ground. They were light yet firm in the glade, younger brothers to the trees in size and color. Between homes, unsure when I would see my mother again, was it possible that some part of me went out of that window and stayed there, a kid by the tracks, wandering about and waiting? At that moment, did I begin some kind of captivity, like the white girl Iron Teeth had rescued and who never left, becoming a mixed-blood in her heart? It serves as a sort of personal origin myth, and it could just be so.

Not long after that memory surfaced I launched into a ten-year study of American Indian architecture. Thirty years after that boy saw those

dwellings I approached the mat-covered winter wikiup of Louis Cuppawhe and his wife, a hundred feet from the freeway outside of Shaw-
nee, Oklahoma. Sunlight mottled its parched cattail mats. When we
pulled aside the door flap, air rushed in and coals licked back to flame.
In here Louis said they were protected from the four Thunders. These
mats were sewn from cattail stalks which The Snake had permitted
Mrs. Cuppawhe to harvest. Two weeks before, they had transferred
them from the summer house's peaked frame to this domed winter
structure, as the Kickapoo culture hero, Wisaka, had instructed long
ago.

By now, however, I had become less surprised by such survivals and
continuities. My years of investigation into Indian house-making and
sacred geography had led me into the heart of histories premised on
spiritual renewal. Not only had available materials been ingeniously
adapted by Indian builders to create shelter for every habitat and
climate, but Indians had also encoded their homes and settlements with
cosmic symbolism and social order. I had learned that architecture
served much the same function as story-telling; it performed as symbolic repository and occasion for spiritual renewal. In territory after
tribal territory I teased out prototype house descriptions from origin
myths. I kept encountering culture heros receiving detailed instructions
for making their first house from an all-creator father, then passing
them on to their human descendants as one of the key indices of tribal
identity. Subsequent structures were consecrated as replicas of this
archetype, and partook of its sanctity, its "aliveness." Where such myths
had the making of primal lodges coincident with the creation of the
world, architectural elements had cosmological correspondences. Floor
was earthly plain. Ceiling was sky. Smokehole was sun. Walls were
cardinal directions. Ladders and sacred posts and trees outside the door
were axes around which the world spun, conduits of power to worlds
above and below. Hearths or pit shrines were navels of creation. With
myriad regional variants and complexities, I discovered cosmic order in
the humblest of spaces. It seemed a universal impulse, expressed in
diverse cultural forms. It tied today to the time of no-time, the pre-
human flux before the birth of history.

So it was historians of religion who helped release me from the trap
of the time-bound traditional. The prophets and sorcerers they studied
had always claimed access across time and space, as they continually
redistilled archaic verities into contemporary creeds. So architecture
was one of the processes that harkened back and brought forth, as the

great festivals in the ceremonial calendar wedded house-building and world-renewing. It was the grandest manifestation in material culture of a cultural longing found the world over: what Mircea Eliade calls the nostalgia for paradise. It was the process of my remembering those wigwams.

I would always feel Deloria's pointing finger. Indians had inherited more responsibilities than renewals throughout their long resistance to cultural annihilation. In the midst of tribal contemporary worlds every bit as precarious and experimental as the world encroaching upon them, but perhaps with mysteries more homegrown to lose, why should they take time to hand over ceremonies for spiritual adaptation by their conquerors? Why should they have patience with the white man's reinvention of them, when they were so desperately struggling to reinvent themselves?

I began to perceive how unnecessary and insulting it was to claim that the years during which our ethnographic pioneers were transcribing tales from the last "traditional" elders, were some finale of tribal culture. Nor did Indians hold any exclusive claim to archaic verities. All our ancestors had reenacted mythic history. It was endurance and renewal that kept societies vital, not credentials of esoteric purity from lost universes. Every cultural cosmos was as many-layered as the East Indian's description of what this world sat on: it sat on the back of an elephant, sir, and that elephant stood on the back of another elephant, and that one on the back of a third, and after that it's elephants all the way. Nor could any of us help joining our own renewal pilgrimages to confront the layers again, as F. Scott Fitzgerald knew by the closing lines of *The Great Gatsby*, "So we beat on, boats against the current, borne back ceaselessly into the past" (1953:159).

Once in Venice I asked a scholar of Hindu music why he had left his native France to take up the life and worship of India. "I found a way of life that made sense," he said, "what else could I do?" Like most Americans, however, I was a mixed-blood caught in a captivity narrative, searching to reinhabit this land. It was within the Indian world where I was finding the ways that made sense. What else could I do? It was in Native American places where I was learning the truth of Paul Radin's conviction, "No progress will ever be achieved, however, until scholars rid themselves, once and for all, of the curious notion that everything possesses an evolutionary history; until they realize that certain ideas and certain concepts are . . . ultimate for man" (1975: 245–46).

In attitudes and stories and house-fronts and cave roofs from this
native land I had come upon such ideas and concepts, meanings and
connections, and they were becoming mine whether I liked it or not.
What the linguist Dennis Tedlock said of the relevancy of American
Indian oral narrative, I could begin to say about the inevitability of
timeless history: "The reopening of the possibilities in our own language
goes hand in hand, or voice in voice, with a new openness to the spoken
words of other traditions, especially those that spring from the same
continent where we are now learning, however slowly, how to become
natives" (1978:xi). Those wigwams that had promised refuge to a boy of
six had let him in, and were sending him out again.

As for my Indian friends, the Penobscot writer of the "wind letter"
and the Crow caller of coups:
When I returned to his house on Indian Island a few weeks after our
talk, I discovered the Penobscot and a woman with a beat-up suitcase
sitting on his cot and passing a bottle of wine back and forth. They
smiled benignly at me and I left them alone.
It took until five years ago for me to see my Crow friend again. The
second volume of my anthology needed some Second World War
material. I had insisted on the word "testimony" in its title, and I hadn't
forgotten one of the best war stories I'd ever heard. I called and he
agreed that I could detour to Billings on a cross-country flight so we'd
have four hours in the airport.
He was waiting and we settled into some plastic seats. I let Indian
etiquette take over as we carefully peeled away the layers of our
friendship and my ties to Crow country, working our way slowly back
to that night in Germany. Once it would have made me antsy, now it
seemed sensible, considerate, civilized, a balm.
I learned who had died in the thirteen years since we'd seen each
other. We didn't exchange many glances; there seemed no need for
affirmation. For me it was important to call up every face that I could.
Past and present telescoped until my fleeting months on the Crow were
soon teeming with life again in the air between my eyes and the buffed
floor. I said silent goodbye to too many people.
When it was time I hosted him in the airport cafeteria and studied his
profile in the foodline as we piled it on our trays. I remembered how
smooth and burnt his skin had been. His face was now a map of kindly
lines. We didn't speak much as we ate. We didn't hurry over dessert and

coffee. Just as it seemed that any residue of information-as-plunder had been dissipated by the time passed together, by two men remembering and joking and eating, he leaned back and sighed with satisfaction. "Good," he said. "Let's plug that thing in somewhere, and I'll tell you"—a deep chuckle seemed to lift him into the remembering ahead— "I'll tell you about those horses."

16

Personal Reflections

N. SCOTT MOMADAY

You ask me to identify and explain, within a brief space, what I consider to be the most crucial, most vital issue at work in the past five hundred years of North American Indian and white relations. That is a very tall order, of course, and a very serious matter. I should like to respond in a personal and a straightforward way.

I believe that there is a fundamental dichotomy at the center of these relations, past and present. The Indian and the white man perceive the world in different ways. I take it that this is an obvious fact and a foregone conclusion. But at the same time I am convinced that we do not understand the distinction entirely or even sufficiently. I myself do not understand it sufficiently, but I may be more acutely aware of it by virtue of my experience than are most. Let me qualify my point of view on the subject in order that my remarks might be taken within a certain frame of reference. I am an Indian. I was born into the Indian world, and I have lived a good part of my life in that world. That is worth something, and it is an indispensable consideration in the argument I wish to develop here. You may recall that Oliver La Farge, in discussing his own, narrative point of view in the novel *Laughing Boy* (1929), drew a distinction between "the thing observed and the thing experienced" (1945:208). La Farge correctly thought of himself as an observer; his point of view was removed from the experience of which he wrote, and the distance of that remove was and is finally immeasurable. That is not to say that his powers of observation were in any way deficient—far from it; nor is it to say that *Laughing Boy* is less than a distinguished work of art. It is merely to remark the existence of intrinsic variables in man's perception of his universe, variables that are determined to some real extent on the basis of his genetic constitution. In the case of my own writing, where it centers upon Indian life, and especially upon an Indian way of looking at the world, I can say with some validity, I think, that I have written of "the thing experienced" as well as of "the thing observed." What this may or may not mean in terms of literary advantage is not a question that I wish to raise here, however. For the time being it is enough to establish that such a distinction is *prima facie* real, and it bears importantly upon the matter under discussion.

What of the dichotomy that I have mentioned? How can we get at it? Let me suppose that my little daughter, Lore, who is not yet three, comes to me with the question, "Where does the sun live?" In my middle-aged and "educated" brain I consider the possibilities of reply. I begin to construct a formula like this: "Well, darling, as you can see, the sun lives in the sky." But already another perception, deeper in the blood, leads me to say, "The sun lives in the earth." I am aware that the first answer is more acceptable to the logic of my age than is the second, and it is more congenial to my learning. The sun is to be observed in the sky and not elsewhere. We are taught beyond any possibility of doubt that the sun and the earth are separated by an all but unimaginable distance. The word "live" we grant to the child as an indulgence, if we grant it at all; it is a metaphor, merely. We certainly do not mean to say that the sun is alive. We mean that, from our point of view the visible sun has its place in the heavens. And we take it for granted that we are speaking of dead matter. But the first answer is not true to my experience, my deepest, oldest experience, the memory in my blood.

For to the Indian child who asks the question, the parent replies, "The sun lives in the earth." The sun-watcher among the Rio Grande Pueblos, whose sacred task it is to observe, each day, the very point of the sun's emergence on the skyline, knows in the depths of his being that the sun is alive and that it is indivisible with the earth, and he refers to the farthest eastern mesa as "the sun's house." The Jemez word for home, *ketha'ame*, bears critical connotations of belonging. Should someone say to the sun, "Where are you going?" the sun would surely answer, "I am going home," and it is understood at once that home is the earth. All things are alive in this profound unity in which are all elements, all animals, all things. One of the most beautiful of Navajo prayers begins "*Tsegi yei!* House made of dawn. . . ." And my father remembered that, as a boy, he had watched with wonder and something like fear the old man Koi-khan-hole, "Dragonfly," stand in the first light, his arms outstretched and his painted face fixed on the east, and "pray the sun out of the ground." His voice, for he prayed aloud, struck at the great, misty silence of the Plains morning, entered into it, carried through it to the rising sun. His words made one of the sun and earth, one of himself and the boy who watched, one of the boy and generations to come. Even now, along an arc of time, that man appears to me, and his voice takes hold of me. There is no sunrise without Koi-khan-hole's prayer.

I want to indicate as best I can an American Indian attitude (for want of a better word) toward the world as a whole. It is an attitude that involves the fullest accomplishment of belief. And I am talking neither about philosophy nor religion; I am talking about a spiritual sense so ancient as to be primordial, so pervasive as to be definitive—not an idea, but a perception on the far side of ideas, an act of understanding as original and originative as the Word. The dichotomy that most closely informs the history of Indian-white relations is realized in language, I believe.

Much has been said and written concerning the Indian's conception of time. Time is a wonderful abstraction; the only way in which we can account for apparent change in our world is by means of the concept of time. The language in which I write and you read upon this page is predicated upon a familiar system of tenses—past, present, and future. In our Western understanding of time we involve the correlative of distance. The past is away in that direction, the future in that, and the present is just here, where I happen to be. But we speak of the passage of time; times come and go, the day will come. We remain in place and observe the flow of time, just as we sit at the cinema and watch, fascinated, as images fly before our eyes. The plane of time is shattered; it is composed of moments, *ad infinitum*, in perpetual motion.

"He loved melons. Always, when we went in the wagon to Carnegie, we stopped at a certain place, a place where there was a big tree. And we sat in the shade there and ate melons. I was little, but I remember. He loves melons, and he always stops at that place." When my father spoke to me of my grandfather, who died before I was born, he invariably slipped into the present tense. And this is a common thing in my experience of the Indian world. For the Indian there is something like an extended present. Time as motion is an illusion; indeed, time itself is an illusion. In the deepest sense, according to the native perception, there is only the dimension of timelessness, and in that dimension all things happen. The earth confirms this conviction in calendars of "geologic time." A few years ago Colin Fletcher wrote a book in which

he described his walk through the Grand Canyon. It was called significantly, *The Man Who Walked Through Time* (1967). In Fletcher's title
we come as close as we can, perhaps, to one of the absolutes of the
Indian world. If you stand on the edge of Monument Valley and look
across space to the great monoliths that stand away in the silence, you
will understand how it is that the mind of man can grasp the notion of
eternity. At some point along the line of your sight there is an end of
time, and you see beyond into timelessness.

> as my eyes
> search
> the prairie
> I feel the summer
> in the spring

In this Chippewa song, time is reduced to a profound evanescence. We
are given a stillness like that of the stars.

Yvor Winters, who was my teacher and my friend, wrote in the
introduction to his final work, *Forms of Discovery*, "Unless we understand the history which produced us, we are determined by that history;
we may be determined in any event, but the understanding gives us a
chance" (1967:xix). It is a provocative, even compelling statement. And
it is eminently wise. But, with respect to our present discussion, there
arises the question, How are we to understand the meaning of the word
"history"?

In the summer of the centennial year, 1876, General George A.
Custer and 265 men of the Seventh Cavalry were killed at the Battle of
the Little Big Horn in Montana. Rutherford B. Hayes and Samuel J.
Tilden were nominated by their respective parties for the office of
President of the United States. Colorado was admitted to the Union.
The Chicago Daily News was founded, and the Dewey Decimal System
was originated.

The summer of 1876 is indicated on the calendar of Set-t'an (a
Kiowa) by the rude drawing of a medicine lodge, below which are the
tracks of horses. This was the "Sun dance when Sun-boy's horses were
stolen." During the dance, which was held that year at the fork of the
Red River and Sweetwater Creek, all of Sun-boy's horses were stolen by
a band of Mexicans. Following the dance a war party was sent in
pursuit of the thieves, but the horses were not recovered. This is the
single record of the summer of that year.

Set-t'an understood history in what can only seem to us extraordinary and incongruous terms. The summer of 1876 was in his mind forever to be identified with the theft of horses. You and I can marvel at that, but we cannot know what the loss of a horse meant to Set-t'an or to his people, whose culture is sometimes called the "horse" culture or the "centaur" culture. We can try to imagine; we can believe that Set-t'an was as deeply concerned to understand the history that produced him as any man can be. My friend Dee Brown wrote in 1966 an estimable study of the year 1876, which he called *The Year of the Century*. Consider that, in some equation that we have yet to comprehend fully, Brown's book is more or less equal to a simple pictograph, the barest of line drawings, on a hide painting of the nineteenth century—or the wall of an ancient cave.

We could go on with such comparisons as these, but this much will serve, I think, as a basis for the main point I wish to make. A good deal has been written about the inequities which inform the history of Indian-white relations in this country, by far the greater part of it from the point of view of the white man, of course. This is the point of view that has been—that can be—articulated in terms that are acceptable to American society as a whole, after all. One of the most perplexing ironies of American history is the fact that the Indian has been effectively silenced by the intricacies of his own speech, as it were. Linguistic diversity has been a formidable barrier to Indian-white diplomacy. And underlying this diversity is again the central dichotomy, the matter of a difference in ways of seeing and making sense of the world around us.

The American Indian has a highly developed oral tradition. It is in the nature of oral tradition that it remains relatively constant; languages are slow to change for the reason that they represent a greater investment on the part of society. One who has only an oral tradition thinks of language in this way: my words exist at the level of my voice. If I do not speak with care, my words are wasted. If I do not listen with care, words are lost. If I do not remember carefully, the very purpose of words is frustrated. This respect for words suggests an inherent morality in man's understanding and use of language. Moreover, that moral comprehension is everywhere evident in American Indian speech. On the other hand, the written tradition tends to encourage an indifference to language. That is to say, writing produces a false security where our attitudes toward language are concerned. We take liberties with words; we become blind to their sacred aspect.

By virtue of the authority vested in me by section 465 of the Revised Statutes (25 U.S.C. #9 [section 9 of this title]) and as President of the United States, the Secretary of Interior is hereby designated and empowered to exercise, without the approval, ratification, or other action of the President or of any other officer of the United States, any and all authority conferred upon the United States by section 403 (a) of the Act of April 11, 1968, 82 Stat. 79 (25 U.S.C. #1323 (a) [subsec. (a) of this section]): provided, That acceptance of retrocession of all or any measure of civil or criminal jurisdiction, or both, by the Secretary hereunder shall be effected by publication in the *Federal Register* of a notice which shall specify the jurisdiction retroceded and the effective date of the retrocession: Provided further, That acceptance of such retrocession of criminal jurisdiction shall be effected only after consultation by the Secretary with the Attorney General.

Executive Order No. 11435, 1968

I have heard that you intend to settle us on a reservation near the mountains. I don't want to settle. I love to roam over the prairies. There I feel free and happy, but when we settle down we grow pale and die. I have laid aside my lance, bow, and shield, and yet I feel safe in your presence. I have told the truth. I have no little lies hid about me, but I don't know how it is with the commissioners. Are they as clear as I am?

Satanta, Kiowa chief

The examples above speak for themselves. The one is couched in the legal diction of a special parlance, one that is far removed from our general experience of language. Its meaning is obscure; the words themselves seem to stand in the way of meaning. The other is in the plain style, a style that preserves, in its way, the power and beauty of language. In the historical relationship in question, the language of diplomacy has been determined by the considerations that have evolved into the style of the first of these examples. It is far removed from the American Indian oral tradition, far from the rhythms of oratory and storytelling and song.

The fundamental difference in ways of looking at the world, as those differences are reflected in the language of diplomacy, seem to me to constitute the most important issue in Indian-white relations in the past five hundred years.

17

White Buffalo Woman
HENRIETTA WHITEMAN

The Grandfather of all grandfathers has existed for all time in all space. He created a universe filled with life and His creation was characterized by beauty, harmony, balance, and interdependence. He considered the Earth Woman to be His most beautiful creation and He intensely loved the human beings. He had made a good world in which His beloved children, the human beings, were to live in a sacred manner.

The Cheyenne Keepers of knowledge, traditions, language, and the spiritual ways maintain a detailed form of this creation story in their oral history. They have taught numerous generations of their children the story of their sacred beginnings. American Indian tribal histories begin with the act of creation. Their unique tribal origins are deeply rooted in the land and in creation, which took place long ago. Unfortunately, the ancient oral histories of these culturally disparate people have been excluded from American history.

To rectify gross historical distortion, White Buffalo Woman and her great-granddaughter will present an oral history and Cheyenne view of history. Their story will cover the important historical events of Cheyennes on their road of life around this island world, which they have walked for thousands of years.

White Buffalo Woman, my great-grandmother, was taught through the oral tradition, just as her mother and grandmothers had been taught. Although White Buffalo Woman began her journey with the people in 1852, she was knowledgeable about their collective tribal experiences beginning with creation. In the way of her people, she, too, understood that the past lives in Cheyenne history. She learned about Sweet Medicine and Erect Horns, the two great compassionate prophets. They had brought the transcendently powerful Sacred Arrows and the Sacred Buffalo Hat and their accompanying ceremonies, the Arrow Renewal and the Sun Dance (Medicine Lodge), as blessings from their Grandfather.

She was taught that the spiritual center of the world was Bear Butte, the lone mountain located near present Sturgis, South Dakota, which is a part of the Black Hills. Cheyennes translate their name for Bear Butte into English as "the hill that gives," or "the giving hill." They call it that because Sweet Medicine brought their Sacred Arrows and way of life from this holy mountain. Throughout time, many individuals have fasted there or made pilgrimages just to experience its sacredness or to receive the blessings that flow from within it.

Cheyenne sacred history dominates all of life. The act of creation is preserved in their two major ceremonials, the Arrow Renewal and the Sun Dance. The teachings of their prophets are made spiritually manifest in these ceremonies. The Keeper of Sacred Arrows, who represents Sweet Medicine, and who is the highest spiritual leader of the tribe, has said that Cheyennes keep this earth alive through their ceremonies.

Tribal historians divide Cheyenne history into four broad periods and remember each period by an outstanding event rather than by dates. They refer to their earliest experiences as the ancient time when they lived in the far northeast. They believe they lived in Canada in the area between the Great Lakes on the south and Hudson Bay on the north. The historian-elders say they lived there for a long time but were decimated by a terrible epidemic, which left many of them orphans.

The grieving survivors moved south, into their second period of history, which Cheyennes say was the time of the dogs. They tamed the huge part-wolf dogs and, thereafter, walked with them on their road of life. After some time, they entered their third historical period, which the aged wise ones refer to as the time of the buffalo. Compared to earlier times, this was a time of abundance, with the buffalo becoming the people's economic base. The tribe pursued this animal deep into the interior of the Plains.

Finally, on the vast northern Plains the Cheyennes entered into the time of the horse, the last period of history. Long before, Sweet Medicine had described a horse to them. He said they would come to an animal with large flashing eyes and a long tail. It would carry them and their arrows on its back to distant places and they, the people, would become as restless as the animals they rode. Within a brief quarter of a century after acquiring the horse, Cheyennes developed into the classic equestrian hunters of American history. Both the horse and buffalo had a strong impact upon their lives.

Sweet Medicine had predicted that white-skinned strangers would cause even more drastic changes in their way of life. He said they would meet them in the direction from where the sun rises, and he described the unfortunate effects of acculturation, primarily the result of education. He told them that these people would make life easier with many good and wonderful things, such as guns and other items made of steel. Tragically, however, the strangers would attempt to superimpose their values of aggressiveness, materialism, rapacity, and egoism, which would cause cultural disorientation among many Cheyenne youth.

The prophet advised them to be cautious in their association with these people, whom they would call *ve?ho?e*. Thus, white people eventually came to be known by Sweet Medicine's name for them, the same Cheyenne term that means spider. Some elders also say their name is a form of the tribal word that means to be wrapped or confined in something, which is based upon the white strangers' tight-fitting clothing. The connotations are noteworthy from a Cheyenne viewpoint. If white people are wrapped up, they are often narrowly exclusive, insular, and illiberal. If they are not liberal, they are often prejudiced, bigoted, and intolerant. If they are intolerant, they limit other people's freedom. The words and actions of *ve?ho?e* are consistent in that white people have been generally intolerant of everything Cheyenne or everything different, as evidenced by the absence of Indians from American history. White egoism has taken precedence over the presentation of authentic Indian history.

Perhaps because of the trauma and disruption to their lives, only fragments of the initial Cheyenne-white contact have been transmitted in tribal oral history. The Cheyennes were divided into ten bands and came together only for their ceremonials. Consequently, each band must have been contacted at different times under different circumstances. White Buffalo Woman stated that many Cheyennes used to flee from white people and the strange odor they had about them. From a pragmatic point of view, this odor, which had the same effect as a murderer's stench, caused game to avoid the Cheyennes, which threatened their survival as a people. More important, however, from a cultural perspective, they remembered the warning of Sweet Medicine and wished to avoid the misfortune that association with whites assuredly would bring.

White Buffalo Woman's daughter, Crooked Nose Woman, who was born in 1887, did not know the exact details of contact. She stated, however, that when some Cheyenne men saw their first white men, a Cheyenne went up to one of them in a spirit of friendship, shook his hand, and using the male greeting for hello, said, "Haahe! Englishman." She also observed that this took place far to the east, on the opposite shore of a big river, which the Cheyennes had to cross in round boats, using sticks as oars. This was probably the Mississippi River, which they refer to as "The Big River." White historians agree that initial Cheyenne-white contact occurred in 1680 in the vicinity of present-day Peoria, Illinois, at Fort Crèvecoeur, La Salle's post near the Mississippi River.

Oral history is a living history in that the learners are involved with the historian on a personal level. They hear, listen, remember, and memorize events expressed in the flowing, soft sounds of their own language, describing the collective experiences of the people just as if they happened only the moment before. Their history is more than cold, impersonal words on pieces of paper. Even today, removed by four generations, I know much of what my great-grandmother White Buffalo Woman knew. I, however, have studied white American history, thereby complementing my oral history background.

Tribal history has no memory as to where White Buffalo Woman was born. We know that she was born in 1852, a year after some of the northern Plains tribes, including the Cheyennes, signed the Fort Laramie Treaty. It has been said that she was a beautiful child, with light brown, naturally curly hair, who matured into a phenomenally beautiful lady. Those who knew her have often lamented that none of her many decendants inherited her striking beauty.

The period around the time of White Buffalo Woman's birth was critical. For several years white emigrants had been streaming across Cheyenne hunting grounds on their way west, carrying strange diseases for which the people had developed no natural immunity. In their rush to find gold they spread the "big cramps" among the Cheyennes, which was so devastating that the band structure was virtually destroyed. It is said that half the tribe died of cholera in 1849.

Disease was only one of the lethal and disorienting results of Cheyenne contact with whites. The *ve?ho?e* acted as Sweet Medicine had predicted, and White Buffalo Woman witnessed their destructive aggressiveness. White land greed rapidly eroded their once vast land holdings, which became smaller with each successive treaty. The southern bands of Cheyennes and Arapahoes signed the Treaty of Fort Wise on February 28, 1861, in which they agreed to live on a small reservation in southwestern Colorado Territory.

Black Kettle led the band to which White Buffalo Woman belonged, and the band included a large number of mixed-blood Cheyennes and Lakotas. In response to Governor Evans's proclamation, they had declared themselves to be friendly by surrendering at Fort Lyons in Colorado Territory. Black Kettle's Cheyennes and Left Hand's band of Arapahoes were camped along Sand Creek, assuming they were there under military protection.

Unfortunately, Coloradans operated on other assumptions. They were anticipating statehood, and wanted to extinguish Indian title to Colorado lands by forcing the removal of all the Indians from the territory. They also feared an Indian uprising. Individuals like John Milton Chivington, a former Methodist minister, had political ambitions. He had become a military officer, and on the morning of November 29, 1864, he led his men in a surprise attack upon the sleeping camp of Cheyennes and Arapahoes at Sand Creek. Black Kettle attempted to stop the soldiers by tying an American flag and a white flag to a long lodgepole.

The ruthless slaughter and savage mutilation of the dead continued unabated, however. When it was over, 137 Cheyennes and Arapahoes lay dead. Only twenty-eight of them were men, the rest women and children. White Buffalo Woman somehow managed to escape. Congressional and military investigations were conducted and, although Chivington and other officers were found guilty, no one was ever punished.

Immediately following the massacre at Sand Creek, Black Kettle took his band south. He hoped to avoid further conflict and, thereby, remain at peace. White Buffalo Woman and her family were among the approximately four hundred Cheyennes, representing about eighty lodges, who followed their peaceable chief south.

Treaty-making intensified. The southern Cheyennes and Arapahoes subsequently signed the Treaty of Little Arkansas on October 14, 1865, agreeing to settle on a reservation in Kansas and the Indian Territory (Oklahoma). Three years later, on October 28, 1867, the tribes negotiated the Treaty at Medicine Lodge, the last they signed with the United States Government. They once again agreed to live in peace, made even more land cessions, and consented to live on a reservation in the Indian Territory. Black Kettle signed both treaties.

Believing they were finally at peace, Black Kettle's band was camped along the Washita River in present southwestern Oklahoma. On the morning of November 27, 1868, the nightmare of Sand Creek was repeated. Lieutenant-Colonel George Armstrong Custer and his men attacked the sleeping camp while the military band played "Garry Owen." Although Custer estimated 103 dead Cheyennes, later figures place the number between twenty-seven and sixty, most of them woman and children. Black Kettle was among the dead. All he had wanted was to be at peace with the whites—the people who killed him.

Again White Buffalo Woman survived. Within her lifetime she had seen the once large island home of her people become very small. On August 10, 1869, President Ulysses S. Grant created by executive order a new reservation for the southern Cheyennes and Arapahoes. It was on that reservation that White Buffalo Woman and her husband, Big White Man, reared their children. One of them, Spotted Horse Fred Mann, was born in 1890. He later married Lucy White Bear and they had two children, the younger, a son name Holy Bird Henry Mann, born in 1915. Henry's mother died when he was seven or nine months old, and White Buffalo Woman reared him and his sister Mariam. Henry married Day Woman Lenora Wolftongue, another full-blooded Cheyenne. In 1934 I became their first child.

White Buffalo Woman told her grandson Henry that her prayers had been answered in getting to see me, her great-grandchild, and that she could now complete her journey on earth happy in the knowledge that I had come to join the Cheyenne people on their road of life. I have been told that just as she had done for many other infants, my aged great-grandmother lovingly took my tiny body in her hands and, using it as one would a pipe, solemnly pointed me headfirst to each of the six sacred directions of the universe. She thus introduced me to the sacred powers of the world, offered me in prayer as one of the people, and microcosmically traced my life journey on earth with the Cheyennes on their road of life.

Through the ritual my great-grandmother acknowledged my life and charged me with contributing to the good ways of the people. Although we were born in different centuries, our cultural foundation was alike in that we were Cheyenne. Our experiences differed, however. White Buffalo Woman was traditional, and Cheyenne-white history in her time was tragic and sad, but the people were sustained by their strong spirituality. I am bicultural, and tribal history in my time has been generally ignored by white America. Cheyenne history, and for that matter Indian history, has been a story of assimilation, unsuccessfully enforced through "civilization," religion, and education.

In 1936 White Buffalo Woman completed her life journey on earth. She taught that understanding was a wonderful thing, and she understood white motivation. She was not cynical but sought only to find the good in people, in the world about her, and in all life. She and I shared two happy years with the people. Nearly half a century later, I only now understand my great-grandmother's death song: "Nothing is hard, only death, for love and memories linger on."

The reservation history of the southern Cheyennes is one of oppression, hunger, broken promises, and rapid environmental degradation. They live solely because of a sheer will to survive. The world in which they once lived in dignity and total self-sufficiency disappeared with the buffalo. Just as Sweet Medicine had predicted, and because of treaty commitments made by their leaders, the Cheyennes as a tribe consented to place their children in the white man's schools in 1876.

From that point on Cheyennes have been subjected to a multiplicity of educational systems. Initially, federally-subsidized schools were operated by the Quakers. The Fort Marion exiles incarcerated in the old Spanish fortress at St. Augustine, Florida, because of their participation in the Red River War of 1874–75, constituted the first Cheyenne adult education class. Lieutenant Richard Henry Pratt was their jailer, and some of them were among his students when he opened the first off-reservation boarding school at Carlisle, Pennsylvania, in 1879. Mennonite mission schools also operated on the reservation, as did federal boarding schools. Their curriculum consisted of industrial training, religion, and academics. Through the Johnson-O'Malley Act of 1934, the Secretary of the Interior was authorized to contract with states for the education of Indian children. With this, Cheyenne children were thrust into the public school system.

Under the provisions of the Indian Allotment Act of 1887, the Cheyenne and Arapaho reservation was allotted in 1891 and was opened to white homesteading in 1892. The Cheyennes' island home was further diminished into 160-acre tracts of individual allotments, checkerboarded throughout seven counties in southwestern Oklahoma. The tribes' traditional forms of governance were supplanted by the adoption of a white form of government in 1937. The Cheyenne-Arapaho Tribes of Oklahoma organized under the provisions of the Oklahoma Indian Welfare Act of 1936, which, like the Indian Reorganization Act of 1934, allowed them to organize for tribal self-government.

In the midst of great environmental, social, political, and educational change, Cheyenne spiritual ways and ceremonies have provided the stability necessary to maintain their uniqueness as a people. Today, just as in earlier times, the Keepers reverently safeguard the Sacred Arrows and the Sacred Buffalo Hat. The Arrow Renewal and Sun Dance are still conducted as they were in the past. Their genesis as a people and the essence of Cheyenneness are preserved in these ceremonies.

This powerful ceremonial life sets the Cheyennes apart as a distinct people with a unique spiritual history. Though their historical genesis extends thousands upon thousands of years back in time, their history is compressed, so that the act of creation is immediate, being preserved in their two major ceremonials. Sweet Medicine and Erect Horns taught them the ceremonies when they brought the transcendently holy tribal symbols to the people as blessings from their Creator. The good teachings of the prophets provide the tribal direction as the people walk their road of life in an historically timeless pilgrimage, following a migration route that extends from the northeastern woodlands of Canada to both the southern and the northern Plains.

In brief, Cheyenne history is a continuum of sacred experiences rooted into the American landscape, with Bear Butte their most sacred and most powerful place. Their continuity as a people requires that they maintain their way of life. Specifically, they must maintain their traditions, beliefs, spiritual life, and, through their ceremonies, maintain their sacred mission to keep the earth alive.

The Cheyenne sense of history is one of power, majesty, mystery, and awe. It is a sacred history, which has been well-preserved in the oral tradition. The people's history and personal history are intertwined in experience. White Buffalo Woman's personal experiences meld into Cheyenne history. Life did not pass her by, nor did history. Her experiences at Sand Creek, the Washita, and at the Little Big Horn all become immediate, personalized history. More important, it is an authentic history, one that reflects her world of personal experiences while simultaneously reflecting the Cheyenne world of sacred experiences.

Cheyenne history is but one tribal perspective. There are many others, all of them constituting authentic American history. Indian history reflects a unique human, spiritual, timeless cosmology. It stands in stark contrast to scientific, secular, dehumanized Anglo-American history. The experiences of Indians and whites reflect two different cosmologies with different missions. As an example, White Buffalo Woman personally suffered the most tragic experiences a people had to tolerate in American history. Yet she maintained her spirituality and did not abandon her sense of history and sacred mission. In the twilight of her life she transmitted this unique sense of history to me as a small child, charging me to keep it alive for the generations of as-yet unborn Cheyennes.

Cheyenne history, and by extension Indian history, in all probability will never be incorporated into American history, because it is holistic, human, personal, and sacred. Though it is equally as valid as Anglo-American history it is destined to remain complementary to white secular American history. In a brief five centuries, Anglo-American experiences have become a secular, scientific history without a soul or direction. The collective stream of American Indian tribal experiences has become a spiritual history with the sacred mission of keeping the Earth Grandmother alive. American Indian history has 25,000- to 40,000-year-old roots in this sacred land. It cannot suddenly be assimilated into American history. Every Indian's personalized experiences today constitute American Indian history of the twenty-first century, just as White Buffalo Woman's history is preserved for all time.

My great-grandmother was a remarkable individual whose life was an historic one and for whom history was life. Our lives together span one hundred thirty years, and being Cheyenne—one of the people—has shaped my distinctive, non-Western view of history. Our history as American Indians is beautiful, rich, valid, and sacred. The challenge lies in understanding and appreciating it as authentic history. The challenge is yours.

18

From a Native Daughter
HAUNANI-KAY TRASK

> *E noi'i wale mai no ka haole, a,*
> *'a'ole e pau na hana a Hawai'i 'imi loa*
> Let the *haole* freely research us in detail
> But the doings of deep delving *Hawai'i*
> will not be exhausted.
>
> KEPELINO
19th-century Hawaiian historian

Aloha kākou. Let us greet each other in friendship and love. My given name is Haunaniokawēkiu o Haleakalā, native of *Hawai'i Nei.* My father's family is from the *'āina* (land) of Kaua'i, my mother's family from the *'āina* of Maui. I reside today among my native people in the community of *Waimānalo.*

I have lived all my life under the power of America. My native country, Hawai'i, is owned by the United States. I attended missionary schools, both Catholic and Protestant, in my youth, and I was sent away to the American mainland to receive a "higher" education at the University of Wisconsin. Now I teach the history and culture of my people at the University of Hawai'i.

When I was young the story of my people was told twice: once by my parents, then again by my school teachers. From my *'ohana* (family), I learned about the life of the old ones: how they fished and planted by the moon; shared all the fruits of their labors, especially their children; danced in great numbers for long hours; and honored the unity of their world in intricate genealogical chants. My mother said Hawaiians had sailed over thousands of miles to make their home in these sacred islands. And they had flourished, until the coming of the *haole* (whites).

At school, I learned that the "pagan Hawaiians" did not read or write, were lustful cannibals, traded in slaves, and could not sing. Captain Cook had "discovered" Hawai'i and the ungrateful Hawaiians had killed him. In revenge, the Christian god had cursed the Hawaiians with disease and death.

I learned the first of these stories from speaking with my mother and father. I learned the second from books. By the time I left for college, the books had won out over my parents, especially since I spent four long years in a missionary boarding school for Hawaiian children.

When I went away I understood the world as a place and a feeling divided in two: one *haole* (white), and the other *kānaka* (native). When I returned ten years later with a Ph.D., the division was sharper, the lack of connection more painful. There was the world that we lived in— my ancestors, my family, and my people—and then there was the world historians described. This world, they had written, was the truth. A primitive group, Hawaiians had been ruled by bloodthirsty priests and despotic kings who owned all the land and kept our people in feudal subjugation. The chiefs were cruel, the people poor.

But this was not the story my mother told me. No one had owned the land before the *haole* came; everyone could fish and plant, except during sacred periods. And the chiefs were good and loved their people.

Was my mother confused? What did our *kūpuna* (elders) say? They replied: Did these historians (all *haole*) know the language? Did they understand the chants? How long had they lived among our people? Whose stories had they heard?

None of the historians had ever learned our mother tongue. They had all been content to read what Europeans and Americans had written. But why did scholars, presumably well-trained and thoughtful, neglect our language? Not merely a passageway to knowledge, language is a form of knowing by itself; a people's way of thinking and feeling is revealed through its music.

I sensed the answer without needing to answer. From years of living in a divided world, I knew the historian's judgment: *There is no value in things Hawaiian; all value comes from things haole.*

Historians, I realized, were very like missionaries. They were a part of the colonizing horde. One group colonized the spirit; the other, the mind. Frantz Fanon had been right, but not just about Africans. He had been right about the bondage of my own people: "By a kind of perverted logic, [colonialism] turns to the past of the oppressed people, and distorts, disfigures, and destroys it" (1968:210). The first step in the colonizing process, Fanon had written, was the deculturation of a people. What better way to take our culture than to remake our image? A rich historical past became small and ignorant in the hands of Westerners. And we suffered a damaged sense of people and culture because of this distortion.

Burdened by a linear, progressive conception of history and by an assumption that Euro-American culture flourishes at the upper end of that progression, Westerners have told the history of Hawai'i as an inevitable if occasionally bitter-sweet triumph of Western ways over "primitive" Hawaiian ways. A few authors—the most sympathetic— have recorded with deep-felt sorrow the passing of our people. But in the end, we are repeatedly told, such an eclipse was for the best.

Obviously it was best for Westerners, not for our dying multitudes. This is why the historian's mission has been to justify our passing by celebrating Western dominance. Fanon would have called this mission- izing, intellectual colonization. And it is clearest in the historian's insistence that pre-*haole* Hawaiian land tenure was "feudal"—a term that is now applied, without question, in every monograph, in every schoolbook, and in every tour guide description of my people's history.

From the earliest days of Western contact my people told their guests that *no one* owned the land. The land—like the air and the sea—was for all to use and share as their birthright. Our chiefs were *stewards* of the land; they could not own or privately possess the land any more than they could sell it.

But the *haole* insisted on characterizing our chiefs as feudal landlords and our people as serfs. Thus, a European term which described a European practice founded on the European concept of private prop- erty—feudalism—was imposed upon a people halfway around the world from Europe and vastly different from her in every conceivable way. More than betraying an ignorance of Hawaiian culture and his- tory, however, this misrepresentation was malevolent in design.

By inventing feudalism in ancient Hawai'i, Western scholars quickly transformed a spiritually-based, self-sufficient economic system of land use and occupancy into an oppressive, medievel European practice of divine right ownership, with the common people tied like serfs to the land. By claiming that a Pacific people lived under a European system—that the Hawaiians lived under feudalism—Westerners could then degrade a successful system of shared land use with a pejorative and inaccurate Western term. Land tenure changes instituted by Ameri- cans and in line with current Western notions of private property were then made to appear beneficial to the Hawaiians. But in practice, such changes benefited the *haole*, who alienated the people from the land, taking it for themselves.

The prelude to this land alienation was the great dying of the people. Barely half a century after contact with the West our people had declined in number by eighty percent. Disease and death were rampant. The sandalwood forests had been stripped bare for international commerce between England and China. The missionaries had insinuated themselves everywhere. And a debt-ridden Hawaiian king (there had been no king before Western contact) succumbed to enormous pressure from the Americans and followed their schemes for dividing up the land.

This is how private property land tenure entered Hawai'i. The common people, driven from their birthright, received less than one percent of the land. They starved while huge *haole*-owned sugar plantations thrived.

And what had the historians said? They had said that the Americans "liberated" the Hawaiians from an oppressive "feudal" system. By inventing a false feudal past, the historians justify—and become complicitous in—massive American theft.

Is there "evidence"—as historians call it—for traditional Hawaiian concepts of land use? The evidence is in the sayings of my people and in the words they wrote more than a century ago, much of which has been translated. However, historians have chosen to ignore any references here to shared land use. But there *is* incontrovertible evidence in the very structure of the Hawaiian language. If the historians had bothered to learn our language (as any American historian of France would learn French) they would have discovered that we show possession in two ways: through the use of an "a" possessive, which reveals acquired status, and through the use of an "o" possessive, which denotes inherent status. My body (*ko 'u kino*) and my parents (*ko'u mākua*), for example, take the "o" form; most material objects, such as food (*ka'u mea'ai*) take the "a" form. But land, like one's body and one's parents, takes the "o" possessive (*ko'u 'āina*). Thus, in our way of speaking, land is inherent to the people; it is like our bodies and our parents. The people cannot exist without the land, and the land cannot exist without the people.

Every major historian of Hawai'i has been mistaken about Hawaiian land tenure. The chiefs did not own the land: they *could not* own the land. My mother was right and the *haole* historians were wrong. If they had studied our langauge they would have known that no one owned the land. But was their failing merely ignorance, or simple ethnocentric bias?

No, I did not believe them to be so benign. As I read on, a pattern emerged in their writing. Our ways were inferior to those of the West, to those of the historians' own culture. We were "less developed," or "immature," or "authoritarian." In some tellings we were much worse. Thus, Gavan Daws (1968), the most famed modern historian of Hawai'i, had continued a tradition established earlier by missionaries Hiram Bingham (1848) and Sheldon Dibble (1909), by referring to the old ones as "thieves" and "savages" who regularly practiced infanticide and who, in contrast to "civilized" whites, preferred "lewd dancing" to work. Ralph Kuykendall (1938), long considered the most thorough if also the most boring of historians of Hawai'i, sustained another fiction—that my ancestors owned slaves, the outcast *Kauwā*. This opinion, as well as the description of Hawaiian land tenure as feudal, had been supported by respected sociologist Andrew Lind (1938).[1] Finally, nearly all historians had refused to accept our genealogical dating of A.D. 400 or earlier for our arrival from the South Pacific. They had, instead, claimed that our earliest appearance in Hawai'i could only be traced to A.D. 1100. Thus at least seven hundred years of our history were repudiated by "superior" Western scholarship. Only recently have archeological data confirmed what Hawaiians had said these many centuries (Tuggle 1979).

Suddenly the entire sweep of our written history was clear to me. I was reading the West's view of itself through the degradation of my own past. When historians wrote that the king owned the land and the common people were bound to it, they were saying that ownership was the only way human beings in their world could relate to the land, and in that relationship, some one person had to control both the land and the interaction between humans.

And when they said that our chiefs were despotic, they were telling of their own society, where hierarchy always results in domination. Thus any authority or elder is automatically suspected of tyranny.

And when they wrote that Hawaiians were lazy, they meant that work must be continuous and ever a burden.

And when they wrote that we were promiscuous, they meant that love-making in the Christian West is a sin.

And when they wrote that we were racist because we preferred our own ways to theirs, they meant that their culture needed to dominate other cultures.

And when they wrote that we were superstitious, believing in the *mana* of nature and people, they meant that the West has long since lost a deep spiritual and cultural relationship to the earth.

And when they wrote that Hawaiians were "primitive" in their grief over the passing of loved ones, they meant that the West grieves for the living who do not walk among their ancestors.

For so long, more than half my life, I had misunderstood this written record, thinking it described my own people. But my history was nowhere present. For we had not written. We had chanted and sailed and fished and built and prayed. And we had told stories through the great blood lines of memory: genealogy.

To know my history, I had to put away my books and return to the land. I had to plant taro in the earth before I could understand the inseparable bond between people and *'āina*. I had to feel again the spirits of nature and take gifts of plants and fish to the ancient altars. I had to begin to speak my language with our elders and leave long silences for wisdom to grow. But before anything else, I had to learn the language like a lover so that I could rock within her and lay at night in her dreaming arms.

There was nothing in my schooling that had told me of this, or hinted that somewhere there was a longer, older story of origins, of the flowing of songs out to a great but distant sea. Only my parents' voices, over and over, spoke to me of a Hawaiian world. While the books spoke from a different world, a Western world.

And yet, Hawaiians are not of the West. We are of *Hawai'i Nei*, this world where I live, this place, this culture, this *'āina*.

What can I say, then, to Western historians of my place and people? Let me answer with a story.

A while ago I was asked to share a panel on the American overthrow of our government in 1893. The other panelists were all *haole*. But one was a *haole* historian from the mainland who had just published a book on what he called the American anti-imperialists. He and I met briefly in preparation for the panel. I asked him if he knew the language. He said no. I asked him if he knew the record of opposition to our annexation to America. He said there was no real evidence for it, just comments here and there. I told him that he didn't understand and that at the panel I would share the evidence. When we met in public and spoke, I said this:

There is a song much loved by our people. It was sung when Hawaiians were forbidden from congregating in groups of more than three. Addressed to our imprisoned Queen, it was written in 1893, and tells of Hawaiian feelings for our land and against annexation. Listen to our lament:

Kaulana na pua a'o Hawai'i	Famous are the children of Hawai'i
Kūpa'a mahope o ka 'āina	Who cling steadfastly to the land
Hiki mai ka 'elele o ka loko 'ino	Comes the evil-hearted with
Palapala 'ānunu me ka pākaha	A document greedy for plunder
Pane mai Hawai'i moku o Keawe	Hawai'i, island of Keawe, answers
Kokua na hono a'o Pi'ilani	The bays of Pi'ilani [of Maui, Moloka'i, and Lana'i] help
Kāko'o mai Kaua'i o Mano	Kaua'i of Mano assists
Pau pu me ke one o Kakuhihewa	Firmly together with the sands of Kakuhihewa
'A'ole a'e kau i ka pūlima	Do not put the signature
Maluna o ka pepa o ka 'enemi	On the paper of the enemy
Ho'ohui 'āina kū'ai hewa	Annexation is wicked sale
I ka pono sīvila a'o ke kānaka	Of the civil rights of the Hawaiian people
Mahope mākou o Lili'ulani	We support Lili'uokalani
A loa'a 'e ka pono o ka 'āina	Who has earned the right to the land
Ha'ina 'ia mai ana ka puana	The story is told
'O ka po'e i aloha i ka 'āina	Of the people who love the land

This song, I said, continues to be sung with great dignity at Hawaiian political gatherings. For our people still share the feelings of anger and protest that it conveys.

But our guest, the *haole* historian, answered that this song, although beautiful, was not evidence of either opposition or of imperialism from the Hawaiian perspective.

Many Hawaiians in the audience were shocked at his remarks, but, in hindsight, I think they were predictable. They are the standard response of the historian who does not know the language and has no respect for its memory.

Finally, I proceeded to relate a personal story, thinking that surely such a tale could not want for authenticity since I myself was relating it. My *tūtū* (grandmother) had told my mother who had told me that at the time of the overthrow a great wailing went up throughout the islands, a wailing of weeks, a wailing of impenetrable grief, a wailing of death. But he remarked again, this too is not evidence.

And so, history goes on, written in long volumes by foreign people. Whole libraries begin to form, book upon book, shelf upon shelf.

At the same time, the stories go on, generation to generation, family to family.

Which history do Western historians desire to know? Is it to be a tale of writings by their own countrymen, individuals convinced of their "unique" capacity for analysis, looking at us with Western eyes, thinking about us within Western philosophical contexts, categorizing us by Western indices, judging us by Judeo-Christian morals, exhorting us to capitalist achievements, and finally, leaving us an authoritative-because-Western record of their complete misunderstanding?

All this has been done already. Not merely a few times, but many times. And still, every year, there appear new and eager faces to take up the same telling, as if the West must continue, implacably, with the din of its own disbelief.

But there is, as there has been always, another possibility. If it is truly our history Western historians desire to know, they must put down their books, and take up our practices. First, of course, the language. But later, the people, the *'āina*, the stories. Above all, in the end, the stories. Historians must listen, they must hear the generational connections, the reservoir of sounds and meanings.

They must come, as American Indians suggested long ago, to understand the land. Not in the Western way, but in the indigenous way, the way of living within and protecting the bond between people and *'āina*.

This bond is cultural, and it can be understood only culturally. But because the West has lost any cultural understanding of the bond between people and land, it is not possible to know this connection through Western culture. This means that the history of indigenous people cannot be written from within Western culture. Such a story is merely the West's story of itself.

Our story remains unwritten. It rests within the culture, which is inseparable from the land. To know this is to know our history. To write this is to write of the land and the people who are born from her.

Notes

1. See also Fornander (1878–85). Lest one think these sources antiquated, it should be noted that there exist only a handful of modern scholarly works on the history of

Hawai'i. The most respected are those by Kuykendall (1938) and Daws (1968), and a social history of the twentieth century by Lawrence Fuchs (1961). Of these, only Kuykendall and Daws claim any knowledge of pre-*haole* history, while concentrating on the nineteenth century. However, countless popular works have relied on these two studies which, in turn, are themselves based on primary sources written in English by extremely biased, anti-Hawaiian Westerners such as explorers, traders, missionaries (e.g., Bingham [1848] and Dibble [1909]), and sugar planters. Indeed, a favorite technique of Daws's—whose *Shoal of Time* is the most acclaimed and recent general history—is the lengthy quotation without comment of the most racist remarks by missionaries and planters. Thus, at one point, half a page is consumed with a "white man's burden" quotation from an 1886 *Planter's Monthly* article ("It is better for the colored man of India and Australia that the white man rules, and it is better here that the white man should rule. . . ," etc., p. 213). Daws's only comment is, "The conclusion was inescapable." To get a sense of such characteristic contempt for Hawaiians, one has but to read the first few pages, where Daws refers several times to the Hawaiians as "savages" and "thieves" and where he approvingly has Captain Cook thinking, "It was a sensible primitive who bowed before a superior civilization" (p. 2). See also—among examples too numerous to cite—his glib description of sacred *hula* as a "frivolous diversion," which, instead of work, the Hawaiians "would practice energetically in the hot sun for days on end . . . their bare brown flesh glistening with sweat" (pp. 65–66). Daws, who repeatedly displays an affection for descriptions of Hawaiian skin color, taught Hawaiian history for some years at the University of Hawai'i; he now holds the Chair of Pacific History at the Australian National University's Institute of Advanced Studies.

19

Socioacupuncture: Mythic Reversals and the Striptease in Four Scenes

GERALD VIZENOR

> There's a battle for and around history going on at this very
> moment. . . . The intention is to programme, to stifle what I've
> called 'popular memory'; and also to propose and impose on
> people a framework in which to interpret the present.
>
> MICHEL FOUCAULT (1974)

> Inventing traditions . . . is essentially a process of formalization
> and ritualization, characterized by reference to the past, if only by
> imposing repetition. The actual process of creating such ritual and
> symbolic complexes has not been adequately studied by histori-
> ans. . . . There is probably no time and place with which historians
> are concerned which has not seen the 'invention' of tradition. . . .
>
> ERIC HOBSBAWM (1983)

Scene One: Release from Captured Images

Roland Barthes shows that the striptease is a contradiction; at the final
moment of nakedness a "woman is desexualized." He writes in his book

All of the contributors to this volume were encouraged to write in a mode that they felt
would best convey their vision of the subject. Thus they were all free to choose their
own literary manner of expression. In this instance, the author chose to write what he
has termed a mythic satire, where he has (in his words) "played" with his sources. Thus
the reader will notice that there are no page numbers furnished for quoted passages
within the text. Vizenor explains that the omission is deliberate — an effort to
unharness the reader from scholarly convention. It is truly another expression of the
striptease. [Editor's note.]

Mythologies (1972) that the spectacle is based on the "pretence of fear, as if eroticism here went no further than a sort of delicious terror, whose ritual signs have only to be announced to evoke at once the idea of sex and its conjuration."

Tribal cultures are colonized in a reversal of the striptease. Familiar tribal images are patches on the "pretence of fear," and there is a sense of "delicious terror" in the structural opposition of savagism and civilization found in the cinema and in the literature of romantic captivities. Plains tepees, and the signs of moccasins, canoes, feathers, leathers, arrowheads, numerous museum artifacts, conjure the cultural rituals of the traditional tribal past, but the pleasures of the tribal striptease are denied, data-bound, stopped in emulsion, colonized in print to resolve the insecurities and inhibitions of the dominant culture.

The striptease is a familiar expression of theatrical independence and social titillation. In the scenes and voices here that delicious dance is a metaphor and in the metaphor are mythic strategies for survival. The striptease is the prime form of socioacupuncture, a therapeutic tease and technique, which is accomplished through tribal trickeries and mythic satire, eternal contradictions that release the ritual terror in captured images.

Ishi, for example, lived alone with one name, loose change, and a business suit, in a corner of an institution, the perfect tribal ornament.[1] The anthropologists at the museumscape declared his private time a public venture; the survivor was collared for a place in an academic diorama until he danced in a striptease.

The inventions and historical plunders of tribal cultures by colonists, corporations, academic culture cultists, with their missions, reservations, deceptions, museum durance, have inhibited the sovereign striptease; racism and linear methods of perception have denied a theater for tribal events in mythic time.

Scene Two: Euphemisms for Linguistic Colonization

Edward Curtis possessed romantic and inhibited images of tribal people in his photographs. Posed and decorated in traditional vestments and costumes, his pictorial tribes are secular reversals of a ritual striptease, frozen faces on a calendar of arrogant discoveries, a solemn ethnocentric appeal for recognition of his own insecurities; his retouched emulsion images are based on the "pretence of fear."

Curtis could have vanished in his own culture, which he strove to understand through tribal civilizations, if tribal people had appeared in his soft focus photographs as assimilated: perched at pianos, dressed in machine stitched clothes, or writing letters to corrupt government agents.

Tribal cultures have been transformed in photographic images from mythic time into museum commodities. "Photography evades us," writes Roland Barthes in *Camera Lucida* (1981). "Photography transformed subject into object, and even, one might say, into a museum object. . . ."

Photography is a social rite which turns the past into a "consumable object," argues Susan Sontag in her book *On Photography* (1977), "a defence against anxiety, and a tool of power." One cannot possess realities, but one can possess images, and "photographs are a way of imprisoning reality. . . . The primitive notion of the efficacy of images presumes that images possess the qualities of real things, but our inclination is to attribute to real things the qualities of image."

Curtis retouched tribal images; he, or his darkroom assistants, removed hats, labels, suspenders, parasols, from photographic prints. In one photograph, entitled "In a Piegan Lodge," the image of an alarm clock was removed. Christopher Lyman in his recent book *The Vanishing Race and Other Illusions* (1982) reveals that the image of a clock, which on the negative appeared in a box between two tribal men, was removed from the gravure print published in the multivolume *The North American Indian* (1907–30) by Edward Curtis.

Lyman writes that the "removal of unwanted detail was certainly not the only end toward which Curtis employed retouching. When it came to pictorialist aesthetics, he was dedicated in his pursuit of dramatic effect."

Curtis invented and then possessed tribal images, while at the same time he denied the tribal people in one photograph the simple instrument of chronological time. The photographer and the clock, at last, appear more interesting now than do the two tribal men posed with their ubiquitous peacepipes. Curtis paid some tribal people to pose for photographs; he sold their images and lectured on their culture to raise cash to continue his travels to tribal communities. He traveled with his camera to capture the neonoble tribes, to preserve metasavages in the ethnographic present as consumable objects of the past.

Photographs are ambiguous, according to the novelist and art critic

John Berger. "A photograph arrests the flow of time in which the event photographed once existed," he writes in *Another Way of Telling* (1982). "All photographs are of the past, yet in them an instant of the past is arrested so that, unlike a lived past, it can never lead to the present. Every photograph presents us with two messages: a message concerning the event photographed and another concerning a shock of discontinuity." Photographs of tribal people, therefore, are not connections to the traditional past; these images are discontinuous artifacts in a colonial road show.

The inventions of the tribes, and denials of the striptease, however, are not limited to emulsion images. Jingoists, historians, anthropologists, mythologists, and various culture cultists, have hatched and possessed distorted images of tribal cultures. Conference programs and the rich gossip at dinner parties continue to focus on the most recent adventures in tribal commodities. This obsession with the tribal past is not an innocent collection of arrowheads, not a crude map of public camp sites in sacred places, but rather a statement of academic power and control over tribal images, an excess of facts, data, narrative interviews, template discoveries. Academic evidence is a euphemism for linguistic colonization of oral traditions and popular memories.

Scene Three: Metasavages in Perfect Opposition

Encyclopaedia Britannica (1980) has sponsored the creation of a dozen tribal manikins, dressed in traditional vestments, for promotional exhibition at various shopping centers.

The sculpted figures, named for Black Hawk, Pontiac, Cochise, Massasoit, and other tribal leaders from the footnotes of dominant cultural histories, stand like specters from the tribal past in a secular reversal of the striptease. What is most unusual about this exhibition of anatomical artifacts is not that tribal leaders are invented and possessed as objects in a diorama to promote the sale of books, but that few of the tribal names celebrated in plastic casts are entered in the reference books published by the sponsor of the manikins.

"The Indian leaders whose likenesses appear in this exhibition represent every major region of the country and span more than four centuries of history," the editors write in the illustrated catalog, which is sold to promote their reference books. "Some were great military leaders who fought valiantly to defend their lands. Others were statesmen, diplomats, scholars, and spiritual leaders." Nine manikins, however, are feathered and the same number are praised as warriors. Black Hawk, the catalog reveals, "established his reputation as a warrior early in life. He wounded an enemy of his tribe at the age of fifteen and took his first scalp the same year." Three invented tribal images bear rifles; but only Massasoit, the manikin who associated with the colonists, is dressed in a breechcloth and holds a short bow. In addition to those mentioned, the other plastic manikins are named Joseph, Cornplanter, Powhatan, Red Cloud, Sequoyah, Tecumseh, Wovoka, and Sacagawea, the one female tribal figure in the collection.

The editors of the catalog and the sculptors of the manikins consulted with "scholars in the fields of Indian history, anthropology, and ethnology," and point out that the tribal biographies in the catalog are the "product of hundreds of hours of research involving scores of sources of information." Such claims seem ironic, even deceptive, because the sponsors were not able to consult entries in the *Encyclopaedia Britannica* for most of the tribal names in the promotion catalog.

The manikin of Wovoka, spiritual founder of the Ghost Dance religion, was created from photographs, while the other manikins, for the most part, were invented as neonobles and metasavages from historical descriptions and from portraits painted by Charles Bird King. "It seems odd," the editors of the catalog write, "that Wovoka is shown dressed in white man's clothes, but this is the costume he typically wore as did many other Indians." The other manikins in this cultural contradiction, however, are dressed in what appear to be romantic variations of tribal vestments, evidence of the denials of the striptease.

The sources of visual information, portraits, and historical descriptions, which the sculptors used to cast the manikins, are colonial inventions, museum-bound. Portrait painters, photographers, explorers, traders, and politicians have, with few exceptions, created a metasavage in perfect racist opposition to the theologies of the dominant culture. The editors and research consultants, even the witnesses at the shopping centers, might vanish if these manikins were embodied in mythic time and participated in a striptease: the structural distances captured in plastic would dissolve in a delicious dance.

Scene Four: Evelybody Is Hoppy in Mythic Time

Tune Browne, mixed-blood tribal trickster from a woodland reservation, and the inspiration behind socioacupuncture, never wore beads or feathers or a wristwatch; he never paid much attention to time or to his image until he became an independent candidate for alderman.

Tune captured his own electronic and emulsion image when he first saw his outsized face and eruptive nostrils on television and in newspaper photographs. He improved his pose from week to week, one image to the next: he cocked his cheeks high at a traditional angle to mimic the old photographs, bought a watch, and dressed in leathers and beads, bits and pieces at first, and then in six months' time he appeared on election eve in braids and feathers, a proud reversal of the striptease. He seldom responded to abstract questions about economies; and in spite of his captured images, he found himself in the oral tradition from time to time. It happened when he removed his watch: he told stories then, myths and metaphors unfurled like blue herons in flight at dusk. Linear time seemed to vanish when he removed his watch.

Tune lost the election, he even lost the urban tribal vote, but he had earned the distinction of being the first tribal person to enter the aldermanic race. Months later in editorial articles, pictures of him in feathers and braids appeared—dubious footnotes to a loser—which he soon recognized as captured images, his image, from the past.

"Who *was* that stranger image?" he asked in a rhetorical pose at the first international conference on socioacupuncture and tribal identities. Tune was dressed in his leather and beads for the conference, redundant beside his photographic image on the right side of the screen behind the podium. "A dreamer who lost his soul for a time and found his families in still photographs," he said as he projected a second photograph on the left side of the screen.

Tune moves in mythic time, an unusual dreamer who tells that he shaves with crows and drives behind bears to the cedar treelines near the cities, hunkers with beaver over breakfast, and walks backwards under fluorescent lights and in institutions without windows. When he cannot see a tree he loses four white faces from his memories, an urban revision of the Ghost Dance.

The lead speaker on tribal identities in the modern world, Tune stands on stage, between two photographic images. On the right is his captured image in braids, sitting on the ground in a tepee with several peacepipes and an alarm clock. The photograph projected on the left side of the screen is "In a Piegan Lodge," by Edward Curtis.

"See here," Tune said as he pointed to the images, "Curtis has removed the clock, colonized the culture games and denied us our time in the world. . . . Christopher Lyman wrote that the clock could have been a medal, a peace medal, but the box is too thick and besides, we *wore* medals then, never museum-boxed medals for a posed picture. . . .

"Curtis paid us for the poses; it was hot then, but he wanted us to wear leathers to create the appearance of a traditional scene, his idea of the past. . . . Curtis stood alone behind his camera, we pitied him there, he seemed lost, separated from his shadow, a desperate man who paid tribal people to become the images in his captured families. We never saw the photographs then and never thought that it would make a difference in the world of dreams, that we would become *his* images."

Tune pushed the podium aside and measured the captured images on the screen with his outstretched hands; from heads to hands he moved his fingers in shadow gestures over the screen. "But it did make a difference, we were caught dead in camera time, extinct in photographs, and now in search of our past and common memories we walk right back into these photographs, we become the invented images as this one did during the aldermanic election, to validate those who invented us on negatives."

He lowered his arms, spread his stout fingers like birds in flight and released several feathers from his vest. The lights were dim, the audience in the conference center was silent. Crows called in the distance, an otter slid down a river bank and snapped back in mythic time like a trickster on a high wire between the woodland and the cities.

"Socioacupuncture is our means of survival on the wire, our strip-tease in mythic time," he said in a deep voice as he untied the ties of the costumes in captured images, unhooked the hooks to museum commodities, and bead over bead he performed a slow striptease, a ritual contradiction between two frozen photographic images from the time-bound past.

"Not satire as shame," Tune explained to the tribal people at the conference, "not social ridicule as a form of social control," he continued as he dropped his bone choker to the floor, "but satire from magical connections with the oral tradition. . . . Robert Elliott writes about a 'mystical ethos' in satire, from ritual dances and tribal trickeries. Mythic satire, not as a moral lesson, but a dream voice out of time like a striptease in the middle of the word wars."

Tune removed his beaded leather vest and dropped it to the floor of the stage. His hands danced as he continued his lecture stories on the ethos of ritual striptease.

"Socioacupuncture reverses the documents, deflates data, dissolves historical time, releases the pressure in captured images, and exposes the pale inventors of the tribes. Lyman tells us that Curtis set out to construct a 'photographic monument to a vanishing race.' Not so, it was the photographer who would have vanished without our images to take as captured families.

"On the frontier, white settlers were offered free guns with the purchase of sewing machines," Tune announced to the conference participants as he untied his moccasins. "The tribes were offered free clocks with a peace medal and a reservation. . . . Curtis stole our alarm clocks and we missed the plane and lost the election, dressed in leather and feathers."

"Take it off," someone yelled from the audience.

"Give him time," someone responded.

"Roy Wagner must have stopped the clocks for a time when he wrote *The Invention of Culture* [1981]," Tune said as he kicked his pinched moccasins with the floral bead patterns into the audience and gestured, at the same time, toward his image on the screen to the right. "He wrote that 'the study of culture is in fact *our* culture'—the dominant culture is what he means here—and 'it operates through our forms, creates in our terms, borrows our words and concepts for its meanings, and re-creates us through our efforts. . . . By applying universal theories naively to the study of cultures we invent those cultures as stubborn and inviolable individualities. Each failure motivates a greater collectivizing effort.'

"We lose the elections in leathers and feathers, failed and fixed in histories, but through mythic satire we reverse the inventions, and during our ritual striptease the inventors vanish."

"Take it off," the tribal audience chanted again and again as Tune unbuttoned his shirt and unbraided his hair and shivered between the captured images at his sides.

"Wagner tells how Ishi, the last survivor of the Yahi tribe in California, 'brought the world into the museum,' where we lived and worked after our capture," Tune confessed, as he threw his shirt and the ribbons from his braids to the audience. "In good weather anthropologists and others would take the two of us from the museum back to the hills where we would demonstrate how to survive with a small bow and wooden arrows. He was the 'ideal museum specimen. . . . Ishi accomplished the metaphorization of life into culture that defines much of anthropological understanding,' Wagner wrote."

"Take it off."

"Take it off."

"Take it off."

"Take it off."

"Tune is the name and the end of the captured game," he chanted as he combed his hair free from braids, and then untied the beaded belt that held his leather trousers erect, "the end of the captured game."

Tune turned the projectors off and the captured images died when he dropped his trousers in a sovereign striptease. The audience burst into wild cheers and peals of animal laughter in the dim light, even the cats and crows called from the crowd. Tune listened to the birds over the trees and when he removed his wristwatch the dichotomies of past and present dissolved one last time. The inventors and colonialists vanished with the striptease; even those whose ideas he had quoted seemed to vanish like petals on a pasture rose. The conference on socioacupuncture was silent.

Tune turned toward the trees in mythic time and told how he and Ishi lived together and worked at the museum to protect the anthropologists, for a time, from vanishing. Then, last summer, "the anthropologists were secure enough in their own culture to recommend that we receive honorary degrees from the University of California at Berkeley."

Tune paused in silence to celebrate the trees in his vision. Then he told stories about the graduation ceremonies in the redwoods: Morning ghosts ride with our dreams over the tribal stories from the past, dark waves, slow waves, water demons under our ocean skin waves, trickeries and turtle memories under the stone waves, under the word gates, through the earth where we hold our origins with the trees and the wind, creation myths with ocean roots. . . . The ghosts dance roundabout in our dreams, clouds dance and burn free in the rituals of the morning sun. . . .

College degrees are degrees in words, with special awards for sentence structure, uniforms in the word wars, which is not much better than being elected to the plastic flower growers' association Hall of Fame, but we must not pluck the carrier pigeons with the documents too soon because the academics might vanish.

Silence.

Gregory Bateson writes in his book, *Mind and Nature* (1979), that in the affairs of living "there are typically two energetic systems in interdependence: One is the system that uses its energy to open and close the faucet or gate or relay; the other is the system whose energy 'flows through' the faucet or gate when it is open." Photographers and colonists are the faucets, historians hold the word-gates, and we are the energies of the tribes that run like dreams in a dance with the morning sun over wet meadows.

Ghosts hover in the tall redwoods roundabout the outdoor amphitheater in the Mather Redwood Grove. Animals and birds soar through the treescapes, dream beasts browse over the mountains. We remember the flood and call the crows back from the cities.

"The imagination is always aware of the present . . . ," writes Mary Warnock in *Imagination* (1976). "Neither understanding alone nor sensation alone can do the work of imagination, nor can they be conceived to come together without imagination. . . . Only imagination is in this sense creative; only it makes pictures of things."

Alfred Kroeber, Thomas Waterman, Edward Sapir, the linguist, Phoebe Apperson Hearst, Regent of the University of California, Robert Sproul, and Benjamin Ide Wheeler were all there for the graduation ceremonies, roundabout in the redwood trees, soaring out of time and place in magical flight.

"The University of California strives not to isolate academic ideas, races and nations on our campus as single population groups. This is not a place of racial separations," asserted Provost Pontius Booker as he pinched the skin under his chin. "Our academic communities are based on trust, research, instruction, fair examinations, and, of course, on excellence. . . .

"This afternoon we are privileged to announce that our very own Ishi, and Tune Browne, will receive honorary Doctor of Philosophy degrees here at the University of California, where these two instinctive native scholars have lived in a museum. . . . It is a distinct pleasure to announce these degrees and to introduce Alfred Kroeber, the famous anthropologist who worked with these two proud and unusual natives."

Kroeber shuffled on stage close to the microphone, leaned over and spoke in a gentle but distant voice: Ishi was the "most patient man I ever knew. I mean he had mastered the philosophy of patience. . . . "

Saxton Pope, our medical doctor and master of bows and arrows, was not present for the graduation but he wrote the following to be read at the ceremonies: Ishi "looked upon us as sophisticated children—

smart, but not wise. We knew many things, and much that is false. He knew nature, which is always true. . . . His soul was that of a child, his mind that of a philosopher."

Phoebe Apperson Hearst came down to the microphone from the right rim of the amphitheater to decorate us with colorful sashes and to present our degrees. "Doctor Ishi Ishi, Doctor Tune Browne, you are both intuitive scholars, we have all agreed . . ." Doctor Kroeber has recorded the first words that Ishi spoke in English. "We are, at last, pleased to imitate this fine man on this special occasion, is 'evelybody hoppy?'"

"The transvaluation of roles that turns the despised and oppressed into symbols of salvation and rebirth is nothing new in the history of human culture," writes Robert Bellah, a sociologist from the University of California at Berkeley, in his book, *The Broken Covenant* (1975), "but when it occurs, it is an indication of new cultural directions, perhaps of a deep cultural revolution."

We danced roundabout on the stage of the amphitheater dressed in our breechcloths and academic sashes with all the animals and ghosts under the redwood trees; a striptease, deep in a cultural revolution.

The fogdogs laughed and barked from the rim.

"Evelybody hoppy?" asked Doctor Ishi.

"Time now for a word striptease," someone chanted.

"Take it off."

"Silence."

"We are what we imagine," wrote N. Scott Momaday, the Kiowa novelist. "Our very existence consists in our imagination of ourselves. . . . The greatest tragedy that can befall us is to go unimagined."

"Evelybody hoppy?" asked Doctor Tune Browne.

Notes

1. Ishi, a Northern California Yahi, became an instant celebrity when, emaciated and frightened, and the sole survivor of his band, he emerged from the brush near Oroville and surrendered to twentieth-century America. It was 1911, and the nation's newspapers trumpeted him as the "last wild Indian of North America." He would live the remaining five years of his life as a ward of the anthropology department at the University of California at Berkeley, succumbing in the end to tuberculosis. See Kroeber (1961). [Editor's note.]

References

The following is a list of those sources which the author wished to acknowledge as having informed his writing but were not explicitly mentioned in the text. The reader should refer to the Cumulative Bibliography at the end of the volume for those titles which the author did cite in his text. [Editor's note.]

Boesen, Victor, and Florence Curtis Graybill
    1977   *Edward S. Curtis: Photographer of the North American Indian.* New York: Dodd, Mead and Company.
Davidson, James West, and Mark Hamilton Lytle
    1982   "The 'Noble Savage' and the Artist's Canvas." In *After the Fact: The Art of Historical Detection.* Pp. 113-38. New York: Knopf.
Drinnon, Richard
    1980   *Facing West: The Metaphysics of Indian-Hating and Empire-Building.* Minneapolis: Univ. of Minnesota Press.
Fromm, Erich
    1981   *On Disobedience.* New York: Seabury Press.
Hawks, Terence
    1977   *Structuralism and Semiotics.* Berkeley and Los Angeles: Univ. of California Press.
Kroeber, Theodora
    1961   *Ishi in Two Worlds: A Biography of the Last Wild Indian in North America.* Berkeley and Los Angeles: Univ. of California Press.
Momaday, N. Scott
    1968   *House Made of Dawn.* New York: Harper and Row.
    1969   *The Way to Rainy Mountain.* Albuquerque: Univ. of New Mexico Press.
Pope, Saxton Temple
    1923   *Hunting with the Bow and Arrow.* San Francisco: James H. Barry.
Vizenor, Gerald
    1978   *Wordarrows: Indians and Whites in the New Fur Trade.* Minneapolis: Univ. of Minnesota Press.
    1979   "The Psychotaxidermist." In *The Minnesota Experience.* Ed. Jean Ervin. Pp. 220-28. Minneapolis: Adams Press.
    1981   *Earthdivers: Tribal Narratives on Mixed Descent.* Minneapolis: Univ. of Minnesota Press.

Epilogue
Time and the American Indian

Old Ben, William Faulkner called it: the "shaggy tremendous" bear who in spirit and flesh roamed and dominated the "big woods" owned by Major Cassius de Spain. Each November the major and a small circle of friends would "keep . . . rendezvous" with the creature in the vain hope of relieving it of its "furious immortality." It was "an anachronism," sensed young Isaac McCaslin, hero of "The Bear," "indomitable and invincible out of an old dead time, a phantom, epitome and apotheosis of the old life which the little puny humans swarmed and hacked at in a fury of abhorrence" (Faulkner 1961:185, 187–88; Utley, Bloom, and Kinney 1971).

The boy was entranced by the thing. "It loomed and towered in his dreams before he even saw the unaxed woods where it left its crooked print"; it "had run in his listening and loomed in his dreams since before he could remember and . . . therefore must have existed in the listening and the dreams of his cousin and Major de Spain and even old General Compson before they began to remember in their turn . . ." (Faulkner 1961:187, 194). The sinew and veritable flesh of the spirit of the place, the keeper of the game and the wilderness precincts, this great sacred beast seemed oblivious of time. "It seemed to him that he could see them, the two of them, shadowy in the limbo from which time emerged and became time: the old bear absolved of mortality and himself who shared a little of it" (1961:197).

There was a lesson in that great creature—the idea took hold of him and would not let go. Or rather, Ike McCaslin realized that he could experience another birth, a spiritual birth, a vision, through encountering Ben. "*So I will have to see him*, he thought, without dread or even hope. *I will have to look at him*" (1961:198).

By now a skilled woodsman, he gathered up compass, watch, and rifle and began his quest in earnest. But Ben refused to be engaged on these anthropological* terms. "'You aint looked right yet,'" Sam Fathers, the old Chickasaw, rebukes him. Sam, who had inducted the boy and then drilled him in the mysteries of the hunt, knew that to see this unearthly animal one had to disavow the logic and terms and instruments of civilization. Sam gently reminds him that Ben doubtless has been watching him the whole time. The bear is omnipresent, tracking him, but the lad can not see the apparition until he makes himself fully vulnerable to it. Only then can he witness the full majesty and awesomeness of its power. "'It's the gun,' Sam said. . . . 'You will have to choose'" (1961:199–200). And so he must.

Ike set off well before dawn the following morning, with compass and watch as guides—but no gun. He was beginning to trust the creature— the one out there and within him. "He had left the gun; by his own will and relinquishment he had accepted not a gambit, not a choice, but a condition in which not only the bear's heretofore inviolable anonymity but all the ancient rules and balances of hunter and hunted had been abrograted." Yet "the leaving of the gun was not enough. He stood for a moment—a child, alien and lost in the green and soaring gloom of the markless wilderness. *Then he relinquished completely to it.* It was the watch and the compass. He was still tainted. He removed the linked chain of the one and the looped thong of the other from his overalls and hung them on a bush . . . and entered it" (my emphasis) (1961:200–1). And quickly became lost. And that was, and is, the point.

The rifle, the compass, the watch—all had to be surrendered if he was to have his vision—on the bear's terms. He was profoundly lost and vulnerable, and the wilderness, as he would discover, would care for him. Before his eyes the scene "coalesced. It rushed, soundless, and solidified—the tree, the bush, the compass and the watch glinting where a ray of sunlight touched them. Then he saw the bear. It did not emerge, appear: it was just there, immobile, fixed in the green and windless noon's hot dappling, not as big as he had dreamed it but as big as he had expected, bigger, dimensionless against the dappled obscurity, looking at him." The two gazed at one another briefly. Then it vanished. "It didn't walk into the woods. It faded, sank back into the wilderness without motion . . ." (1961:202).

To fully understand and incorporate *the primordial and eternal*

*See note at bottom of page 8 for my definition of the term "anthropological."

symbol of the bear Isaac McCaslin believed that he had to confront the beast. And Ben obliged him, but, again, on the creature's terms. Terms not anthropological. Ike had to make himself vulnerable, become a true supplicant. Time, the compass, and the rifle were all irrelevant and antagonistic categories of thought and symbol in this realm, in the world defined in such a manner. They alienate it, and alienate us from it. When he finds the nerve to leave them behind he does indeed find his vision; he witnesses the personification of that wilderness, the creature housing its power and intelligence—the creature (power) which takes care of and inspires him. Nature nurtures the child on his vision quest, and forever more. As Thoreau would have put it, Ike has had intelligence with the place by communing with the bear—the animal that existed both in the timeless recesses of the boy's imagination and in the timeless dimension possessed by the wilderness. The bear was symbol of that eternal human-Nature dance.

"The Bear" is surely a fitting ending to this collection of essays. With the death of the bear, the wilderness ceases to exist as a vibrant, spiritual place. A timber company now fastens its vision and its will upon it, defining it in terms of "board feet." Faulkner's "big wood" thus slips into time's coma, into the "practical" agenda of the people of history. There lies America in microcosm. And there lies, as well, the tale of the American Indian.

There are two types of time in operation in "The Bear." The one is eternal, cyclical, endlessly repetitive, powered by Nature, and cosmogonic. The other, a linear segment, remorselessly historical, profane, and anthropological. Ike McCaslin can imagine himself and Old Ben, "the two of them, shadowy in the limbo from which time emerged and became time: the old bear absolved of mortality and himself who shared a little of it" (1961:197). Mircea Eliade makes an identical distinction in *Cosmos and History: The Myth of the Eternal Return*. There are, he declares, "two distinct orientations" of time in human society, "the one traditional, . . . that of cyclical time, periodically regenerating itself *ad infinitum*; the other modern, that of finite time, a fragment (though itself also cyclical) between two atemporal eternities" (1959:112). Herein lies "the chief difference between the man of the archaic and traditional societies and the man of the modern societies with their strong imprint of Judaeo-Christianity": "the former feels himself indissolubly connected with the Cosmos and the cosmic rhythms, whereas the latter insists that he is connected only with History" (1959:vii).

People of myth and people of history. In North America, this translated into the people of myth trying to comprehend and adjust to the people of history, and vice versa. Or, just as correctly, the people of biological orientation attempting to adjust to the people of anthropological orientation, and vice versa.

Mythic people hold that all of life's effective and responsible acts exist as "paradigms," or "exemplary models," that were "revealed . . . in mythical times," more specifically, at creation. These "tremendous events that occurred at the beginning of time," comprising as they do "all the important acts of life . . . revealed *ab origine* by gods or heroes," form the archetypes (models) of human activity and behavior (Eliade 1959:viii, 32). The aim is thus to arrange one's life so that these sacred acts, these archetypes, can be experienced (conjured up) as frequently as possible. "Every act which has a definite meaning— hunting, fishing, agriculture; games, conflicts, sexuality,—in some way participates in the sacred. . . . Profane activities are those which have no mythical meaning, that is, which lack exemplary models" (Eliade 1959:27–28). Hunting, fishing, agriculture, games, etc., when performed after the fashion dictated by the archetypes, whose terms have been handed down faithfully from generation to generation, become by definition rituals (Eliade 1959:28). Ritual, then, involves "the imitation of archetypes and the repetition of paradigmatic gestures" (Eliade 1959:35). By executing a particular act exactly as it was done originally, at Creation, one can actually project oneself into "that same primordial mythical moment" (Eliade 1959:35). "Every sacrifice," for example, "repeats the initial sacrifice and coincides with it. All sacrifices are performed at the same mythical instant of the beginning; through the paradox of rite, profane time and duration are suspended. And the same holds true for all repetitions, i.e., all imitations of archetypes; through such imitation, man is projected into the mythical epoch in which the archetypes were first revealed" (Eliade 1959:35).

Marshall Sahlins reiterates the point in *Historical Metaphors and Mythical Realities*, where he explains how the Native Hawaiians sought to insert Captain James Cook into their mythic system as the returned deity Lono. In effect, they were seeking to transform (translate) emergent history into myth.

Mythical incidents constitute archetypal situations. The experiences of celebrated mythical protagonists are re-experienced by the living in analogous circumstances. More, the living *become* mythical heroes. Whakatau was the paradigmatic avenger. He who would now avenge himself "puts on Whakatau." The dying die the primordial death of Maui, who failed in an heroic attempt to conquer death; the mourners thereupon sing the lament of Apakura, whose son was the prototypical sacrificial victim. It is not exactly that the living are "like" the ancients, or even that they "repeat" the latter's deeds and words: "We are so apt to insert in thought a 'like' and in this way make all of it very simple according to our presuppositions. We find it quite obvious that when an event has happened, it never returns; but this is exactly what happens" (1981:14).

History, for mythic peoples, is "sacred history," confined exclusively to the time and act of Creation, and its vehicle (voice) of recollection, preservation, and narration is myth. Notice, too, that such history is an endlessly repeating phenomenon: "It is a 'history' that can be repeated indefinitely, in the sense that the myths serve as models for ceremonies that periodically reactualize the tremendous events that occurred at the beginning of time. The myths preserve and transmit the paradigms, the exemplary models, for all the responsible activities in which men engage. *By virtue of these paradigmatic models revealed to men in mythical times, the Cosmos and society are periodically regenerated* [my emphasis]. . . . It is not difficult to understand," concludes Eliade, "why such an ideology makes it impossible that what we today call 'historical consciousness' should develop" (1959:viii).

Nor, by the same token, is it difficult to understand why the concept of "progress," the corollary to "historical consciousness," should prove alien to such people. "The Yuin tribe of Australia know that Daramulun, the 'All Father,' invented, for their especial benefit, all the utensils and arms that they have employed down to today. In the same way the Kurnai tribe know that Mungan-ngaua, the Supreme Being, lived among them, on earth, at the beginning of time, in order to teach them to make their implements, boats, weapons, 'in fact, all the arts they know' " (Eliade 1959:32). As with Nabokov's sacred architecture, the making and use of these artifacts was revealed at the beginning of time, for all time, by sacred individuals under sacred conditions, and to continue using them is to revive that time and occasion and continue the power then conferred upon them.

"Progress" is an inapt term for the adaptation and cultural borrowing and change that mythic societies engage in. As Neal Salisbury makes plain in his essay in this volume, North American Indian societies were hardly static aboriginally in their cultural patterns and social relations.

They adapted to changes in their habitat, they selectively borrowed ideas and technology introduced from points near and far, and they have retained this capacity up to the present. The point to be emphasized is that the changes which they made in their lifestyle, including their technological inventory and general material culture, were fit within their overarching mythic structure. Change, in whatever form it occurred or appeared—whether as steel fishhook, steel trap, steel knife, or copper kettle, or whether it was the concept of maize agriculture deriving ultimately from Mexico—was interpreted within and reconciled to their vibrant mythic system. This meant that items of foreign origin were often defined in ways the donor society would have considered, or did consider, novel, in order to fit them into the mythic circuitry of the native society in question. We see this very clearly, for example, in the case of the copper cooking vessels which the French introduced to eastern Canadian Indians in the seventeenth century (Martin 1975).

To say that exotic items or ideas were folded within the mythic system is to say that they became part of myth; they were mythologized. The use of such an item or idea might make certain activities easier, more convenient, yet its use did not normally remove these people from their mythic realm—did not normally result in their being propelled through time, through history. On occasion, however, perturbations did occur that could not be fit easily within the mythic structure, the mythic view—as with European epidemic diseases in the early contact and colonial period. Such acute infectious diseases, coupled with the corrosive and muting forces of Christian missionary teaching, coupled with an alien technology, coupled often with displacement from ancestral lands—all these taken together did mount a powerful assault on the Indians' traditional philosophical system, and it appears that many were stymied in their efforts to reconcile these novelties to the familiar mythic structure. Many thus lost faith (more or less) in that mythic commitment, as the historical literature confirms (Martin 1978). In apostatizing, they fell into history and history's offspring, "progress."

The thing to keep in mind on the matter of "progress" is the philosophical matrix within which it is taking place for native societies. Viewing the world through mythic eyes, there was no powerful incentive to dream up new technologies and associated strategies to assist human survival. The biological outlook on life does not spawn that sort of mentality or behavior. It is the anthropological outlook which does. When new items or concepts did appear, they were not rejected for being foreign, but rather were inserted into the biological (mythic) model, and if they seemed attractive within that context, in those clothes, they might then indeed be resorted to and assimilated. If repugnant, they were rejected. What I am saying is that they took on a new definition—one within the existing mythic pattern. Thus, in a sense, they were not new. They became original; they entered myth. For us to call such a process, such a phenomenon "progress" is to misconstrue it—that is, to see it inappropriately in historical, developmental, evolutionary terms.

As with "progress," so "history," as we Westerners conceive of the term, becomes an ill-fitting concept for such traditional societies, including traditional North American Indians, who have always tried to duck it: "The man of archaic cultures tolerates 'history' with difficulty and attempts periodically to abolish it" (Eliade 1959:36). Eliade writes that anything not partaking of or participating in the archetypal models is an "unusual" event, representing "novelty," deriving from "profane time," "concrete time," "duration," and is rejected out of hand (Eliade 1959:xi, 35, 84–85, 154). Our Western version of historic time is repellent because of its "corrosive action" in "revealing the irreversibility of events"; time of this sort must be annulled, combusted, refused, devalued, left unrecorded, forgotten (Eliade 1959:74-75). By rejecting such history, primal man shows "his thirst for the real and his terror of 'losing' himself by letting himself be overwhelmed by the meaninglessness of profane existence" (Eliade 1959:92). The operating principle in all of this is a steadfast "belief in an absolute reality opposed to the profane world of 'unrealities,'" resulting in "a desperate effort not to lose contact with *being*" (Eliade 1959:92). Again, archaic societies reject the "novelties" of experience (what we call "historical events") as being "either meaningless conjunctures or infractions of norms (hence 'faults,' 'sins,' and so on)"—either way as dangerous events which have "to be expelled (abolished) periodically" (Eliade 1959:154). "'If we pay no attention to it, time does not exist,'" so goes the logic; "'furthermore, where it becomes perceptible—because of man's "sins," i.e., when man departs from the archetype and falls into duration—time can be annulled'" (Eliade 1959:85–86). Basically, then, "the life of archaic man. . . , although it takes place in time, does not bear the burden of time, does not record time's irreversibility. . . . Like the mystic, . . . the primitive lives in a continual present" (Eliade 1959:86).

The grid upon which mythic people structure their lives, their time, is Nature's pattern, one of endlessly repeating cycles of birth, growth, senescence, and death, followed by rebirth (Eliade 1959:74). Moreover, the forces operating in Nature, and the lives of animals, are thought to be changeless; the elements and creatures with which these people so strongly identify, and the myriad cycles they witness in this grand symphony, are the same, in behavior and form and power, as they were at Creation. By welding themselves to this spectacle and pattern and conviction, they transfigure "history into myth": "the myth of eternal repetition," of the eternal present (Eliade 1959:37, 153). Such is the biological paradigm which serves as the primary symbolic locus for their entire existence.

Repeating the archetypes in one's daily life goes a long way toward annulling time, as we have seen, but that is not always enough. Periodically, at least annually, profane time must be repudiated/combusted on a grand scale, in the manner of the lunar or seasonal cycle. Writes Eliade:

> The death of the individual and the death of humanity are alike necessary for their regeneration. Any form whatever, by the mere fact that it exists as such and endures, necessarily loses vigor and becomes worn; to recover vigor, it must be reabsorbed into the formless if only for an instant; it must be restored to the primordial unity from which it issued; in other words, it must return to "chaos" (on the cosmic plane), to "orgy" (on the social plane), to "darkness" (for seed), to "water" (baptism on the human plane . . .). . . . We may note that what predominates in all these cosmico-mythological lunar conceptions is the cyclical recurrence of what has been before, in a word, eternal return (1959:88).

"Placed between accepting the historical condition and its risks on the one hand, and his reidentification with the modes of nature on the other, he [primal man] would choose such a reidentification," asserts Eliade (1959:155). Through renewal ceremonies of various sorts, all founded on the renewal scheme observed in Nature and the universe around them, traditional societies, as with traditional Native American societies, managed to achieve the ultimate regeneration, freedom, and creation: "We know that the archaic and traditional societies granted freedom each year to begin a new, a 'pure' existence, with virgin possibilities. And there is no question of seeing in this an imitation of nature, which also undergoes periodic regeneration, 'beginning anew' each spring, with each spring recovering all its powers intact. . . . Nature recovers only itself, whereas archaic man recovers the possibility of definitively transcending time and living in eternity. . . . He retains the freedom to annul his faults, to wipe out the memory of his 'fall into history,' and to make another attempt to escape definitively from time" (Eliade 1959:157-58). Thus "he is free to be no longer what he was, free to annul his own history through periodic abolition of time and collective regeneration. This freedom in respect to his own history . . . cannot be claimed by the man who wills to be historical" (Eliade 1959:157).

In sum, "Every year . . . archaic man takes part in the repetition of the cosmogony, the creative act *par excellence*" (Eliade 1959:158). Modern men and women, on the other hand, having fallen from this "paradise of archetypes and repetition" into "history and progress" (Eliade 1959:162), are free merely to create history—a terrifying act since it is something we, individually and even collectively, seem unable to control, or comprehend. The "catastrophes and horrors" resulting from "the blind play of economic, social, or political forces, or, even worse, . . . the 'liberties' that a minority takes and exercises directly on the stage of universal history" (Eliade 1959:151, 153-54, 156-57)—these Eliade calls the terrors of history (1959:139-62). The more biologically rootless and abstracted (disengaged) it has become, the more frightening and absurd does history appear. Eliade attributes our fall into "history and progress" to our "resistance to nature, the will of 'historical man' to affirm his autonomy" (1959:154), a tragic illusion. Or, one might say, it is a result of our furious determination to be anthropological. And so in our conceit we create anthropological history, which is biological madness. Yet the final Word is surely biological, not anthropological.

For "we are rag dolls made out of many ages and skins," Loren Eiseley reminds us, "changelings who have slept in wood nests or hissed in the uncouth guise of waddling amphibians. We have played such roles for infinitely longer ages than we have been men. Our identity is a dream. We are process, not reality, for reality is an illusion of the daylight—the light of our particular day. In a fortnight, as aeons are measured, we may lie silent in a bed of stone, or, as has happened in the past, be figured in another guise" (1978:175). One finds this conviction embedded in the cosmology and behavior of primal people the world over, from stories of the trickster, to *Homo*'s powerful identification and kinship with animals, to the shape-shifting that occurs during a vision quest, to the fluid identity of sorcerers and the awesome powers of conjurors, to the imitation of animals in dances and masks, to the mythic origin of clans. On and on. As a species we may indeed be process. But note that mythic people, American Indians for example, do not define themselves as a distinct and separate species from other creatures. Theirs is a view that transcends the evolutionary perspective, the evolutionary squeeze; they seek (to recall their) kinship with all of the power and life of creation, not just the human vessel that happens to contain some portion of it at that moment in time. Drinnon calls this the "principle of affirmation," where ties of kinship and acts of communion spill over from the "family and clan and tribe to all other beings and things in a universal embrace."

Eiseley goes on to warn that we, in the West, must discard our anthropologically blindered view of the world if we are going to succeed as a species. "We are too content with our sensory extensions," he reproaches, "with the fulfillment of that Ice Age mind that began its journey amidst the cold of vast tundras and that pauses only briefly before its leap into space. It is no longer enough to see as a man sees. . . . It is not enough to hold nuclear energy in one's hand like a spear, as a man would hold it, or to see the lightning, or times past, or time to come, as a man would see it. If we continue to do this, the great brain—the human brain—will be only a new version of the old trap, and nature is full of traps for the beast that cannot learn." Our salvation, he believes, lies in our enormous capacity for imagination and creation: "Beyond lies the great darkness of the ultimate Dreamer, who dreamed the light and the galaxies. Before act was, or substance existed, imagination grew in the dark. Man," he declares, "partakes of that ultimate wonder and creativeness." Indeed we do. Man "can create the web but not hold it together, *not save himself except by transcending his own image*" (my emphasis) (1978:120, 128).

Transcending our image. Our Western myth is narcissistic: we see ourselves in the reflecting pool. So much of our great literature is heroic, so much of our philosophy humanistic (Meeker 1972). Even our God is a man. Our thoughts, as we gaze into that pool, are anthropological.

Imagination is the key to transcendence—an order of magnitude of imagination rarely encountered in Western culture. Momaday defines it as "the fullest accomplishment of belief. And I am talking neither about philosophy nor religion; I am talking about a spiritual sense so ancient as to be primordial, so pervasive as to be definitive—not an idea, but a perception on the far side of ideas, an act of understanding as original and originative as the Word." It constitutes, he says, "my deepest, oldest experience, the memory in my blood." The salient issue in this particular exercise of imagination is that it is being used in the service of

discerning and gaining access to a truth, a relationship, a realm that is
genuinely there: our profound connection with other biological life, as
well as with non-life forms and the various and sundry phenomena of
Nature. Such connection is no fabrication, no fantasy. No figment of
someone's imagination. There is no scientist alive who would dispute
that relationship. What is awesome is the uncanny and extraordinary
ability of mythic people to merge themselves, in what is for them a
convincing and practicable way, with the stuff of creation around them.
Again, no educated person would deny that the connection exists; it's
just that mythic people make it in such an astonishingly palpable and
literal and vivid manner. They seem genuinely to envision and conduct
themselves as practicing musicians in the grand symphony of Nature:
"The mountains, I become part of it . . . / The herbs, the fir tree, I
become part of it. / The morning mists, the clouds, the gathering
waters, / I become part of it. / The wilderness, the dew drops, the /
pollen . . . / I become part of it." Writes Joseph Epes Brown in com-
menting on this passage: "And in the context of other chants, there is
always the conclusion that indeed, I *am* the universe. We are not
separate, but are one" (1982:12).

It is interesting to see this same force of imagination being employed
by professional magicians. David Abram is an individual who has had
extensive training in the serious art of magic. In describing the magician's philosophy, he reveals that the magician "moves down, deeper
into the earth, into the material world which he is in love with. If and
when he is successful, the magician discovers himself to be an animal,
wholly and fully an animal. The successful magician is not a transcendent being, he is a creature of the earth." And on the power of
imagination: "I cannot really make a coin disappear. I can, however, set
up the situation so that a coin will seem to disappear. I try to create a
paradoxical or enigmatic situation that calls out the imagination
through the eyes of the person who is watching. After working this way
for many years I have begun to get a sense that perception is a very
active and engaging work by which we constantly move out of ourselves
through our eyes, our ears, our mouths, into the world and dance in
that world, and shape it." One recalls the power of dance described by
Drinnon, as well as the creative power of Momaday's sun-watcher in his
daily act of praying up the sun.

The magician knows that everything we perceive is really a grand work of
the imagination, much grander than one would at first think because it is

> not simply my imagination. . . . When we see things we are also being seen
> by them. When we hear things we are also being heard. Perception is a type
> of communication that precedes language. Perception is what gives rise to
> speech and to language because perception is itself and always was a
> reciprocal interchange between this body that I am and the big body of the
> world that surrounds me[,] so that perception is communication. . . . Tra-
> ditional magicians seem to be able to flood the world which surrounds them
> with their imagination, to let their imaginations out (Abram 1983).

For the professional magician all of creation is a product of imagination, of thought, and the things "out there" are equipped with imaginations just as functional and powerful as ours. Moreover, I can join
my imagination to theirs. We and they live in the same matrix, are part
of the same fabric and material and logic and system, part of the same
mind. The same act of imagination, same dream. Indeed, we can
imagine ourselves into one another since ours is a single, unified story
and performance.

Notice the similarities between Abram's perspective and performance
as a trained magician, and traditional Navajo philosophy, so brilliantly
described by Gary Witherspoon in *Language and Art in the Navajo
Universe*. "In the beginning matter existed in a neutral, unordered, and
unformed condition. Thought [imagination] and speech transformed
matter into an ordered and formed condition." Elsewhere, he puts it this
way: "In the beginning were the word and the element, the symbol and
the symbolized" (1977:77, 180-81). Through language we participate in
and manipulate the cosmos, so traditional Navajos believe. "It is language through which man harmonizes with the blessedness of his
environment, and through which he restores this blessedness when it
has been disrupted. Without language man is impotent, ignorant, isolated, and static. He is, in fact, an inactive part of a cosmos in which he
cannot find any meaning for his being. With language man is an active,
creative, and powerful part of his universe. Through language, the
meaning that he finds in his being and that he creates and expresses
through his being is fused with the omniscience, omnipotence, and
omnipresence of air, the source of all life, beauty, and harmony"
(Witherspoon 1977:62).

Witherspoon is here referring to language as vocalized ritual—ritual
deriving its potency from its "ordered ways of thinking, speaking, and
acting" (1977:77). Things tend to run down toward evil (chaos), ugli-
ness, and disharmony, while ritual, in language and art, is capable of
reversing this metaphysical entropy through its power of control.

"Thought is of primary importance in the Navajo world, for it is not only the source of control but the means by which the goal of control may be atttained. The goal of control is the creation of form, order, harmony, balance, and beauty." Hence "language not only classifies experience, it also controls it; it not only defines situations, it also determines them" (Witherspoon 1977:180, 114). Ritual, here, deals in primordial symbols—images retained and reached through the exercise of imagination. Explains Witherspoon: "Everything in the universe cannot be materially constituted or reordered in the mind, but mental ordering and reordering of the universe can take place through symbols. Symbols come in both linguistic and nonlinguistic forms, for in ritual both language and art are utilized in efforts to reorder the universe and restore it to the condition of *hózhó* [beauty]. . . . Symbols antedate the existence of people and are a prerequisite to the creation of form and beauty in the world. Symbols are primordial, for in the beginning were the word and the element, the symbol and the symbol-ized" (1977:180-81).

Through the controlling power of these primal symbols expressed in oral and kinetic ritual, humankind believes that it commands the attention of the cosmos and shapes (controls) it. Momaday's Koi-khan-hole, "Dragonfly," presumed to "stand in the first light, his arms outstretched and his painted face fixed on the east, and 'pray the sun out of the ground.' His voice, for he prayed aloud, struck at the great, misty silence of the Plains morning, entered into it, carried through it to the rising sun. His words made one of the sun and earth, one of himself and the boy who watched, one of the boy and generations to come." For Momaday's Kiowa, language ("the rhythms of oratory and storytelling and song") is power, the power of the place. It utters the power, speaks to the power, of Nature about us. It is directed at and heard by people as well as by the cosmos. Words are thus used to express, appeal to, and converse with an animated and mythic world. A timeless world: "There is only the dimension of timelessness, and in that dimension all things happen." Whereas words for non-Indians, Momaday is convinced, are addressed to and depict a very different world; the message and purpose of discourse are vastly different for Indians and whites.

Oral ritual (myth) "roots its actions in place, not dates," echoes Nabokov. "It neglects time to inject energy instead into the human and supernatural neighborhoods of its tales. . . . It nurtures the family and community and cosmic continuities of which it speaks." Myths are "designed as actions, not pieces of evidence"—actions which invoke the cosmogony through symbol. The point is vividly illustrated in Indian architecture. "Indians," he discovers, "encoded their homes and settlements with cosmic symbolism and social order." House-building, like myth, "performed as symbolic repository and occasion for spiritual renewal." The idea was to hew to the blueprint revealed at the time of creation, adhere to the archetype. "Subsequent structures were consecrated as replicas of this archetype, and partook of its sanctity, its 'aliveness.' " To construct in this cosmic fashion thus "tied today to the time of no-time, the pre-human flux before the birth of history. . . . Architecture was one of the processes that harkened back and brought forth, as the great festivals in the ceremonial calendar wedded house-building and world-renewing. It was the grandest manifestation in material culture of a cultural longing found the world over: . . . the nostalgia for paradise."

Yet there is more here than mere human renewal, for humans are under an obligation to renew the cosmos, as well. This we do by virtue of our ability to connect things through our thoughts, speech, and art (in the broadest sense of the term). Momaday's Koi-khan-hole "made one of the sun and earth, one of himself and the boy who watched, one of the boy and generations to come" when he prayed "the sun out of the ground." This individual was not speaking *of* the sunrise, he was *speaking the very act itself*, and in so doing he was effecting (re-effecting) the sun's primal and eternal connection to the earth; he was reaffirming (renewing) the unitary nature of creation by projecting himself through great force of imagination into that awesome spectacle in the eastern sky. It's not that he was responsible for the sunrise, rather, in giving voice to that performance he was daily affirming the profound affinity of all parts of that scene. By reaffirming the connections he was renewing the cosmos.

Witherspoon says much the same thing in his discussion of beauty. Man and woman are the keepers of beauty, so the Navajo believe. "In the Navajo world . . . the creation of beauty and the incorporation of oneself in beauty represent the highest attainment and ultimate destiny of man." The beauty he speaks of is "in the mind of its creator and in the creator's relationship to the created (that is, the transformed or the organized). . . . Beauty is not 'out there' in things to be perceived by the perceptive and appreciative viewer; it is a creation of thought. The Navajo experience beauty primarily through expression and creation, not through perception and preservation." "To the Navajo . . . beauty is an essential condition of man's life and is dynamic. It is not in things so much as it is in the dynamic relationships among things and between man and things. Man experiences beauty by creating it." This leads him to conclude: "Navajo culture is not just a food-gathering strategy; it is an artistic way of life. One is admonished to walk in beauty, speak in beauty, act in beauty, sing in beauty, and live in beauty. All things are to be made beautifully, and all activities are to be completed in beauty" (1977:151, 152, 153).

Beauty, as implied, is ephemeral; it is axiomatic in Navajo philosophy that movement always returns eventually "to rest, life to death, and beauty to plainness," this owing to the cyclical nature of creation. "That is why life cannot be forever prolonged, movement cannot be forever perpetuated, order cannot be forever maintained, and beauty cannot be forever preserved. Thus life must be regenerated, movement rejuvenated, order restored, and beauty renewed and recreated" (Witherspoon 1977:201). The point is that the Navajo feel it is they, it is humans, who have the power and solemn responsibility to do just this: regenerate life, rejuvenate movement, restore order, and above all, renew and recreate beauty—in short, renew themselves and the cosmos through the connecting power of oral and artistic symbol. To live otherwise is to live frivolously and pointlessly, even dangerously (Witherspoon 1977:179–80).

The Cheyennes also see themselves as directly involved in creation— not just for their own sake, their own welfare, but for the welfare of creation in whose uterus they thrive. Through the Arrow Renewal and Sun Dance ceremonies the Cheyennes "keep this earth alive." And they have been doing it for many thousands of years, reminds Whiteman, "keeping the Earth Grandmother alive." Trask says the same thing about her people, the Native Hawaiians: "In our way of speaking, land is inherent to the people; it is like our bodies and our parents. The people cannot exist without the land, and the land cannot exist without the people."

Mircea Eliade wrote that mythic people recreate themselves "through the paradox of rite," by which they conjure up, then and there, the archetypes of creation (1959:35). They may supplement this with deliberate and conscious renewal ceremonies aimed at further repudiating time. It seems that the impetus for all of this activity derives from the astounding (to us) conviction that humans can and must keep the cosmos intact, vibrant, and lucid through ceremony. Time is the focal issue in all of this because it is the ultimate symbol of disconnection. A sense of time's passing produces a sense of distance from the grand unity which prevailed in the act of original creation and which indeed prevails still in the creation witnessed in one's lifetime. Rituals that conjure up the archetypes give the lie to any such sense of discontinuity. The genius of man and woman is that they have the imagination to discern that original and eternal unity of Nature. Yet we are supposed to go beyond merely recognizing this cosmic unity (connection), go beyond voyeurism; we are to give voice to it, give it form in art and architecture and technology, so as actually to restore and recreate that unity. Thus American Indians see themselves as a kind of cosmic mucilage (see Meeker 1972:146), connecting *Homo* to animals, plants, and the elements, and connecting all of these forms to one another, in the manner of the original relationship. Humans, they feel, are the glue holding it all together, the agency that keeps it coherent and ordered and beautiful, because we (as a species) remember and constantly invoke—at least they did—those original terms of connection. *This* is our true and best role as historians.

For American Indians it begins with the act of imagining themselves out of themselves and into the larger personality of Nature enveloping them. It starts with an image of interpenetration. Japasa experienced it "in the searing transformation of his vision quest." At nine, he threw himself on the mercy and care of Nature, knowing it would care for him. He made himself fully vulnerable to it; he was cold and wet in the night rain. He was lost—though "lost" only in anthropological terms. A pair of silver foxes "found" him and began his transformation from human to fox-human. They fed him, and he learned "'their language. He said they taught him a song.' At this point in the narrative," recalls Ridington, "the old man sang the boy's song. He sang his medicine song." Before his vision was through Japasa would consort with rabbits, too, and with wind and rain. "He can call the wind. He can call the rain. He can also make them go away." And eventually he would live with frogs "on the bottom of a lake."

Japasa let himself be metamorphosed into fox-rabbit-wind-rain-frog-human; "he obtained power by joining his own life force to theirs. He knew them in the bush away from the society of other humans. . . . He became their child, one of their kind. He saw them clothed in a culture like his own. He carried them through to the end of his life, and then he let them go." "I can be a frog or a fox and still be a person," insists Ridington. "I can know them as I know myself. If I am Indian I can be led toward a place where this knowledge will come naturally."

The key here is one's cultural conception of time. Archaic societies

maintain their strikingly vivid relationship with Nature because of their
a priori commitment to living in mythic, rather than in historic, time. In
mythic time one truly can "be a frog or a fox and still be a person," one
can indeed have a hyphenated identity and existence, because one
continues to live in the time of origins, the time when biological
connections are most pronounced and fluid, when species distinctions
and diversity were (and are) inconsequential. The male and female
silver foxes in Japasa's experience "looked after him as if they were all
the same." Cosmogony, for these people, stresses relationships, not
disconnections—seemingly not the case in the Judeo-Christian Genesis
story, where disconnections are paramount. Humans, so these people
believe, have the genius to discern these primal and eternal connections;
we, and we alone, have the power of intellect necessary to learn and
then fashion the symbols and images with which to express the connections. We can learn Nature's songs: "My dad said he could understand
their language," whispered the old man's son, "he said they taught him a
song"—the fox song, which would become Japasa's inspiration and
power for the rest of his life.

We are, after all, *Homo sapiens sapiens*, the magnificent imager, the
creature whose formidable brain allows it to dream into (conceptualize)
the calculus of creation, from the level of ecological system, to species
behavior within the system, to the physiology of individuals within the
species, magnifying on down to tissue and cell structure, until ultimately we reach the molecular scaffolding of life. The creature endowed
with an anatomy and physiology permitting it then to recapitulate that
cosmogonic wizardry through symbol. Thus, not only can we think the
symbol, but we can express it through speech and language, dance and
movement, and material, mechanical, and technical dexterity. What
sets mythic societies apart is their insistence that humans are under an
obligation to express those connections in a life of oral and kinetic and
technological artistry. The art of cosmic connections. As they see it, by
affirming the connections we renew the system.

Notice that mythic people are not pretending that humans create the
(archetypal) structures and phenomena of Nature in their ritual activities—Momaday's sunwatcher did not literally make the sun come up—
rather, through ritual (in speech, art, architecture, tool-making, and so
forth) we give voice and movement and even tangible form—in short,
affirmation—to the connections, the relationships, between the organized structures, forms, and phenomena of Nature. *This* is how we
recreate and renew. Again, they believe they *must* recreate and renew if

the universe is to remain coherent, vibrant, lucid, and interpenetrating—if it is to remain patent. Humans are obliged to forge and forge again the links for all of Nature to see, feel, hear, and savor. For Nature knows us, so they believe; it perceives us, they are convinced, much as the magician David Abram said it does. Nature, aware of our formidable intellectual endowment and anatomical capacity, expects us to celebrate the complex circuitry and patterns of the system. In return for a life of celebration, a life of exquisite attention and affirmation, Nature promises to sustain us. The relationship is actually a compact: if I celebrate and affirm and renew, Nature will take care of my physical and spiritual needs. But the watch and compass and rifle and other anthropological terms must first be jettisoned before we can see and hear and know who and what we are dealing with and what the fundamental terms are. It all begins, as it did for Faulkner's Ike McCaslin, with a vision quest on other-than-human terms. And it results, as it did aboriginally for North American Indians, in a life of biological orientation and commitment.

There is something in all of this which does not square with Eric Wolf's Marxist postulate that "social life is shaped by the ways human beings engage nature through production," that "ideology-making . . . occurs within the determinate compass of a mode of production deployed to render nature amenable to human use" (1982:386, 388). I objected strenuously to that formula in my introduction since it appears to me that it perverts the peculiar relationship these mythic societies held with Nature. Wolf is furnishing his "people without history" with the wrong point of departure in their "social life" and "ideology-making." By living and acting in mythic time, by renewing the cosmos through innumerable acts of affirmation of perceived cosmic connections, they in fact never did set themselves apart from Nature. In a sense there was no departure. Nature was never conceived of as "out there," as a separate article from which to wrest a living. Never did they believe that they had to make it "amenable to human use." Nature and *Homo* were too interpenetrating for that. Which means that there was never any question about the latter's survival. It was only the ethnographers who worried about that. Humankind was always there, and will always be there, in one form or another, always taken care of—as long as we lead a life of celebration and affirmation. According to this view, our chief function and priority as humans is not to busy ourselves searching for and refining new and ingenious strategies for survival. To define life in this manner is faithless, tedious, unnecessary, alienating, dehumanizing, and dangerous. Survival, life and death, were not oppressive, burning issues for them. They were epiphenomena: secondary issues growing out of a more fascinating and engrossing, more important discourse with Nature. The issue, rather, was a life of appreciation, of affirmation, to keep the whole thing going. A life of responsibility, of vigilance. A life committed to making the connections.

The ethnologists who recently completed the Northern Algonkian Project among the Cree and Ojibwa went north expecting to find a society and culture at war with its environment (as I put it in my review of their book) and instead found environment and people "embracing one another in an intimate dance"—"a living art" is the phrase they used in summing up the elegant manner in which these people deal with winter's bitter cold (Steegmann 1983:322, 318). Adaptation to cold (the principal focus of the project) was but a fragment of a broader, more comprehensive adaptation to this sprawling boreal environment. That, too, the anthropologists found awesome. "The habits and fluctuations of its wildlife, the ways of water (as solid and liquid), the geography and virtues of plants, etc."—the Cree and Ojibwa knew it all "intimately and with supreme confidence. The land, they believe, will take care of them. And it genuinely does, in part at least because of this deep knowledge of its performance coupled with what is to Western eyes a peculiar willingness to work with and in the spirit of that medium" (Martin 1985b:147).

Humankind and Nature engaged in a living art. "Navajo culture is not just a food-gathering strategy," underscores Gary Witherspoon, "it is an artistic way of life" (1977:153). One must realize that this artistry of North American Indians was timeless, that they lived a life of timeless art, this indeed being judged the only responsible way to live. In fact, the reason the whole thing was appealing and satisfying was because it was timeless—anthropologically timeless. Time of the sort that takes humankind, alone, on a journey we know not whither, a time whose meaning and trajectory we attempt to compute by watching its wake roiling behind us, is anthropological. The temptation to measure, to time one's life in such fashion had to be repudiated repeatedly. And it was. Opting for biological time—mythic time—American Indians found that they were neither alone in this enterprise nor launched on a journey of uncertain destiny with a receding, irreclaimable past.

That was their great discovery: that time, anthropological time, can have a stop, or, more accurately, need never begin. It was an American eternity that began unraveling when Europeans assigned it dates: Christendom's calendar. October 12, 1492: Columbus encountered the Bahamas and hailed America and its "Indians" for European history. Cartographers would soon correct the admiral's error of location, and put him properly in a new place: America. As for the aborigines being forever more stuck with the wrong name, "Indians," it did not matter much since they were usually rendered in caricature anyway.*

America as *terra firma* was now finally discovered and, in time, accurately mapped by European civilization, although let it be emphasized that it was for a European agenda, a European time. Like the crocodile in *Peter Pan* that had swallowed the clock, Europeans were a creature propelled by an obsessive mission, and they ticked wherever they went. In the pursuit of a gilded destiny America would be recalibrated to anthropological time—time spent in a poignant search for a physical paradise, the Garden, a salvation here and now for a restless creature, *Homo*. After the manner of the Old Testament deity, they would gather up the dust of this new land and breathe into it their terms, their message, their blueprint, in the hope of making it into a place compatible with and conformable to themselves. It worked, more or less; the land was transformed. "So God created man in his own image," reads Genesis (1:27), and that creature in turn went on to create this landscape in his own image which, after all, was God's image. So reads our North American history: we set the terms after the fashion of our species and our history, rather than look for the Bear and its terms. There was no vision quest on other-than-human terms.

American Indians, too, were re-calibrated according to anthropological time, to make them conform also to our God-like image. But here we met with notably less success. "The Indian is hewn out of a rock," snapped Francis Parkman. "It is this fixed and rigid quality which has proved his ruin. He will not learn the arts of civilization, and he and his

---

*I think it prudent to underscore here that the American Indians I am referring to in my discussion of "time" and "history" throughout this and the introductory essay are those of North America exclusively. By way of contrast, we see in pre-Columbian Mesoamerica, for example, the rise and fall of architecturally flamboyant civilizations several of which, at least, seem to have combined a linear, historical vision and mission with what appears to have been a more ancient mythic round. The Aztecs conducted themselves thus, and one might argue it as well for the Maya. The former invoked their powerful sense of historical destiny to terrorize or swallow surrounding city-states— "those still in the grip of myth are never military matches for those devoted to a historical mission" (F. Turner 1980:158)—while simultaneously they kept faith with myth, in particular the myth of Quetzalcoatl. Cortes would exploit their leaders' inability to reconcile the two (F. Turner 1980:156–65; see also León-Portilla 1963).

forest must perish together" (1898:48). It was a piece of literary extrava-
gance, for neither the Indian nor his forest perished altogether. Where
Parkman saw only an "irreclaimable son of the wilderness" (1898:48),
Mary Young sees plenty of adaptation—to white religion, white political and economic institutions, Old World diseases, and, in general, all
efforts to assimilate them. Young is struck by the fluidity of it all: fluid
spiritual beliefs, fluid geographical location, fluid ideals and ambitions,
even fluid ethnic composition. There were numerous metaphysical systems in operation among these people, she maintains, and these were
constantly mutating. Indians survived, through accommodation and
flexibility, all the while surviving *as* Indians and *to be* Indians. Their
history since European contact is a process of hybridization.

The above is true only as far as it goes. Young dodges the big issue, I
believe. Granted, there was accommodation, there was adaptation.
When a tidal wave hits, the survivors swim. What Young fails to see is
that those multifarious, white-derived, white-inspired circumstances
were being creatively reconciled to a tenaciously guarded, overarching,
and suffusing biological orientation and commitment which does indeed yield itself to gross analysis and which has served from time
immemorial as the mainspring of all North American Indian cultures
and societies. The point is that it continued to hold their attention even
as they sought to hang on amid the maelstrom of white conquest and
domination. What is most instructive is what they refused to surrender,
and how they fit the terms and paraphernalia of white civilization to
that backboard.

Witherspoon puts his finger on it when he describes the Navajo
adaptive strategy. "Many aspects of Navajo culture have been adopted
from other cultures and incorporated into Navajo life. This has been
done creatively, so that the essence and core of Navajo life and culture
have not been disrupted or destroyed but have been enhanced. Many
writers and historians have commented on the ability of the Navajo to
absorb without being absorbed. This ability is derived from a capacity
to make creative syntheses" (1977:182). This ability is seemingly shared
by all North American Indians, which should not surprise us, for, after
all, that was what they had been doing since time out of memory under
the mythic, biological paradigm: making "creative syntheses." They are
unsurpassed at such art. In truth it is this ancient and finely tuned skill
that has enabled them to hold on to what they deem a saner, more
responsible, and far more engaging vision of life: the biological commitment. In Chapter 3, Salisbury quite rightly acknowledges this tenacious

retention of what he unfortunately terms "traditional norms" in the face of pressure to change and modernize, yet, like Young, does not specify just what it was they were holding on to and why.

To write about American Indians without making the biological connections, that is, to write about them exclusively in anthropological terms, is to lose not only an integral part of the narrative but lose its ethic as well. Washburn, Dobyns, and Jaenen have each fallen into this trap, I believe. "Those who decry the intrusion of the white presence in Indian history are often simply unwilling to recognize that Indian history is, for good or ill, shaped by the white presence, whether physically, in terms of European immigrants, or intellectually, in terms of Western historical or anthropological theories." Dobyns carries this (Washburn's) advice to its limit: "If the history of Native American interactions with invaders is to be anything more than mere chronicle written by authors with literary pretensions, it must become a social science. To do so, historical analysis must accumulate understandings that accord with interpretive theories of anthropology, sociology, economics, and demography." Dobyns is hard on the trail of "scientific history," which in his mind means "replicability of analysis." For him, the most cogent issues of Indian and white relations are demographic: the cold realities of microbial infection, malnutrition, and forced and voluntary migration. In his mind, the more abstract realm of ideas and perceptions should be keyed to these fundamental phenomena, which in many respects influenced peoples' thoughts and behavior. Demographics are to be studied first, ideas second. Jaenen, in a similar vein, warns against the "tendency on the part of many native leaders and some of their academic defenders to overdo the spiritual aspects of Amerindian cultures to the detriment of their practical and materialistic contours."

I am troubled by the dictum that all our inquiries into the subject of North American Indians, whether considered alone or in association with whites, should bend the knee to academic orthodoxy. Galileo received similar advice. One is reminded of Robin Ridington and his "anthropological [indeed] rite of passage known as fieldwork" undertaken in the mid-1960s. The young Harvard ethnologist set up shop in a Beaver hunting camp and began firing questions at his hosts in an effort to fit and fix them into an elaborate personality structure he had packed in with him, till it dawned on him that what he was looking for was really quite irrelevant to life as they perceived and lived it. "Preliminary analysis indicated they were severely withdrawn if not virtually autistic,

but they did not act that way outside of the test situation," confesses he.
"From time to time they suggested that they knew 'Indian stories,' much
more interesting than the ones I wanted them to make up in response to the set of standardized pictures I had brought with me. For
a long time I rejected their suggestions. These stories were not the
scientific data I required." Scientific data. Scientific history. Their
stories were replicable, but unconfirmable through literary and other
documentation. "One day a tiny, frail old man was led into our camp by
his grandson. . . . His name was Japasa—'Chickadee,'" and he was
dying of heart disease. "As the attacks became more frequent and more
severe" he had thought to check himself out of the Fort Nelson hospital,
for "he wished to be in the bush with his people. He needed moosemeat,
wind, stars, his language, and his relatives, rather than the narrow white
bed on which I had seen him perched cross-legged, like a tiny bird."
Japasa was not a practical man. Indeed, as Ridington would quickly
discover, he was not an anthropological man at all.

His "history," if we can call it that, was to a certain degree obviously
"shaped by the white presence." Washburn is right about that. Shaped
mostly by the physical, demographic forces Dobyns talks about and
Washburn and Jaenen allude to. But Dobyns, it seems, would like to
end the matter there. Though claiming to support the study of Native
American micro-cosmologies, he seems to deprecate them. Dobyns
finds the spiritual-philosophical commitment of his Indians pretty well
eclipsed, as far as explanatory value is concerned, by the physical and
demographic forces of contact. "To understand Native American interaction with invaders, scientific historians must reconstruct demographic trends first, and then relate other events to them." Though
admittedly furnishing a version of their "history," these "demographic
trends" most assuredly constitute an insufficient version. Ridington
mentions that the "son told a story about how he and the old man
survived the terrible flu of 1918–19 that had killed many people." Here,
presumably, is the raw stuff of "scientific history": an extrinsic event
over which these people had little or no control that had a confirmable
date affixed to it. Japasa lived despite that extraneous historical lesion.
The purpose and performance of his life in fact had very little to do with
that momentous event, which was but a searing aberration.

The old man was not particularly moved by the influenza pandemic
of 1918–19; he did not dwell on it, nor did he allow it to change the
course of his life. For Japasa was possessed by a different story, the one
he "began speaking softly, apparently to himself, as if he were looking

back into a dream to find the words. His son whispered a simultaneous translation into English for my benefit. It must have been important to him that I share this event. He wanted me to understand enough of what was going on at the time that I could discover its meaning later in my life. This is the essence of Japasa's revelation as related to me by his son." The time he lived with the silver foxes, the first time he entered mythic time, the time when he was transformed into fox-human, the time by which he would calibrate the rest of his time on earth—this, the dying man insisted, was the absolutely essential core of his story, his history if you will.

We are left wondering whose story we are going to tell (as Berkhofer asks in his wonderfully searching essay), and "from whose categories of reality should the facts of history be derived?" How much of their story are we going to tell, one might add, and how much are we equipped to tell? It is this final question that exercises me most.

The animal and elemental stories were crucial to Japasa because he gained power from them. "The wind came to him as a person, the foxes wore clothes and spoke in a language he could understand, the frogs gathered to drum and gamble. They gave this boy their songs as guides to the powers he would have as a man. Throughout his life he returned in his dreams to that visionary time-out-of-time." He derived no power from the influenza experience. That, indeed, was not a part of his overall scheme of life. It did occur, and he coped with it—as an aberration. A lesion. But his terms, his interests, his role and meaning lay elsewhere, lay with the biological commitment—with the wind, foxes, frogs, and other beings who somehow conferred their prodigious power on him, in a manner he understood and accepted and could use. Ridington puts it succinctly when he declares: "His powers were forces within him as well as forces of nature. His experience was always within nature." Herein lies the solution to the historian's dilemma.

As long as the Japasas of this land insist on linking their life-force to that of Nature around and within them, we historians are obliged to write about them in just those terms. In a sense it is irrelevant whether we believe in talking animals or not. If they believe it, or did, and if they make their lives conformable to that belief, then to write about the Japasas we have no choice but to write about the animals ("animal-persons") as well. What is more, we must take care to describe a hyphenated existence and identity: Japasa as fox-frog-rabbit-wind-human. For he did, orally, and so must we, orally and in print. The first and most potent question is, What were these people doing with their

lives? What was *their* metaphysics? Everything we write about them
should follow from this seminal question.

The answer is the biological commitment, I believe. That is what they
were doing with their lives. "On the evening when Japasa gave up his
medicines" he narrated two stories. Ridington recorded and credited
both. One was about the people congregating "in the prairie country
near the Peace River to dry saskatoon berries," also to sing and dance
and play the hand game. "The other story was about frogs who play-
gamble, just like people. He said he knew frogs because he once lived
with them on the bottom of a lake." Written records verify that Indians
came together where Japasa said they did "to sing, dance, and gamble."
Whereas "there is no documentary or scientific evidence to indicate that
frogs really sing and dance and gamble beneath the waters of a pond,
but the old man said he experienced this, too." The point is that "both
of Japasa's stories were true to his experience," where the tutelage of
frogs, foxes, and wind, and the "songs" they gave him, powered and
inspired his life from thenceforth.

The other point worth noting is that the apparently "historical"
recollection of periodic congregation near the Peace River occurred, for
Japasa, within the larger context, larger envelope, of a life of mythic, of
biological orientation. Japasa was obviously inspired by and hence
concentrated on participating in and recalling the biological realm to
which he had become indissolubly joined. The "historical" event had
significance only insofar as it occurred and performed within the larger
sphere of his biological attention. To the extent that these people
traditionally recalled "historical" events, their context and terms and
meaning were patently mythic. We see this in the life of Japasa, and
elsewhere, as with Whiteman's four stages, or "broad periods," of
Cheyenne "history." The danger is that we can make too much of these
so-called historical recollections; we must place our emphasis where
these people put theirs: on the larger context within which such recollections were tendered.*

In the end, Ridington declares emphatically that "the true history of
these people will have to be written in a mythic language. Like the
stories of Japasa, it will have to combine stories of people coming

*The existence of pictographic calendars, such as those produced by the Dakota and
Kiowa in the last century, might appear to contradict what I have just said, though
in fact this is not so. Such pictorial records are still to be interpreted within a larger
mythic structure and commitment—one that was in the process of being compromised
and tempered by white influence. See Thurman (1982) and Mooney (1979).

together with other people, and those that tell of people coming together with animals." They fathomed themselves, their psyche, even their physiology, by absorbing Nature about them. Eschewing the conceit and circularity of inventing themselves anthropologically, they looked for their creation in a biological sphere—surely a far more sophisticated and saner approach to living. Even more, they realized and assumed a splendid role for themselves in that realm, the role of celebrant—celebrating the myriad and dazzling connections ramifying throughout.

Surely this is what Trask is describing in Native Hawaiians when she dismisses the *haole* (white) record of Hawaiian history as a fraud. "To know my history, I had to put away my books and return to the land. I had to plant taro in the earth before I could understand the inseparable bond between people and *'āina*. I had to feel again the spirits of nature and take gifts of plants and fish to the ancient altars. I had to begin to speak my language with our elders and leave long silences for wisdom to grow. . . . There was nothing in my schooling that had . . . hinted that somewhere there was a longer, older story of origins, of the flowing of songs out to a great but distant sea." "Historians," she implores, "must listen, they must hear the generational connections, the reservoir of sounds and meanings. They must come, as American Indians suggested long ago, to understand the land . . . in the indigenous way, the way of living within and protecting the bond between people and *'āina*."

Our failure as scholars has been in failing to see and understand this effort at making and maintaining biological connections. We have simply not understood the enormous and profound dimensions of this activity, of this ambition and pursuit. So many aspects of American Indian performance and existence, including their aboriginal technology and the manner in which they married European technology to existing inventories, their architecture, their ways of clothing and adorning themselves, their intimate relationship with animals and the elements, their rituals and narratives, their longing for native food, their conduct vis-à-vis whites in innumerable contexts, their reluctance to alienate their land and the crushing sense of loss when that land was lost to them—so much in the past five hundred years makes sense when seen against this backdrop of seeking to maintain those biological connections. At the same time one must admit that the white intrusion severed many of those connections, sometimes permanently and sometimes only temporarily, as with the sundering of the spiritual bond between humans and animals (when it was claimed that animals no longer conversed with them, and when hunt dreams failed to reveal vital information [Martin 1978]), or the bond between people and the land (in the process of removal and dispossession), or even the powerful nutritional bond with the plants and animals eaten not only to nourish but also to stimulate and manipulate their distinctive physiology (Martin, forthcoming). If Europeans carried alarm clocks, they also wielded scythes, such as the scythe of infectious disease, which undermined belief in a nurturing and benevolent Nature, or the scythe of Christianity, which taught that Nature practices were deranged and heathenish.

Despite it all they went about reforging the connections as best they could, so to mend the broken hoop. Reforging in ways ingenious and often subtle or clandestine, reforging to maintain a web of biological connections. It is interesting to picture the Europeans becoming enveloped within this mythic plexus right from the start, as with the raucous reception given Jacques Cartier in the shallows of Chaleur Bay (Baie des Chaleurs) in the summer of 1534, or that accorded Francis Drake forty-five years later on the other side of the continent, when the Miwok mistake "the English for ancestral ghosts and set up an unholy howling accompanied by appalling self-mutilation. Drake and his men frantically seek to end the bedlam and gore by praying, singing hymns, and physically restraining the berserk flagellants. Drake puts it down to demon possession; the Miwok . . . are honoured and at the same time totally unnerved by the unexpected appearance of their departed loved-ones" (Martin 1980:369). Sailing into Kealakekua Bay in 1779, James Cook gets comparable treatment from his Hawaiian hosts, who confer on him the mantle of the returned god-chief Lono, prompting Marshall Sahlins to observe: "The incidents of Cook's life and death at Hawaii were in many respects historical metaphors of a mythical reality" (Sahlins 1981:11). In each instance Europeans were being systematically "cosmicized" (Eliade 1959:10). And the Europeans "cosmicized" them in turn.

As historians, we also "cosmicize," as these essays amply demonstrate. By rendering Native Americans (and Hawaiians) as a "people of history," a people of anthropological time and errands, we cut the biological umbilical cord they had so carefully established and maintained over the millennia, and in many respects still insist on maintaining. Is it surprising, then, that Trask should declare, "*Our* story remains unwritten"? "It rests within the culture, which is inseparable from the land. To know this is to know our history. To write this is to write of the land and the people who are born from her." I suppose that as long as the prevailing ethic is to twist such matters into an anthropological commitment and perspective, the approach urged by Ridington and Trask and others herein will strike many in this profession as an exercise in poetry. No doubt there are those who will say just that—and more. Like all academics, historians maintain a formidable arsenal of high holy curses with which we effectively police our ranks; it is a normal part of professionalization.

But there is too much at stake here to let ourselves be turned back by the charge of heresy. "Unless we can find some way to understand the reality of mythic thinking we remain prisoners of our own language, our own thoughtworld," warns Ridington. "It is no longer enough to see as a man sees," Eiseley cautions. "If we continue to do this, the great brain—the human brain—will be only a new version of the old trap, and nature is full of traps for the beast that cannot learn" (1978:120). We have proven ourselves adept at human-serving recollection, at narrating anthropological history. Yet there is a biological recollection, too, a biological recollection and connection within which the human-serving recollection and human connection form but a subset. Surely no one would dispute that. The challenge is to learn the terms, the meter of the "song," of that biological connection, to understand not only American Indians better, but to understand ourselves differently, and better, as well.

It has been often remarked that historians are the new high priests of our collective consciousness, the keepers of the sacred memory. Yet we are derelict by our silence on the memory of our sacred relationship to the Bear—the biological sphere that embraces and courses through us. We concentrate our instruments and thoughts on our kind above all—our rise to civilization, our conquest of Nature, our progress, our affairs—rendering the rest as cultural landscape. The achievements we chronicle are truly awesome, as are the costs of those achievements, and we understand the full implications of neither. The flaw lay in defining the remainder as cultural landscape—the definition that was both illusion and justification. For the "achievements" of our species earn that name only in the language of history, which is but a category of anthropology. Historians must now find another language, another symbolic grid, another category, by which to render ourselves and our habitat, one that does not disfranchise and disarticulate the latter. The problem, I believe, lies in our enslaving philosophy of time—enslaving us and Nature in separate spheres. We need to discard anthropological time for biological time, which means finding ourselves in the Bear in biological time. It means viewing creation and its creature on other-than-human-serving terms. That, for me, is the ultimate message of these essays.

Cumulative Bibliography

Abram, David (1983). "Natural Magic." In *Minding the Earth: Newsletter of the Strong Center for Environmental Values (Berkeley, California)* 4 (June).

Adler, Joyce (1972). "Melville on the White Man's War against the American Indian." *Science and Society* 36 (Winter):417-42.

Akwesasne Notes (1978). *A Basic Call to Consciousness: The Hau de no sau nee Address to the Western World.* Roosevelt Town, N.Y.: Akwesasne Notes.

Axtell, James (1981). *The European and the Indian: Essays in the Ethnohistory of Colonial North America.* New York: Oxford Univ. Press.

Bailyn, Bernard (1982). "The Challenge of Modern Historiography." *American Historical Review* 87 (Feb.): 1-24.

Barthes, Roland (1972). *Mythologies.* New York: Hill and Wang.

—— (1981). *Camera Lucida: Reflections on Photography.* New York: Hill and Wang.

Bateson, Gregory (1979). *Mind and Nature.* New York: E. P. Dutton.

Bellah, Robert (1975). *The Broken Covenant: American Civil Religion in Time of Trial.* New York: Seabury.

Benson, Lee (1981). "Doing History as Moral Philosophy and Public Advocacy: A Practical Strategy to Lessen the Crisis in American History." Paper delivered at the Annual Meeting of the Organization of American Historians, Detroit, Mich., 1 April.

Berger, John, and Jean Mohr (1982). *Another Way of Telling.* New York: Pantheon.

Berger, Thomas (1964). *Little Big Man.* New York: Dial.

Berkhofer, Robert F., Jr. (1965). *Salvation and the Savage: An Analysis of Protestant Missions and American Indian Response, 1787-1862.* Lexington: Univ. of Kentucky Press.

—— (1969). "Barrier to Settlement: British Indian Policy in the Old Northwest, 1783-1794." In *The Frontier in American Development: Essays in Honor of Paul Wallace Gates.* Ed. David M. Ellis *et al.* Pp. 249-76. Ithaca: Cornell Univ. Press.

—— (1971). "The Political Context of a New Indian History." *Pacific Historical Review* 40 (Aug.):357-82.

—— (1973). "Native Americans and United States History." In *The Reinterpretation of American History and Culture*. Eds. William H. Cartwright and Richard L. Watson, Jr. Pp. 37-52. Washington, D.C.: National Council for the Social Studies.

—— (1978). *The White Man's Indian: Images of the American Indian from Columbus to the Present*. New York: Knopf.

—— (1981). "The North American Frontier as Process and Context." In *The Frontier in History: North America and Southern Africa Compared*. Eds. Howard Lamar and Leonard Thompson. Pp. 43-75. New Haven: Yale Univ. Press.

Bingham, Hiram (1848). *A Residence of Twenty-one Years in the Sandwich Islands*. 2nd ed. New York: Converse.

Black, Lydia T. (1981). "The Nature of Evil: Of Whales and Sea Otters." In *Indians, Animals, and the Fur Trade: A Critique of Keepers of the Game*. Ed. Shepard Krech, III. Pp. 109-53. Athens: Univ. of Georgia Press.

Borah, Woodrow (1964). "America as Model: The Demographic Impact of European Expansion upon the Non-European World." *Actas y Memorias, XXXV Congreso Internacional de Americanistas, Mexico, 1962*. 3 vols. 3:379-87. Mexico: Editorial Libros de Mexico.

Boucher, Philip (1979). "French Images of America and the Evolution of Colonial Theories, 1650-1700." *Proceedings of the Sixth Annual Meeting of the Western Society for French History* (1978) 6:220-28.

Bowden, Henry Warner (1981). *American Indians and Christian Missions: Studies in Cultural Conflict*. Chicago: Univ. of Chicago Press.

Bradley, David (1982). *The Chaneysville Incident*. New York: Avon.

Brown, Dee Alexander (1966). *The Year of the Century: 1876*. New York: Scribner's.

Brown, Joseph Epes (1976). "The Roots of Renewal." In *Seeing with a Native Eye: Essays on Native American Religion*. Ed. Walter H. Capps. Pp. 25-43. New York: Harper and Row.

—— (1982). "Becoming Part of It." *Parabola* 7 (Summer):7-14.

Bruner, Edward M. (1986). "Ethnography as Narrative." In *The Anthropology of Experience*. Eds. Victor Turner and Edward M. Bruner. Pp. 139-55. Urbana: Univ. of Illinois Press.

Cahill, P. Joseph (1977). "Aspects of Modern Cree Religious Tradition in Alberta." *Studies in Comparative Religion* 28 (Nov.):208-12.

Canary, Robert H., and Henry Kozicki, eds. (1978). *The Writing of History: Literary Form and Historical Understanding*. Madison: Univ. of Wisconsin Press.

Clifton, James A. (1977). *The Prairie People: Continuity and Change in*

  Potawatomi Indian Culture, 1665–1965. Lawrence: Regents Press of Kansas.

Cook, Sherburne F. (1945). "Demographic Consequences of European Contact with Primitive Peoples." *Annals of the American Academy of Political and Social Science* 237 (Jan.):107-11.

Cronon, William (1983). *Changes in the Land: Indians, Colonists, and the Ecology of New England.* New York: Hill and Wang.

Crosby, Alfred W., Jr. (1972). *The Columbian Exchange: Biological and Cultural Consequences of 1492.* Westport, Conn.: Greenwood.

—— (1976). "Virgin Soil Epidemics as a Factor in the Aboriginal Depopulation in America." *William and Mary Quarterly* 33 (April): 289-99.

Curtis, Edward S. (1907–30). *The North American Indian: Being a Series of Volumes Picturing and Describing the Indians of the United States, and Alaska.* Ed. Frederick Webb Hodge. 20 vols. Seattle: E. S. Curtis.

Daws, Gavan (1968). *Shoal of Time: A History of the Hawaiian Islands.* Toronto and New York: Macmillan.

De Belmont, Abbé François Vachon (1840). *Histoire de l'eau-de-vie en Canada.* In *Collection de Mémoires et Relations sur l'histoire ancienne du Canada.* Québec: Cowan et fils.

De la Roche-Tilhac, M. (1784). *Almanach Américain, ou Etat physique, politique, ecclésiastique et militaire de l'Amérique.* Paris: Lamy.

Deloria, Vine, Jr. (1973). *God is Red.* New York: Grosset and Dunlap.

—— (1980). "Foreword/American Fantasy." In *The Pretend Indians: Images of Native Americans in the Movies.* Eds. Gretchen M. Bataille and Charles C. P. Silet. Pp. ix–xvi. Ames: Iowa State Univ. Press.

De Pauw, Corneille (1770). *Recherches philosophiques sur les Américains.* Vols. 1 and 2. London.

De Premonval, M. (1770). *Défence des Recherches philosophiques sur les Américains.* Berlin.

Dibble, Sheldon (1909). *History of the Sandwich Islands.* Honolulu: Thrum.

Dobyns, Henry F. (1964). *Social Matrix of Peruvian Indigenous Communities.* Ithaca: Cornell Univ., Dept of Anthropology, Cornell Peru Project.

—— (1972). *The Papago People.* Phoenix, Ariz.: Indian Tribal Series.

——, and Paul L. Doughty (1976). *Peru: A Cultural History.* New York: Oxford Univ. Press.

——, and Robert C. Euler (1976). *The Walapai People.* Phoenix, Ariz.: Indian Tribal Series.

Drinnon, Richard (1980). *Facing West: The Metaphysics of Indian-Hating and Empire-Building.* Minneapolis: Univ. of Minnesota Press.

Duffy, John (1953). *Epidemics in Colonial America.* Baton Rouge: Louisiana State Univ. Press.

Eastman, Charles Alexander (1977). *From the Deep Woods to Civilization.* Lincoln: Univ. of Nebraska Press.

Eccles, William J. (1972). *France in America.* New York: Harper and Row.

Eiseley, Loren (1978). *The Star Thrower.* New York: Times Books.

Eliade, Mircea (1959). *Cosmos and History: The Myth of the Eternal Return.* Trans. Willard R. Trask. New York: Harper and Row.

Elliott, Robert (1960). *The Power of Satire: Magic, Ritual, Art.* Princeton: Princeton Univ. Press.

Encyclopaedia Britannica (1980). *Great American Indian Leaders.* [A pamphlet distributed nationally by the publisher.] Chicago.

Evans-Wentz, W. Y. (1981). *Cuchama and Sacred Mountain.* Eds. Frank Waters and Charles L. Adams. Chicago: Swallow.

Fanon, Frantz (1968). *The Wretched of the Earth.* New York: Grove, Evergreen Edition.

Farb, Peter (1978). *Man's Rise to Civilization: The Cultural Ascent of the Indians of North America.* rev. 2nd ed. New York: E. P. Dutton.

Faulkner, William (1961). "The Bear" [1942]. In *Three Famous Short Novels.* Pp. 185–316. New York: Random House, Vintage.

Fire, John [Lame Deer], and Richard Erdoes (1972). *Lame Deer: Seeker of Visions.* New York: Simon and Schuster.

Fitzgerald, F. Scott (1953). *The Great Gatsby* [1925]. New York: Scribner's.

Fletcher, Colin (1967). *The Man Who Walked Through Time.* New York: Knopf.

Forbes, Jack D. (1981). *Native Americans and Nixon: Presidential Politics and Minority Self-Determination, 1969–1972.* Los Angeles: Univ. of California, American Indian Studies Center.

Fornander, Abraham (1878–85). *An Account of the Polynesian Race: Its Origin and Migrations and the Ancient History of the Hawaiian People to the Times of Kamehameha I.* 3 vols. Vol. 1. London: Trübner.

Foucault, Michel (1974). "Anti-Retro: Entretien avec Michel Foucault." *Cahiers du Cinéma*, nos. 251–52. (July–Aug.):5–15. See also as "Film and Popular Memory: An Interview with Michel Foucault." Trans. Martin Jordin. *Radical Philosophy* 11 (Summer 1975):24–29.

Frame, Donald H., ed. (1963). *Montaigne's Essays and Selected Writings.* New York: St. Martin's.

Fuchs, Lawrence (1961). *Hawaii Pono: A Social History.* New York: Harcourt, Brace and World.

Gardner, Howard (1981). *The Quest for Mind: Piaget, Lévi-Strauss, and the Structuralist Movement.* 2nd ed. Chicago: Univ. of Chicago Press.

Gates, Merrill E. (1897). "Address of President Merrill E. Gates." *Proceedings of the Fourteenth Annual Meeting of the Lake Mohonk Conference of Friends of the Indian, 1896.* Lake Mohonk, N.Y.: Lake Mohonk Conference.

Gibson, Arrell Morgan (1980). *The American Indian: Prehistory to Present.* New York: D. C. Heath.

Greenblatt, Stephen J. (1976). "Learning to Curse: Aspects of Linguistic Colonialism in the Sixteenth Century." In *First Images of America: The Impact of the New World on the Old.* Ed. Fredi Chiappelli. 2 vols. 2:561–80. Berkeley and Los Angeles: Univ. of California Press.

Harrison, G. B., ed. (1962). *King Henry the Fourth, Parts I and II.* Part I. New York: Harcourt, Brace and World.

Highwater, Jamake (1981). *The Primal Mind: Vision and Reality in Indian America.* New York: Harper and Row.

Hobsbawm, Eric, and Terence Ranger, eds. (1983). *The Invention of Tradition.* Cambridge: Cambridge Univ. Press.

Holden, Madronna (1976). "Making All the Crooked Ways Straight: The Satirical Portrait of Whites in Coast Salish Folklore." *Journal of American Folklore* 89 (July–Sept.):271–93.

Horsman, Reginald (1982). "Well-Trodden Paths and Fresh Byways: Recent Writing on Native American History." *Reviews in American History (The Promise of American History: Progress and Prospects)* 10 (Dec.):234–44.

Horton, Donald D. (1943). "The Functions of Alcohol in Primitive Societies: A Cross-Cultural Study." *Quarterly Journal of Studies on Alcohol* 4 (Sept.):199–320.

Hoxie, Frederick E. (1985). "The Indians Versus the Textbooks: Is There Any Way Out?" *Perspectives: American Historical Association Newsletter* 23 (April):18–22.

Hudson, Charles (1970). *The Catawba Nation.* Athens: Univ. of Georgia Press.

Indian Law Resource Center (1979). *Report to the Hopi Kikmongwis and Other Traditional Hopi Leaders on Docket 196 and the Continuing Threat to Hopi Land and Sovereignty,* March 1979. Washington, D.C.: Indian Law Resource Center. (TS, 200 pp. A version without footnotes published in *Akwesasne Notes* 11, nos. 2, 4, and 5, 1979, under the title, "The Erosion of Hopi Land Rights.")

Jackson, Helen Hunt (1881). *A Century of Dishonor: A Sketch of the United States Government's Dealings with Some of the Indian Tribes.* New York: Harper and Bros.

Jacobs, Wilbur R. (1971). "The Fatal Confrontation: Early Native-White Relations on the Frontiers of Australia, New Guinea, and America— A Comparative Study." *Pacific Historical Review* 40 (Aug.):283-309.

—— (1974). "The Tip of an Iceberg: Pre-Columbian Indian Demography and Some Implications for Revisionism." *William and Mary Quarterly* 31 (Jan.):123–32.

Jaenen, Cornelius J. (1978). "Conceptual Frameworks for French Views of America and Amerindians." *French Colonial Studies* 2:1–22.

—— (1980). "L'Amérique vue par les Français aux XVIe et XVIIe Siècles."

In *Rapports: XVe Congrès International des Sciences Historiques* 2:272–78. Bucarest: Editura Academiei Republicii Socialiste România.

Jaulin, Robert (1970). *La paix blanche: Introduction a l'ethnocide*. Paris: Editions du Seuil.

Jennings, Francis (1975). *The Invasion of America: Indians, Colonialism, and the Cant of Conquest*. Chapel Hill: Univ. of North Carolina Press.

—— (1984). *The Ambiguous Iroquois Empire: The Covenant Chain Confederation of Indian Tribes with English Colonies from Its Beginnings to the Lancaster Treaty of 1744*. New York: W. W. Norton.

Jones, Dorothy V. (1982). *License for Empire: Colonialism by Treaty in Early America*. Chicago: Univ. of Chicago Press.

Kesey, Ken (1962). *One Flew over the Cuckoo's Nest*. New York: New American Library, Signet.

Kip, W. I., ed. (1846). *The Early Jesuit Missions in North America*. New York: Wiley and Putnam.

Kroeber, Theodora (1961). *Ishi in Two Worlds: A Biography of the Last Wild Indian in North America*. Berkeley and Los Angeles: Univ. of California Press.

Kuykendall, Ralph S. (1938). *The Hawaiian Kingdom, 1778–1854*. Honolulu: Univ. of Hawaii Press.

La Farge, Oliver (1929). *Laughing Boy*. New York: Pocket Books.

—— (1945). *Raw Material*. Boston: Houghton Mifflin.

LaFeber, Walter (1980). "From Redskins to Gooks." *Inquiry* 3:25–26.

Langer, Susanne K. (1957). *Problems of Art: Ten Philosophical Lectures*. New York: Scribner's.

Le Guin, Ursula K. (1974). "The Author of the Acacia Seeds and Other Extracts from the *Journal of the Association of Therolinguistics*." In *Fellowship of the Stars: Nine Science Fiction Stories*. Ed. Terry Carr. Pp. 213–22. New York: Simon and Schuster.

Leland, Joy (1976). *Firewater Myths: North American Indian Drinking and Alcohol Addiction*. New Brunswick, N.J.: Rutgers Center of Alcohol Studies.

León-Portilla, Miguel (1963). *Aztec Thought and Culture: A Study of the Ancient Nahuatl Mind*. Trans. Jack Emory Davis. Norman: Univ. of Oklahoma Press.

Lévi-Strauss, Claude (1966). *The Savage Mind*. Chicago: Univ. of Chicago Press.

Lind, Andrew (1938). *An Island Community: Ecological Succession in Hawaii*. New York: Greenwood.

Lurie, Nancy O. (1971). "The World's Oldest On-Going Protest Demonstration: North American Indian Drinking Patterns." *Pacific Historical Review* 40 (Aug.):311–32.

Lyman, Christopher (1982). *The Vanishing Race and Other Illusions: Photo-

     graphs of Indians by Edward S. Curtis. New York: Pantheon/Smithsonian Institution Press.

Lyons, Oren (1980). "An Iroquois Perspective." In *American Indian Environments: Ecological Issues in Native American History.* Eds. Christopher Vecsey and Robert W. Venables. Pp. 171–74. Syracuse: Syracuse Univ. Press.

McNickle, D'Arcy (1971). "Americans Called Indians." In *North American Indians in Historical Perspective.* Eds. Eleanor B. Leacock and Nancy O. Lurie. Pp. 29–63. New York: Random House.

McNeill, William H. (1976). *Plagues and Peoples.* Garden City, N.Y.: Anchor.

Marquis, Thomas Bailey (1976). *Keep the Last Bullet for Yourself: The True Story of Custer's Last Stand.* New York: Two Continents Publishing Group.

———, comp. (1973). "Iron Teeth: A Cheyenne Old Woman." In *Cheyenne and Sioux: The Reminiscences of Four Indians and a White Soldier.* Ed. Ronald H. Limbaugh. Pp. 4–26. Stockton, Calif.: Pacific Center for Western Historical Studies, Univ. of the Pacific.

Martin, Calvin (1975). "The Four Lives of a Micmac Copper Pot." *Ethnohistory* 22 (Spring):111–33.

——— (1978). *Keepers of the Game: Indian-Animal Relationships and the Fur Trade.* Berkeley and Los Angeles: Univ. of California Press.

——— (1979). "The Metaphysics of Writing Indian-White History." *Ethnohistory* 26 (Spring):153–59. Reprinted in this volume as Chapter 1.

——— (1980). Review of H. C. Porter, *The Inconstant Savage: England and the North American Indian, 1500–1660. Canadian Historical Review* 61 (Sept.):368–70.

——— (1982). "The Metaphysics of Writing Indian-White History: A Book Proposal." 3 pp. Sent to prospective contributors to this volume.

——— (1984). Review of William Cronon, *Changes in the Land: Indians, Colonists, and the Ecology of New England. Pacific Historical Review* 53 (Nov.):506–8.

——— (1985a). "The Covenant Chain of Friendship, Inc.: America's First Great Real Estate Agency." Review of Francis Jennings, *The Ambiguous Iroquois Empire: The Covenant Chain Confederation of Indian Tribes with English Colonies from Its Beginnings to the Lancaster Treaty of 1744. Reviews in American History* 13 (March):14–20.

——— (1985b). Review of A. Theodore Steegmann, Jr., *Boreal Forest Adaptations: The Northern Algonkians. Journal of Interdisciplinary History* 16 (Summer):146–47.

——— (forthcoming). *The Biological Conquest of the North American Indian.* New York: Oxford Univ. Press.

Meek, Ronald L., ed. (1973). *Turgot on Progress, Sociology and Economics.* Cambridge: Cambridge Univ. Press.

Meeker, Joseph W. (1972). *The Comedy of Survival: In Search of an Environmental Ethic.* Los Angeles: International College Guild of Tutors Press.

Melville, Herman (1954). *The Confidence-Man: His Masquerade* [1857]. Ed. Elizabeth S. Foster. New York: Hendricks House.

Momaday, N. Scott (1968). *House Made of Dawn.* New York: Harper and Row.

—— (1980). Commencement Address, Hobart and William Smith Colleges, Geneva, N.Y., 1 June.

—— (1981). "The Man Made of Words." In *The Remembered Earth.* Ed. Geary Hobson. Pp. 162–73. Reprint. Albuquerque: Univ. of New Mexico Press.

Mooney, James (1928). "The Aboriginal Population of America North of Mexico." *Smithsonian Miscellaneous Collections* 80, no. 7 (Feb.).

—— (1979). *Calendar History of the Kiowa Indians* [1898]. Washington, D.C.: Smithsonian Institution Press.

Morin, Françoise, and Jacques Mousseau (1971). "La Paix Blanche: A Conversation with French Anthropologist Robert Jaulin." *Akwesasne Notes* 3 (Oct./Nov.):16–17.

Morison, Samuel Eliot (1942). *Admiral of the Ocean Sea: A Life of Christopher Columbus.* Vol. 1. Boston: Little, Brown.

——, ed. (1963). *Journals and Other Documents on the Life and Voyages of Christopher Columbus.* New York: Heritage.

Nakai, Irene (1980). "Bridge Perspective." In *The South Corner of Time.* Ed. Larry Evers. P. 91. Tucson: Univ. of Arizona Press.

Nash, Gary B. (1974). *Red, White and Black: The Peoples of Early America.* Englewood Cliffs, N.J.: Prentice-Hall.

Neihardt, John G. (1972). *Black Elk Speaks: Being the Life Story of a Holy Man of the Oglala Sioux.* New York: Simon and Schuster, Pocket Books.

New York (State) Commissioners of Indian Affairs (1861). *Proceedings of the Commissioners of Indian Affairs, Appointed by Law for the Extinguishment of Indian Titles in the State of New York.* By Franklin B. Hough. 2 vols. Albany: J. Munsell.

Normandin, Joseph (1732). "Journal de Joseph Normandin." Public Archives of Canada, MG 7, I, A-3, Bibliothèque Nationale, Nouvelles acquisitions françaises, Collection Margry, vol. 9275, pp. 1–171.

Parkman, Francis (1898). *The Conspiracy of Pontiac and the Indian War after the Conquest of Canada* [1851]. 3 vols. Champlain Edition. Vol. 1. Boston: Little, Brown.

—— (1899). *The Jesuits in North America in the Seventeenth Century* [1867]. 2 vols. Vol. 1. Toronto: George N. Morang.

Powell, Peter J. (1969). *Sweet Medicine: The Continuing Role of the Sacred*

Arrows, the Sun Dance, and the Sacred Buffalo Hat in Northern Cheyenne History. 2 vols. Norman: Univ. of Oklahoma Press.

—— (1979). *People of the Sacred Mountain: A History of the Northern Cheyenne Chiefs and Warrior Societies, 1830–1879.* With an Epilogue, 1969–1974. New York: Harper and Row.

Public Archives of Canada (1730). "Mémoire sur l'état présent du Canada, 1730." MG 4, Archives de la Guerre, Paris, C 2, Bibliothèque du Comité technique du génie, vol. 3.

Radin, Paul (1975). "Monotheism among American Indians" [1924]. Reprinted in *Teachings from the American Earth: Indian Religion and Philosophy.* Eds. Dennis Tedlock and Barbara Tedlock. Pp. 219-47. New York: Liveright.

Ray, Arthur J. (1977). "Fur Trade History as an Aspect of Native History." In *One Century Later.* Eds. Ian A. L. Getty and Donald B. Smith. Pp. 7-19. Vancouver: Univ. of British Columbia Press.

——, and Donald Freeman (1978). *"Give Us Good Measure": An Economic Analysis of Relations between the Indians and the Hudson's Bay Company before 1763.* Toronto: Univ. of Toronto Press.

Ridington, Robin (1971). "Beaver Dreaming and Singing." In *Pilot Not Commander: Essays in Memory of Diamond Jenness.* Eds. Pat and Jim Lotz. Pp. 115-28. *Anthropologica,* Special Issue, n.s., 13 (1 and 2).

Rogers, Katharine M. (1966). *The Troublesome Helpmate: A History of Misogyny in Literature.* Seattle: Univ. of Washington Press.

Rogin, Michael Paul (1975). *Fathers and Children: Andrew Jackson and the Subjugation of the American Indian.* New York: Random House, Vintage.

Sahlins, Marshall (1972). *Stone Age Economics.* Chicago: Aldine/Atherton.

—— (1976). *Culture and Practical Reason.* Chicago: Univ. of Chicago Press.

—— (1981). *Historical Metaphors and Mythical Realities: Structure in the Early History of the Sandwich Islands Kingdom.* Association for Social Anthropology in Oceania Special Publications No. 1. Ann Arbor: Univ. of Michigan Press.

Sandoz, Mari (1953). *Cheyenne Autumn.* New York: McGraw-Hill.

Sayre, Robert F. (1977). *Thoreau and the American Indians.* Princeton: Princeton Univ. Press.

Schell, Jonathan (1982a). "The Fate of the Earth I." *New Yorker,* 1 Feb., 97.

—— (1982b). "The Fate of the Earth II: The Second Death." *New Yorker,* 8 Feb., 48.

Sekaquaptewa, Emory (1976). "On Approaching Native American Religions— A Panel Discussion." In *Seeing with a Native Eye: Essays on Native American Religion.* Ed. Walter H. Capps. Pp. 107-25. New York: Harper and Row.

Sheehan, Bernard W. (1980). *Savagism and Civility: Indians and Englishmen in Colonial Virginia.* Cambridge and New York: Cambridge Univ. Press.

——— (1981). Review of Richard Drinnon, *Facing West: The Metaphysics of Indian-Hating and Empire-Building. Western Historical Quarterly* 12 (Oct.):433–34.

Simpson, Howard N. (1980). *Invisible Armies: The Impact of Disease on American History.* Indianapolis: Bobbs-Merrill.

Slickpoo, Allen P., Sr., Project Director, and Deward E. Walker, Jr., Technical Advisor (1973). *Noon nee-me-poo (We, the Nez Perces): Culture and History of the Nez Perces.* Vol. 1. Lapwai, Idaho: Nez Perce Tribe of Idaho.

Sontag, Susan (1977). *On Photography.* New York: Farrar, Straus and Giroux.

Speck, Frank G. (1935). *Naskapi: The Savage Hunters of the Labrador Peninsula.* Norman: Univ. of Oklahoma Press.

Spicer, Edward H. (1969). *A Short History of the Indians of the United States.* New York: Van Nostrand Reinhold.

Stanley, Sam (1977). "American Indian Power and Powerlessness." In *The Anthropology of Power: Ethnographic Studies from Asia, Oceania, and the New World.* Eds. Raymond D. Fogelson and Richard N. Adams. Pp. 237–42. New York: Academic.

Steegmann, A. Theodore, Jr., ed. (1983). *Boreal Forest Adaptations: The Northern Algonkians.* New York: Plenum.

Tedlock, Dennis, trans. (1978). "Preface." In *Finding the Center: Narrative Poetry of the Zuni Indians.* Lincoln: Univ. of Nebraska Press, Bison Book Edition.

Thurman, Melburn D. (1982). "Plains Indian Winter Counts and the New Ethnohistory." *Plains Anthropologist* 27 (May):173–75.

Thwaites, Reuben Gold, ed. (1896-1901). *The Jesuit Relations and Allied Documents: Travels and Explorations of the Jesuit Missionaries in New France, 1610-1791.* 73 vols. Cleveland: Burrows Bros.

Tuggle, H. David (1979). "Hawaii." In *The Prehistory of Polynesia.* Ed. Jesse D. Jennings. Pp. 167–99. Cambridge, Mass.: Harvard Univ. Press.

Turner, Frederick (1980). *Beyond Geography: The Western Spirit against the Wilderness.* New York: Viking.

Turner, Frederick Jackson (1963). *The Significance of the Frontier in American History* [1893]. Edited, with an introduction, by Harold P. Simonson. New York: Frederick Ungar.

Turner, Katharine C. (1951). *Red Men Calling on the Great White Father.* Norman: Univ. of Oklahoma Press.

Tyler, Daniel, ed. (1976). *Red Men and Hat-Wearers: Viewpoints in Indian History.* Papers from the Colorado State Univ. Conference on Indian History, Aug. 1974. Boulder, Colo.: Pruett.

Utley, Francis Lee, Lynn Z. Bloom, and Arthur F. Kinney, eds. (1971). *Bear,*

Man, and God: Eight Approaches to William Faulkner's "The Bear."
2nd ed. New York: Random House.

Vaughan, Alden (1965). *New England Frontier: Puritans and Indians, 1620-1675*. Boston: Little, Brown. See the introduction to the revised edition, published by W. W. Norton and Co. (New York, 1979).

Wade, Mason (1969). "The French and the Indians." In *Attitudes of Colonial Powers towards the American Indian*. Eds. H. Peckham and C. Gibson. Pp. 61–79. Salt Lake City: Univ. of Utah Press.

Wagner, Roy (1981). *The Invention of Culture*. Chicago: Univ. of Chicago Press.

Warnock, Mary (1976). *Imagination*. Berkeley and Los Angeles: Univ. of California Press.

Washburn, Wilcomb E. (1957). "A Moral History of Indian-White Relations: Needs and Opportunities for Study." *Ethnohistory* 4 (Winter):47–62.

—— (1973). "James Adair's 'Noble Savages.'" In *The Colonial Legacy*. Ed. Lawrence H. Leder. 3:91–120. New York: Harper and Row.

—— (1976). "The Clash of Morality in the American Forest." In *First Images of America: The Impact of the New World on the Old*. Ed. Fredi Chiappelli. 2 vols. 1:335–50. Berkeley and Los Angeles: Univ. of California Press.

—— (1979). "On the Trail of the Activist Anthropologist: Response to Jorgensen and Clemmer: *JES* 6:2, 6:3." *Journal of Ethnic Studies* 7 (Spring):89–99.

—— (1981a). "The Indian Symbol: A Positive Stereotype." *Dartmouth Review*, 9 Feb., 13.

—— (1981b). "Symbol Must Emanate from College Culture." *Dartmouth Review*, 1 June, 9.

—— (1981c). "The Russell Tribunal—Who Speaks for Indian Tribes?" *Indian Truth: The Newsletter of the Indian Rights Association*, no. 240 (July–Aug.):8.

—— (1982). "Leftist Academics and Ethnic Minorities." *Washington Times*, 30 Dec., 10A.

—— (1983). "A Rollback of Left in Nicaragua Too?" *Washington Times*, 20 Dec., 1C.

—— (1984a). "Skins as Free Speech Defenders." *Washington Times*, 20 Jan., 1C.

—— (1984b). "The Shaping of an American Ideology." *Washington Times*, 11 Sept., 1C.

—— (1985a). "Pulling the Plug on the Sandinistas." *Washington Times*, 2 Jan., 2C.

—— (1985b). "Expand U. S. Policy against Nicaragua." *Miami News*, 5 Sept., 11A.

Watts, Pauline Moffitt (1985). "Prophecy and Discovery: On the Spiritual

Origins of Christopher Columbus's 'Enterprise of the Indies.' " *American Historical Review* 90 (Feb.):73–102.

Weeks, Philip, and James B. Gidney (1981). *Subjugation and Dishonor: A Brief History of the Travail of the Native Americans*. Huntington, N. Y.: Robert F. Krieger.

Whorf, Benjamin Lee (1956). *Language, Thought, and Reality: The Selected Writings of Benjamin Lee Whorf*. Ed. John B. Carroll. Cambridge, Mass.: M.I.T. Press.

Williams, William Carlos (1925). *In the American Grain*. New York: Albert and Charles Boni.

Winters, Yvor (1967). *Forms of Discovery: Critical and Historical Essays on the Forms of the Short Poem in English*. Chicago: A. Swallow.

Witherspoon, Gary (1977). *Language and Art in the Navajo Universe*. Ann Arbor: Univ. of Michigan Press.

Wolf, Eric R. (1982). *Europe and the People without History*. Berkeley and Los Angeles: Univ. of California Press.

Wood, Douglas Kellogg (1982). *Men against Time: Nicolas Berdyaev, T. S. Eliot, Aldous Huxley, and C. G. Jung*. Lawrence: Univ. Press of Kansas.

Yazzie, Ethelou, ed. (1971). *Navajo History*. Chinle, Ariz.: Navajo Community College Press for the Navajo Curriculum Center, Rough Rock Demonstration School.

Young, Mary Elizabeth (1961). *Redskins, Ruffleshirts, and Rednecks: Indian Allotments in Alabama and Mississippi, 1830–1860*. Norman: Univ. of Oklahoma Press.

—— (1975). "Indian Removal and the Attack on Tribal Autonomy: The Cherokee Case." In *Indians of the Lower South: Past and Present*. Ed. John K. Mahon. Pp. 125–42. Gainesville: Univ. of Florida Press.

—— (1981a). "The Cherokee Nation: Mirror of the Republic." *American Quarterly* 33 (Winter):502–24.

—— (1981b). Review of Richard Drinnon, *Facing West: The Metaphysics of Indian-Hating and Empire-Building. New Mexico Historical Review* 56 (Oct.):413.